MARINER'S LAUNCH

DR. RAY SOLLY

Whittles Publishing

Published by
Whittles Publishing Limited,
Dunbeath Mains Cottages,
Dunbeath,
Caithness, KW6 6EY,
Scotland, UK
www.whittlespublishing.com

Typeset by
Samantha Barden

ISBN 1-904445-03-9

Printed by
Bell & Bain Ltd., Glasgow

*To Merchant naval deck cadets – many had (and have)
much with which to contend*

"I'm sure that cadet gets enough from the Mate without you!"

(courtesy NUMAST Telegraph)

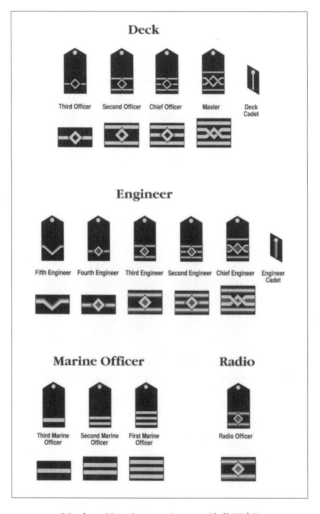

Merchant Navy Insignia (courtesy Shell IT&S)

CONTENTS

——

FOREWORD

Queen Mary 2
The Greatest Ocean Liner of Our Time

Over fifty years has passed since the author made his maiden voyage to sea. Since that time, ships have changed dramatically, not only in size and technology but also in the way they are manned, and how they are operated by their owners.

In the last few decades I have seen numerous cruise ships come into service, each one bigger and grander than the last. Whist this is good news for the Merchant Navy and those of us who still serve afloat, their existence, and the publicity they attract, tends to overshadow the history of shipboard life. Those earlier days in our careers are pushed by the passage of time, further and further to the background. Accordingly, in this, the "Year of the Sea" it is fitting that Dr Solly has described life at sea as it was over half a century ago. Having also served my 'time' in the cargo ships during the same era, some of his recollections and experiences are very similar to my own. They are so close in fact, that in some of the chapters, I felt as though I was reading my own diary.

This book presents a rich tapestry of life at sea in a bygone era and at the same time provides an important historical record of our country's Maritime Heritage. It will be of interest to anyone who enjoys maritime and modern history.

Commodore R W Warwick
Master
Queen Mary 2
At Sea – January 2005

Commodore R W Warwick
Master – Queen Mary 2
Cunard Line - Richmond House - Fourth Floor - Terminus Terrace - Southampton - SO14 3PN - UK

PREFACE

Jonathan Caridia, narrator of this book, does not entirely exist. 18th-Century Magistrate William Mansfield's assertion: 'the greater the truth, the greater the libel' hints at a bridle preventing our author writing too freely. Time may well demonstrate Mansfield's truth yet, because much encountered by Caridia was experienced, a danger remains embarrassing litigation could still arise from these pages. Thus, a narrator finds himself co-opted.

Keddleston Navigation School, and Ellerton Shipping Company are also semi-fictitious. As the narrator's split personality is divided between author and two seafaring colleagues, so Keddleston appears as a composite of two pre-sea officer cadet training establishments of the mid-1950s. Ellerton's represents a number of highly reputable ship-owners (each alas, no more) with whom he sailed. The Merchant Navy alone has genuine authenticity; but does not emerge unscathed, for its honour is painted with more than slightly tarnished humour.

This book is not just another 'service memoir'. The author believes it to be a social and historical document possessing genuine educational value. It depicts a way of life forever lost. 1950s' cargo ships were differently constructed from today's container and bulk carriers; each carried a forest of 'sticks' or derricks, and mariners moved in a highly labour intensive world whose very nature created a slow, indeed leisurely, pace of life. Cargo delays and strikes world-wide, frequently running into weeks, were patiently accepted as the norm. Although these factors indicate that many incidents as they are described could not occur today, collectively they capture the atmosphere of what it meant to serve as a navigating cadet in yesterday's Merchant Navy. Events may sometimes appear surprisingly incredible, but it remains true that seafaring is very different to life ashore.

Using a 'persona' is the safest medium in which to write but, incidental to the narrative (and almost imperceptibly) is chronicled the growth of a youth, captured initially through the innocent thoughts of a very naïve sixteen year old. Sailing with him we observe, sometimes cynically, his development into a mature young man – capable eventually of accepting grave responsibilities entrusted to a watch-keeping officer on the bridge of an ocean-going ship. We are there as he learns; observe him slide into pitfalls, and see him ambushed by escapades – created largely of his own making.

It has always intrigued me why Mansfield failed to complete his thought by adding: 'so the greater the humour'. After all as a magistrate, few people were better placed to witness the funnier aspects of life often accompanying the seriousness of his 'greater truth'; a fact equally applicable to service at sea. This story line has to evoke an occasional chuckle because it reflects life seen through the eyes of a teenager and thus, although lived fairly responsibly, had its own light-hearted impetus. His often long-suffering seniors needed their unique brand of clinical detachment, but for them, this was easier because they had been cadets themselves in an earlier age, so were fully aware of the ingenious foibles to which youngsters following in their footsteps were necessarily prone.

It follows therefore, that apart from photographs attributed 'Author's Collection' all others serve only as representations illustrating situations described in the text. They do not portray people, places or ships actually served with or in: consequently there is no direct connection between text and attributed copyright holders.

ACKNOWLEDGEMENTS

———

My publisher and I are indebted to individuals and organisations who have supplied photographs. Every effort has been made to trace all copyright holders but, as some images extend over fifty years, it has simply not been possible always to establish exact ownership. Some photographs (from 'unknown/untraceable sources') have been ascribed to suppliers. I apologise for – and should be extremely grateful of the opportunity to redress – any errors. A considerable number of people and organisations have assisted collation by generously giving their time, expertise, and kindness. The following are particularly worthy of acknowledgement and are people to whom I express grateful thanks:

Mr. Robert Wine, BP Media/External Affairs Manager at Hemel Hempstead, and Mrs Jo Wong, Archive Assistant at the BP Archive at the University of Warwick.

Mr. D.A. Belson, Crown Copyright Administrator, Ministry of Defence ILS, on behalf of Her Majesty's Stationery Office, covering Crown Copyright photographs.

Professor John Millican, and his Personal Assistant, Therese Barker, of Southampton Institute's Maritime Centre at Warsash.

Captain D. Salmon, Operations Manager, together with Mr. Alan Doig and Ms. Stephanie Varsani of Photographic Services, Shell International Limited.

Mr. Bob Aspinall, Former Historian and current Archivist, at the Port of London Authority's Museum in the Docklands.

Mr. G. Wilson, Headmaster, and Mr. N. Cann, Bursar, of the London Nautical School.

Mr. A. Linington, Editor, *The Telegraph*, House Magazine of NUMAST.

Mr. Paul Taylor, ex-2nd Officer BP Tanker fleet, for much encouragement.

I am grateful also to Her Majesty's Stationery Office for permission to quote from their *Channel Pilot, Volume One* and to Brown, Son and Ferguson for a quote from the *Nautical Almanac*.

Chapter 1

FITTING OUT

———

I left school under a cloud. Not the heavily-laden thunder-storm type, but more of a whimsical cumulus. The prefect's summons to my Head of Fifth Year interrupted lunch one Monday shortly after the Michaelmas term had commenced. Immediately on crossing the carpet, and seeing those red faced features across his desk contorted with irritation; and my French master standing next to him, a more than judicious 'two and two' were put correctly together. I knew immediately the import of this particular interview.

His opening exclamation that textbooks did not grow on trees was thrown even before I had stopped. It was clear anger clouded any awareness of ambiguity, although a quick glimpse was caught of the French master struggling to retain a passive countenance and just managing to smother his wry amusement. Under the circumstances, my dutiful reply managed the right balance between politeness and humour, even though I realised, on this matter, there would be no relenting.

He declared the issue of a lost textbook should not have reached him and it ought to have been replaced when I was asked to do so by the subject master. Abruptly cutting short my explanation, concerning how the book had been stolen by a group responsible for continued bullying (of which my school were well aware), he merely reiterated that I would still have to pay for it. The interview terminated with his passing an open letter across the desk for delivery to my parents explaining the circumstances as the school viewed them which, I was bemused to note, instructed them to refund the loss. Imagining my father's delighted reaction to this particular missive created a series of wildly fluctuating thoughts.

Travelling home that afternoon, with the envelope smouldering in my prep bag as strongly as in my mind, came the realisation I might just as well have kept quiet. My anger was fuelled by a sense of truly volcanic injustice: flamed by the school's inability to deal effectively with some mild bullying which had been my lot since entering the Fifth year, a couple of months earlier, when I fell foul of Thornton, the classroom moron, and his equally spineless henchmen. Class tests placed me well within the top strand so this it seemed had made me vulnerable. Certainly, up to then, my very traditional grammar school had been attended with pride and pleasure. It was true sports and gymnastics were never strong points – in fact, had hated both – but at least I had made an effort to 'go along for the ride'. The Head of Fifth Year was also director of sports and games at my highly competitive school, although I could not see that had any bearing upon the issue … much.

Mum saw immediately all was not well with son and heir and, without preamble, shot her own penetrating questions putting a finger on the root cause, identifying Thornton as a probable involvement in an on-going problem. I related what had happened, highlighting the foul temper which being bothered had created in my head of year. She read the offending letter, pursed her lips, and quietly said it should be discussed with my father upon his return from work later that evening.

Whilst supposedly working on my prep, more dominant and far from charitable ideas prevented serious study. There was a feeling in my bones this incident might develop into a situation: although not sure how far things would go – or even the extent to which I would allow them. New, disturbing thoughts seeped into my musings – causing me to tingle slightly. My resolve become unshakable: I was definitely *not* going to pay for the book, from money saved from my (until recent) Saturday greengrocery round, and would not allow father to do so. As determination hardened so additional decisions followed: either the school backed off or I would leave and not enter the sixth form. It was true circumstances had led me to question authority occasionally, but my nature was really quite timid: I could hardly be labelled habitually a rebellious youth and had never acted directly in opposition. Current events were therefore unnerving – yet curiously exciting. It seemed prudent however not to mention these thoughts immediately, but wait and see how things developed. Catching sight of the unheeded trigonometry prep awakened my often described 'bizarre gift of humour': I realised things were turning into a right-tangle.

As surmised, father, smothering an obvious irritation, wrote a cheque and, as his own subtle snub, returned the master's letter crossed through with a large tick in the same envelope, which he handed to me. Sucking a deep breath and, with a severe attack of what my biology master would have called 'palpitations', I told him I was not going to fork out for the stolen book, would not allow him to do so and simultaneously put the offending envelope back into a surprised hand. Then, somewhat clinically, I watched my parents' expressions develop and change as they confronted a novel situation.

The outcome was inevitable. Letters winged home and back with neither side relenting. Amidst this joyfully acrimonious exchange, late one evening after yet another tension filled supper, I felt enough was enough and dropped a bombshell on my astonished parents so precipitating a course of events, which completely altered my future. Drawing yet another deep breath I told them, although my feelings towards them were deeply affectionate, continued wrangling and uncontrolled bullying were becoming too much for me. I no longer cared about any rights or wrongs; was not going to school anymore, but would leave at the end of the current term in a few weeks time, without returning to complete my 'O' levels, and definitely not entering the sixth form.

My bald statement led to more heated exchanges. Father said bluntly my course of action was 'totally unacceptable' and he could not allow me to take it. I detected however a slightly bemused tone in his voice, which was interpreted as an initial weakening of defences, giving me that necessary impetus to stick to my guns.

Mother's reaction was fairly predictable. In a voice of unbridled concern she exclaimed her mystification at my attitude; recalled how I had always been a reasonably quiet and acquiescent son; lamented my sudden awkwardness and foundered lamely into silence, murmuring something indefinable about possible associations with my age.

'Quietly acquiescent son' listened as father continued the process of adult reasoning, explaining how he and mother had signed a legally-based undertaking to keep me in grammar school until I was eighteen years of age. This, he stressed, was in order for me to develop and not waste, the keen mind which their reports reckoned I possessed. He stated how important it was for me to take academic examinations and go to university.

That idea was not convincing so, drawing upon my newly found confidence, I explained it was not *me* who had signed the agreement and compared it, somewhat unfairly perhaps, with how they had arranged my baptism as a baby, but the decision to delay confirmation had been mine, two years previously at thirteen. I reminded them how readily they had then agreed to my postponing this until later when maturity allowed acceptance.

My parents looked intently at me, clearly detecting a flaw in logic somewhere, but more concerned about current events in our normally uncomplicated family life for this to be demonstrated. Their expressions became even more agitated as 'dutiful son' stirred the waters of equanimity again by reiterating his blunt intention to leave school regardless.

In the quiet which followed, I watched my parents individually begin the process of coming to terms with a new decisiveness in my demeanour and voice. I watched as Father absent-mindedly played with the tea-spoon in his cup of rapidly cooling coffee. For me, a new road to learning had been discovered. Unbelievably, it seemed previously recognised authorities in the shape of school and parents (of all people), were not quite so self-confident as they outwardly appeared, but were open to successful challenge.

My father expressed his fears with a hitherto unseen openness and gave Mum a simultaneous side glance as if seeking her confirmation. He told me he did not like the way events were developing and they both detected the emergence of a hitherto unsuspected force of character within me. His voice broke slightly as he made a last ditch stand to impose reason. He said point blank the situation was becoming ridiculous and they would not allow me to break my education over such comparatively trivial incidents.

In the face of my unrepentant stance, he tried a different tack by proposing I should enter a further education college. This would eliminate the bullying and allow completion of my 'O' level and 'A' level courses. Consistent with newly found form, unreasonable son simply rejected his suggestion out of hand. Then followed the inevitable question expressing their concerns about the course of action I intended; there clearly had to be some way forward.

I took another deep breath. This was to be an evening of surprises for my suddenly disillusioned parents. I explained that, now being fifteen, leaving school would be quite legal and how thoughts had lurked at the back of my mind for some time about joining the Merchant Navy.

My father looked at me speechlessly whilst taking in such an astounding piece of news. It was as if I had suddenly grown two heads. This avenue was completely unforeseen by them, as such a nautical enterprise had previously neither been mentioned nor even hinted at by me. Mum, still in a state of shock, was not so silent. In fact, I thought she was going to faint. I had never heard before such sheer horror as was expressed in her voice. She floundered on, stumbling over thoughts, as she wondered where on earth such an idea had come from. She clearly envisaged my capture – possibly to be sold somehow to the Zanzibar slave trade – a facet of recent media interest. Inevitably, her mind turned to occasional London dock visits I had recently started making; and Saturday trips on the River Thames with my Uncle 'Wag' working out of Gravesend. I was quick to shift any blame from that direction by re-asserting promptly how the idea was entirely of my own making.

I maintained a reflective silence as my father took second wind and came back for another attack. He emphasised, sensibly it seemed, that entry into a nautical college would require five 'O' levels and, leaving school as threatened, would render this route impossible.

With such bouncing newly found confidence, I could not be deterred now, so simply explained my intention of writing to a shipping company enquiring if they could make any suggestions. I felt my parents had clearly arrived at something the French (appropriately enough) would term an *impasse*.

The next round also was undoubtedly mine. I targeted a major passenger/cargo liner company in nearby central London who specialised in the round-Africa trades.

This was a continent I had secretly yearned to visit after seeing a lurid adventure film which featured, amid a long-forgotten plot, numerous deliciously naked, pertly uplifted, female breasts. These had proved a lucrative source of many delightfully erotic thoughts so it was no wonder, perhaps, I had felt it inappropriate to respond truthfully to Mum's reaction. The only way of getting to Africa – my long hidden Conradian dark continent – was to become a seafarer.

M.L. Rosherville on the River Thames (Author's collection).

Three days after my letter, a form arrived inviting me to apply for a post as messenger boy at the Company's Head Office, in Fenchurch Street. A reply to my application cordially invited me, accompanied by parents, to attend an interview the following week.

Opening the heavy wooden and glass front door, we were confronted by a receptionist in an ornate box who offered assistance. Looking at our letter of appointment he directed a messenger, dressed in a black suit with the name of the shipping company embossed in gold across his high collar, to lead us towards the Personnel Manager's office. As we crossed a patterned mosaic floor, and ascended a marble staircase, the thought came that I also might soon be showing visitors around this impressive building.

Once seated, the manager explained my job would last until I was old enough to apply through the Shipping Federation to enter sea training school on a course for deck boy trainees. He said I would need formal academic qualifications both for a permanent junior clerk's post in the Company and for entry to a navigation college and that, in the absence of these, a ratings' sea school was the only method of entry into the Merchant Navy.

Mother and I both nodded sagely, but doubtless with different thoughts. Dad had been unable to take time off work so, as I was under age, Mum had filled the gap.

"Of course, if you complete the sea school course we shall consider offering you the choice of going away aboard one of this Company's liners, if that option is still one you then wish to pursue," the manager had continued – in tones which I casually thought unnecessarily pompous for a schoolboy interview. My mind was really flying in other directions for I felt a quick stirring within at the thought of those breasts gleefully, perhaps frighteningly, coming closer to realisation.

Mother quickly expressed on my behalf her satisfaction with the progress of the interview so far, having apparently noticed (as she explained afterwards) an inexplicably dreamy sort of look crossing my countenance.

More surprises were revealed as the manager stated that he had noticed my extremely neat handwriting and thought this could be more usefully employed as a junior clerk rather than in a purely messenger capacity. And, as I had made a good impression in the interview so far, he could offer me immediate promotion to such a post in their Letter department, which attracted a higher salary. He explained that, subject to satisfactory behaviour, the job could last until embarking upon my sea training. An additional option was stressed: for, were I to change my mind and decide to stay ashore and study through evening classes for five ordinary level subjects, then they would consider making the clerical post permanent.

I was delighted at the way things had progressed and quickly agreed. Already I was not over-enamoured by the office idea, but felt it not quite the right time to mention this. My interview terminated with the manager explaining that the Company would write confirming all that had been discussed, and offering me a starting date for the Monday following official ending of the current term.

Overjoyed, I returned home and watched as father wrote to the grammar school explaining this decisive turn of events. The two-lined reply indicated they had written off me, my parents, and the cost of replacing the textbook. Presumably however, at some stage, they must have supplied a suitably satisfactory reference to the shipping company.

Delivering urgent personal cables brought me into direct contact with the senior managers. After about a month, during a slack late Friday afternoon, the Chief Marine Superintendent stopped me as I was preparing to rush from his office towards my next adventure. He invited me to take a seat and asked about my plans for the future. I told of the continued visits to docks and river at weekends, and my hopes of being sponsored by the Company for the sea school course and perhaps a deck boy's job aboard one of the liners. His very direct look (the first of many to come my way in my sojourn through life) was followed by enquiries concerning what I foresaw myself doing at sea, and whether or not any longer-term plans had been made. I was able to answer decisively, having thought constructively about my future – within my limitations – and explained my intentions of working from rating towards officer status, and then hopefully becoming captain of a ship.

There was a pause, after which he enquired if I had ever considered going to sea as a navigating officer cadet. I told him that although cadetships had been heard about vaguely in the course of my work, I had never really considered myself a likely candidate, being still only fifteen, and having left school without any qualifications. My response implied a crop of problems might grow in that particular academic field.

The superintendent rapidly assimilated this information, but had clearly detected an interested questioning in my voice as he told me, equally bluntly, that if I really wanted to become a navigating officer, and then a master mariner proceeding to ultimate command in the Merchant Navy, a cadetship would be the only realistic way forward. He stressed the benefits of structured and supported training, which I would be unlikely to receive as a rating, and how the life-style would be considerably better for me living with ships' officers than with the crew.

I listened fascinated as navigating officer cadetships, and the various methods of entry were explained, and felt an enhanced sense of excitement as he took me through the necessary stages. My immediate reflection was the bullies might have unwittingly done me a very big favour. I homed in again as he – obviously something of a realistic cynic – concluded by stressing how his Company would be unable to offer a cadetship, pointing out that their trainee officers were taken only from public schools, after which they were required to follow nautical training at a navigation college. He paused for a moment and offered me another very direct look before agreeing that in one respect I was correct; my lack of exams did present a potential problem, but this was not necessarily one that would prevent cadet entry. I had age on my side and it could well be worth my sounding out a nautical college, but I might have to face studying for exams at evening classes for a year, or even two, before going away to sea. He added this latter thought with a speculative smile.

I took in this information with the rueful thought that yet again the question of examinations and night school had popped up. Nevertheless I was most impressed by the fact that this obviously important man had taken the trouble to be so extremely helpful. This had been reinforced by the interest also shown in my future by my departmental manager. I presumed that it probably resulted from help they might have received themselves when at a similar stage.

There were additional factors which my father explained very much later. I was of an age close to children of the superintendent's and manager's own. Possibly, the experienced master mariner could see potential and some latent talent within me, of which I was blissfully unaware, but the school had clearly identified, and had led additionally to my promotion at the interview. Knowing the rigours of lower deck life he probably assessed that the chances of my survival in the rough and tumble associated with deck boy training might perhaps be limited. Although many similar boys had successfully made the transition he obviously felt I was potentially officer cadet material.

Even in my innocence, having seen the lunch-time antics of messenger boys bound for the same training as me, I had looked ahead trying to imagine mixing with them in the jungle which passed for sea school. Already I had become involved in a fight over a trivial incident but luckily, after a brief affray, had (as much to my surprise as the other boys) given my opponent a bloody nose. We were now the best of friends, but I was treated with a new measure of respect. There was an initiation test which had also been survived, that consisted of being locked in a pitch black safe for a while during the lunch hour. I had not been all that worried concerning this incident, working on the reasonable theory as they were inside with me, nothing too horrific could happen. Additionally and more worrying, were repeated tales from elder brothers who had successfully completed, or merely given up their courses, but either way had passed on horrific stories of life at Sharpness or Gravesend sea schools. Whilst allowing for exaggeration and embellishments, I had wondered occasionally whether I possessed the physical, mental, emotional or spiritual toughness (which covered just about all options) to survive this training, let alone the rigours of a deckhand's life onboard ship. Although not a snob, I was concerned about sustaining long periods at sea with an obviously rough and ready deck crowd. Secretly, I had felt there might well be something of a struggle ahead. The advice about cadet training was therefore very much worth further investigation so, working on the not unreasonable principle that 'a word to the wise is sufficient', I studied carefully the booklet about navigating officer cadet entry he gave me, which included a list of nautical colleges.

To say my enthusiasm was fired put things very mildly and I rushed home from work to inform Dad and Mum about these latest developments. My father, with perhaps an inevitable eye on less romantic and far more prosaic aspects of life, asked about the costs – even assuming my acceptance. I pointed out the brochure stated the Local Education Authority would supply a training grant to cover all aspects. Mum, predictably, enquired about the idea of studying for the five ordinary subjects and remaining in the office; uttered, it must be said, in a recognisable mood of her own last-ditch stand hopelessness.

I killed that one stone dead by telling her how, having been in the office a couple of months and continually seeing and hearing reports of the movements of their thirty liners and cargo ships, I was adamant working ashore was really not for me. I think such a firm response conveyed to them both a very 'positive negative' – a phrase I felt my ex-English master would have thoroughly enjoyed.

Carefully we studied the booklet and that night I sent a letter to the principal of Keddleston Navigation School. Within a couple of days, we received a prospectus and application form. Events were becoming interesting. My eye was captured immediately by a paragraph in the accompanying college reply. This stated clearly:

'Applicants not possessing formal academic qualifications can nevertheless be considered for potential navigating officer-cadet entry. They may normally be offered a place on our one-year course but, in special circumstances, *might* be accepted for the three-month accelerated course. In the latter case, they have to follow an extremely strict selection procedure.'

I focused on this immediately and told father earnestly how much I should really like to have a stab at the latter option. His reaction was whole-heartedly supportive as he wisely suggested a covering letter to the college, advising my background and asking specifically what was meant by 'special circumstances', would lead them to indicate the best way forward.

In view of the distance, the information continued, I would have to take an initial battery of selection tests, including English, mathematics and physics, lasting an entire morning, after asking permission for these to be supervised by my last school. The nautical college would send the test booklets directly to them once the application form had been processed and references pursued.

I was quite aghast after reading this part of the letter. It would mean writing to my headmaster asking permission for his school to supervise the tests. It seemed a 'bit of a cheek perhaps', as Dad said. Two thoughts, therefore, simultaneously crossed my mind: the necessity of coping with the humiliation of contacting them, although this was not such a horror as the second, concerning the action which could be taken if, remembering the way I left them, they refused to help. Allowing this notion to run its mental course led to my decision that, in this latter event, I would enquire if the things could be taken at Keddleston; draw some pocket money and travel at my own expense, going back again later if called for the second stage interview. Encouraged by putting that thought to bed, I continued to read, learning:

'You will also have to send a preliminary Shipping Federation (Officers) medical report, on a pro-forma provided, and take also the Board of Trade (Marine) Eyesight Test.'

The letter offered information concerning these previously unheard of documents and how they could be obtained. Assuming all was well, the college would call me for a series of specialised aptitude tests and an interview with the Captain-Superintendent, to complete processing my application. They assured me free overnight accommodation would be available. My parents clearly shared my view that things were moving at an alarming rate through a process apparently both efficient and thorough.

Parental reactions were becoming interesting in other ways. Father was again quietly bemused by the various directions matters were taking, but readily counter-signed the form, whilst Mother was quietly worrying (a lot can be transmitted in occasional glances). Pensively, I wrote to my former school about my plans, bluntly asked for a reference to be sent and requested permission to use their premises for the tests. I remember, against all the Christian tenets in which I had been brought up, crossing my fingers and kissing the sealed letter on its way.

Their response was agreeably cordial, but they did remind me, very gently, that a certain book cost 'appeared outstanding'. There was no suggestion of course that this should be paid, but by now I was beginning to discover how things worked in varying adult environments, so sent a cheque, along with (somewhat sardonically) my thanks.

The day of my selection process and interview soon arrived. First impressions invariably possess their own importance, if not always charm, for as the train swerved gently from the main line to a secondary track, curving alongside the southern bank of a river estuary, I caught a distant sighting of the navigation school. My glance focused on a tall, distinctive set of white flag masts, with indistinguishable blobs flying in the breeze. These contrasted strongly with the background variety of brown-red buildings, black and green hues of trees and a stretch of overgrown fields and hedgerows.

The complex seemed rambling. It was situated inland, quite a few miles from the water, but with an unimpeded distant northward view of the river. To me, the college appeared a romantic setting overlooking the mud-flats, amidst rustic woods, shrubs and bushes. It had a quietly nautical air, which (I was to find) varied considerably from the hectic life-style within. I noticed also an array of waders and herring gulls digging in the mud, undisturbed by the proximity of the passing train.

Everything proceeded smoothly and my impressions of the set-up proved favourable. I was kindly received, enjoyed a substantial supper and spent a comfortable overnight stay in the cadets' guest-room. I was totally relaxed whilst taking a battery of aptitude tests the following morning (in fact, quite enjoyed doing them). After lunch, I was shown into the office of Captain Mobbs, the Superintendent of the nautical college – or 'the Boss' as he was colloquially (if not very originally) known – and seated opposite his large desk for that all-important, in fact vital, interview.

Things began rather disconcertingly. I caught sight of my school reference across the desk and, not very sensibly but overcome with a burning desire to know what they had said about me, could not resist reading the thing upside down across the desk. My action was noticed and, to my chagrin, the ensuing conversation remains embedded in my memory.

"You know, Caridia, or perhaps you do not," the great man had explained, simultaneously moving the offending document from my line of vision. "All references are strictly confidential; otherwise we should willingly allow you to read it, without you endeavouring to give yourself astigmatism. A disastrous affliction, I might add, for any potential navigating officer – let alone an embryo cadet."

"Pardon, Sir?" came my query, horrified at being detected, and needing time to think.

"Perhaps I should add deafness to your eyesight problem," came his response with, it should be added, far more promptness than I had shown. "But I notice your medical report states you are perfectly sound…?" His voice tailed off in a mystified questioning tone, as he leafed myopically through my application file, apparently disbelieving what was written.

He glanced across the desk, and followed his observations with an open grin, thus defusing the situation and letting me off the hook. I was grateful for that action and suspected it represented a case of authority taking the initiative to practice its own version of gentle teasing, with me – justifiably – on the receiving end.

There was only one thing left to do. I caved-in, admitted myself beaten and apologised, having the grace to blush ashamedly. My grammar school, surprisingly – considering the circumstances – had been strongly supportive. My progress there had apparently been extremely promising and I learnt of their disappointment at my decision to leave earlier than originally planned upon initially joining them.

Very close questioning followed concerning my reasons, not only for breaking my education before the age of eighteen, but why I had left at fifteen without even waiting the extra year to take 'O' levels. Shyly and diffidently, I explained about the bullying and stolen book, gaining confidence from reading something indefinable in Captain Mobbs' attentive expression.

As it happened, my misdemeanour could not have proved too detrimental for, on leaving the interview, I noticed a twinkle in his eye as he called in his secretary to direct me to the waiting room, whilst he presumably reflected on my application. I occupied my thoughts by thinking back to the college parade glimpsed whilst having breakfast. The cadets had looked extremely smart and well disciplined as they responded to barked commands from divisional officers. It was easy to visualise myself amongst their ranks – if *only* I could do well – with so many odds against me.

Daily parade at the college (courtesy Southampton Institute Warsash Maritime Centre).

My reverie was broken by the secretary's voice calling me back into the inner sanctum.

"Right, Caridia," the Superintendent commenced. "I'll put you out of your misery. I really do think you should remain at school for 'A' levels, but that is your decision. So far as I am concerned, having discussed your papers with my Deputy, I am delighted to offer you a place on our short, three-month, navigating officer cadet training course and, if you wish to accept, then we shall expect you here next term – after Easter. I'll write to your parents, confirming both our advice and this decision."

I felt an indescribable raft of emotions sweep over me; relief, yes, but mixed with apprehension and a sense of having taken an irrevocable step along an unknown path. I recall my thoughts as we shook hands and, leaving his office, noticed a photograph of a large tanker on the study wall which nervousness had prevented my seeing before – presumably it was a ship upon which Captain Mobbs had served.

Metaphorically at least, I hugged myself with excitement on the train home. Leaning out of the window, glancing backwards, I caught again that distant glimpse through thick train smoke, as the college disappeared from my line of vision. My thoughts remained in an excited turmoil, knowing next time this view appeared, I would be on my way to join as a potential officer-cadet.

Relating events to my parents, words tumbled out in a wave of infectious enthusiasm, although I suspected their obvious pleasure on my behalf was tinged with varying unspoken thoughts.

My departmental manager at the shipping company sounded genuinely sorry – yet pleased for me – as he complimented me on my efforts during the very short time I had been employed by them. He did express his rueful thought that I might have stayed a little longer. My favourite Chief Marine Superintendent however was clearly delighted at my news; he asked me to keep in touch, hinting that his Company might one day change its officer recruitment policy.

Lying snugly in bed on the evening prior to leaving home, with suitcases packed ready for departure, my thoughts churned over the previous few months. Events had moved so quickly, I had not really had time to come to terms with a situation not foreseen even a few months previously. Now the moment of reckoning loomed over the immediate horizon my outward self-assurance was paper thin. I was aware, getting up next day, of a variety of emotions – foremost of which was an ever present sense of apprehension.

For the initial step in the journey, I was accompanied by my parents. They wanted to see me launched (as Dad said, with re-assuring dry humour) and would travel from my home in south London, seeing me off on the main-line train.

The immediate journey was uneventful, apart from an incident which happened when we arrived at Charing Cross, prior to catching the tube for the main line

London terminus. There was suddenly a muffled crash and, in a flurry of movement and luggage, Dad fell over his feet and landed in a heap at the bottom of the steps leading to the underground platform. I raced to his assistance. Mum, who was very much preoccupied with her son venturing towards a new career very much away from home and her abiding influence appeared to focus only slowly on the occurrence. As it happened, he had fallen just two steps and there was no damage. Finding him still in one piece, I smiled my thanks to the man who had helped father up and was now, impatiently, holding the offending suitcase. The remainder of this significant journey to the concourse was made without further mishap, but I wondered if the tumble was the result of Dad also being moved by events of the moment? A question best perhaps left unasked.

Amongst the station bustle, three other boys were visible at the terminus. I judged by their ages, luggage, lost looks, and embarrassment over equally fond parental farewells, they were also Keddleston bound. I joined them as they crossed the ticket barrier and, as a group, we settled into a single compartment of the train carriage, mutually introducing ourselves. Working on the theory of safety in numbers, comfort was obtained from the others' presence. Our three hour journey passed rapidly but, even whilst I conversed animatedly with them, I detected evidence of their barely controlled nervousness.

My rambling thoughts crystallised intermittently as the scenery flashed by. I was totally committed now and resolved to make the most of things, although aware it might prove the sea was not to be for me after all. Certainly I would give it everything before taking the major decision of bailing out. It was impossible for me even to visualise spending the remainder of my life in that office, especially having seen the − I tried to analyse − respectability almost, of those who had spent thirty years or more there, however kind they were to me.

An air of relaxed joviality from the driver of the school bus meeting our train was comforting as, after a short drive, he deposited us in the courtyard immediately opposite the administration block. An immaculately uniformed duty officer opened the door and urged us into the office. His authoritative air, yet warmly welcoming smile, helped put our troubled minds to rest.

Following general admittance procedures, my travelling companions and I were immediately separated into different Watches, the 'family unit' of the school structure. Other than occasional meetings at musters and meal-times we saw very little of each other for the remainder of the course, making a mockery of our fervent vows, during the train journey, of sticking together for mutual support.

The collection of huts comprising our cadet accommodation was across the parade ground, whose towering white masts I had seen from my train. Access was by a gate entrance, in one side of a quadrangle holding tutors' accommodation and studies, with the administration offices and some classrooms forming the three other sides. Anson Watch was easily found.

An openly engaging smile and warm relaxed welcome introduced me to Peter Dathan. I caught sight behind him of two other members of Anson, 'Ginger' Fulbright and Jeremy Woodley. They both came over and we chatted generally about the places from which we had travelled, sharing casual pleasantries to break the ice. Other cadets gradually joined the cabin and general conversation until we were twelve in number and all of the made-up single-tiered bunks had been taken.

My first impressions of the Nissen style hut were not over impressive. I was far from enamoured of its Spartan appearance – with stark shortage of carpets, limited heating and permanently open windows. Our gear was stowed in a battered array of tall, metal bunk-side lockers, whilst the pungent aroma of polish and antiseptic floor wash stood out amongst other novel smells. The six unmade bunks in the hut indicated that our Watch at least was to be under manned. I wondered whether or not this might have had some bearing on the rapidity of my entrance procedure.

Amongst mutual fencing and weighing-up, we seemed to be settling into a friendly enough group, but already I was making some reservations personality-wise concerning Woodley. It was nothing really definite – more a vague sense of unease that was as negative as the feelings reciprocated between Dathan, myself and the others, seemed positive. Wisely, I decided to allow time to make the final decision.

By the time we had assembled, our Watch officer, Second Mate Fred Mitcham entered and, sitting casually on the end of my bunk, introduced himself and told us about the College rules, procedures and routines; meal arrangements and other essentials regarding our course. He explained that the original building, whose arch we had come through on the bus, used to be Trinity House headquarters for this area of the coast and extra Nissen huts had been added when the site was developed into a Second World War Royal Naval training camp. These formed the basis of the college Watch system and, in deference to the former function, each was named after a famous admiral. Tradition had been maintained by offering us cadets the option of applying to join the Royal Naval Reserve during our training which was strongly recommended to us, we thought rather lamely, as 'a good thing'. Mr. Mitcham finished by appointing Fulbright to be our Watch leader and delegating to him the task of drawing a roster for us to undertake a weekly round of cleaning duties on a daily basis. Already we were not over-enamoured by Mr. Mitcham.

Going over later to the mess hall, I felt quite relaxed about things, and guessed that probably another fifty youngsters contributed towards the murmur of voices which met our Watch as we joined others assembled in the mess. I caught fragmentary sight of only one of my travelling companions. We were still in civvies and collectively constituted the three-month 'short' course new entries for this particular term. There were additionally a number of uniformed regular cadets well established on the one-year course. Had I failed my specialised entrance tests, a place on this longer course might have been offered me the following September, but I was heartily glad I had not. Training for all commenced the following Monday.

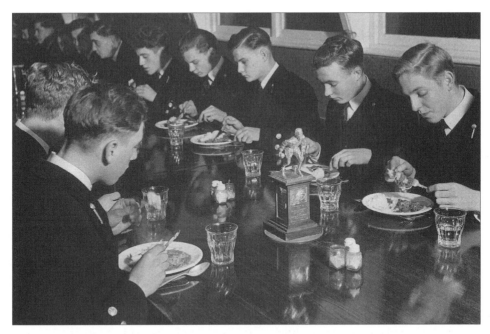

Formal dinner with table silver (courtesy Southampton Institute Warsash Maritime Centre).

We sat at long polished wooden tables and tucked into a well-cooked and plentiful supper. Meal-times were to prove grand and quite civilised – with even silver centre-pieces on formal occasions. At this our initial meal, however, it was more relaxed but, afterwards, once the Captain-Superintendent had given his welcoming address, I received the first of many minor shocks that were to come my way. We were dismissed and told to re-assemble in PE shorts and join one of five queues in the main hall. As directed, we then received a medical examination from a team of local colleagues who had joined the college doctor. For me, it was the very first time I had stood publicly naked, with shorts around my ankles, and proved mildly disconcerting.

Everything proved rather difficult over the first few days and I soon found myself explaining very hesitatingly to Peter, after taking my courage in both hands, that I was feeling homesick. It was my first time away from parents and family; my mind was bedevilled with memories of ministrations from a certain set of school bullies, amidst uncertainties regarding my current situation. Peter's response was warmly supporting. He explained how he had been sent away to boarding school at just three years of age, due to his father's work as export director for a large company in the Far East. In some respects, boarding had proved good training for this stage of his life, because our Watch system was not too dissimilar from the boarding house set-up to which he had been accustomed in public school. He invited me, hesitatingly, to discuss things with him and his tone encouraged sufficient humility for me to relate the unexpected intensity of my feelings. I explained it was not only receiving and writing letters home that triggered the most vicious attacks, but small apparently insignificant things, such as the playing of a familiar tune on the radio, or smelling rubbish being burned by a grounds man – subtle things which slipped, like a knife, under my guard.

His advice was sensible and sensitive as he suggested I should keep as busy as possible and always try to be with other people. He promised to help where he could and suggested it might be unwise to mention anything to the others as this might lead to a bit of unnecessary teasing. True to his promise, Peter, an older and much more experienced lad proved a tower of strength during those early days, cementing a friendship that was to last fragmentarily, in the way of seafaring life, for many years.

I wisely took advantage of the novelty of never being on my own – of having people around virtually all of the time, and made extra efforts to mingle with other cadets and create friendships as widely as the college restrictions of the almost fetish observance of Watch-life insularity permitted. I suspected, from their demeanour, that others were suffering equally quietly and possibly as painfully.

Homesickness did take its toll however when a cadet from Nelson left, after eleven days residence, to return home. This was despite genuine efforts by the staff and, to give them their due, encouragement from his fellow Watch cadets to remain. My first reaction on hearing this was to consider how very fortunate I had been by meeting, in Anson, someone as sensitively supportive as Dathan. Guessing that I might well have survived on my own, my lack of confidence made me glad I did not have to put things to the test.

I was to find, after that first evening, nudity proved totally natural and soon became a matter of course – upon realising my body was little different to that of fellow cadets. I found the variety of male human nakedness was quite staggering really, not having given over much thought to this aspect of development. Each day commenced with us rushing into the icy water of showers or running a return trip of what seemed like miles to the river tributary for an equally freezing swim. I soon became used to these novel ideas, but could never really work up much enthusiasm for the cold dunking into icy water.

True to his role as Watch leader, Fulbright was most vociferous of our morning ritual and commented, frequently, that it took his mind off sex for all of at least ten minutes. I thought ruefully, dressing rapidly and thankfully into my comfortably warm blue working gear, that his comment was all too appropriate. As the course continued I soon cottoned on, and followed the example of other cadets by staying as much out of the shower as possible, putting only head and shoulders into the stream, whilst pretending, to the supervising duty officer, thorough enjoyment of the experience. Occasionally, of course, boys were sometimes caught out and had then to endure prolonged supervised drenching after the others had finished. In this respect we looked forward to those days when Fred was there for, as Woodley announced – with predictable accuracy – our esteemed Watch officer was pretty easy to fool.

Breakfast followed this rude awakening, after which quarters were cleaned, and at eight hundred precisely, the daily parade commenced. We cadets stood to attention – or, at least initially what passed for attention – as two flags were hoisted; the Blue Ensign, defaced with the college coat of arms, and a training flag. The latter was not hoisted on days following those when training conditions were defaulted. This proved a source of much consternation to the staff and guaranteed a communal rocket to all, administered by the Boss.

It was more an element of cynical amusement to us cadets who, not unnaturally, were far more interested in the reasons *why* conditions had been broken. Usually these occurred when a cadet had been caught illicitly smoking or drinking alcohol; although there were other instances, such as the occasion when the tuck-shop was breached one dark night and the entire stock removed. The first Peter and I knew about this was when a cadet from Hood came into our hut lavishly distributing a generous portion of the spoils on a purely 'no questions asked' basis. Rigorous staff investigations failed to find the culprits and resulted in closure of the shop for a couple of days.

A personal uniform inspection followed during which, once I had been passed, my thoughts wandered happily around our professional academic studies. The process invariably ended abruptly as we were called to attention, and a quick side-kick on the ankle from Dathan invariably brought me back to realms of reality. On alternate days the Bosun, an ex-Royal Naval chief petty officer, took the combined school for drill sessions. Some days, we remained on the parade ground for short sessions, practising semaphore with hand held flags.

Practical semaphore (Crown copyright/MOD).

Following dismissal, a varied diet of lectures and impromptu tests took up the remainder of our weekday and (most) Saturday mornings. These covered maths, navigational theory, seamanship, signals, ship construction and associated maritime matters. Tuition was intermingled with swimming instruction, and the inevitable PE and sports (with which I was not over enamoured). We were allowed a thirty-minute interval for coffee and biscuits, followed by two more classroom sessions. A welcome one-hour lunch break, at thirteen hundred hours, led into afternoon practical work spent usually on seamanship and boating (which I found very interesting and therefore loved).

Launching cutters on a Saturday (courtesy Southampton Institute Warsash Maritime Centre).

We Ansonites mixed with short-course cadets from other Watches (or 'shorties' as we were ambiguously known to the longer serving cadets) for all training – and quite a varied bunch we turned out to be. I was not only the youngest but, it transpired, the only entrant without academic qualifications. This did not seem to matter to my fellow cadets but made me, I quickly noted, the recipient of occasional questioning looks from instructors during classroom lessons. A penetrating glance often came my way when we were asked if things had been understood and whether or not we had any questions.

Afternoons spent sailing a cutter made a welcome break from classroom teaching (courtesy Southampton Institute Warsash Maritime Centre).

Overtures of friendship towards Woodley – try as I might – always seemed fated to disaster, thwarted largely by the superior attitude he displayed towards any younger boys. He had been a police cadet for a while – not that this excused his extreme arrogance – although his career change was never satisfactorily explained. Dathan probably put his finger close to the reason, on an occasion when his target was absent, by pointing out how Woodley's colleagues and superiors had probably just became fed-up with his obnoxious manner towards people – as well as his capacity for subtle stirring; a remark which was received with varying comments of approbation.

Other boys had had different jobs for varying periods, with a few entering directly from a range of grammar and independent schools. Some even had 'A' levels in maths and sciences. Overall, we were a very mixed lot, with 'all sorts and conditions' of boys – as the church Litany so aptly described the human condition.

Fulbright had 'A' levels and worked previously as a trainee surveyor – work he found 'boring beyond description'. He was a strange mixture; electing to clean the toilet part of our block himself for a double weekly stint, yet enforcing objections to his leadership with a good clout, rather than charm. He ignored me in the main, largely because of my age, but more probably because I did what he told me, so causing few problems.

In class, I enjoyed an unexpected aptitude for navigational theory and was able to respond quickly and accurately to solving problems. This was possibly due to a 'well developed ability in the visualising of spatial concepts', as the result to one of my entrance tests had stated, in a language then quite outside my understanding – even if not my eyesight. I was a bit nosy, I suppose, and never lost any opportunity to see comments lurking in official files unwisely left open on unguarded desks.

My progress on other practical aspects of seamanship was not quite so hot. Fair enough, I was competently proficient on things like sailing, compass work and steering the college's motor cruisers, but knots and splicing were definitely not my forte. In fact, the verdict delivered after a frustrating personal tuition session by Bosun Elvett, the college's long-suffering seamanship and drill instructor, was that I had 'two left hands and two right feet'. It was a remark which might well have held for both areas of my instruction with him. Much of the practical work was helpful and quite serious, but learning to climb a rope ladder in preparation for a task frequently undertaken at sea – we were told – was also quite amusing.

It was interesting to watch personalities emerge both from staff and cadets. Our Watch officer, described by Greerson as 'a right secret plonky', soon earned his nickname, 'Boozy Fred'. Although not over blatant, he occasionally smelled distinctly of stale beer and some afternoons after lunch was decidedly unsteady on his feet. He was the perfect target for Kelly's god-given talent for imitation, which had us in fits, even when we ourselves were on the receiving end. It was universally agreed amongst us that Kelly was humorous, but fortunately lacking entirely in malice. Apart from the boat work team, the staff were all ex-Master Mariners and professionally extremely good. They knew their subjects, both theoretically and from the hard school of experience, and were (excluding our *bete noir*) efficient approachable teachers, taking genuine interest in the progress of their cadets. I was not over impressed by the fates landing us with Fred. He had early on taken a distinct dislike to me which Peter, again with perspicacity, probably attributed to my being the only cadet without 'O' levels coming in on the College's specialised entry conditions – something with which he found difficulty.

Woodley, inevitably perhaps, soon fell foul of many of the instructors simply by 'winding-them up' and even occasionally being downright rude. He was up for frequent punishment and finally – by the beginning of only the third week – achieved the accolade of being called before 'the Boss'. Captain Mobbs took a strictly firm line and dealt with him in a 'seamanlike' manner. He was officially cautioned for insolence, told point blank and given notice in writing that he would be sent home immediately following the next incident. Unwisely, he left the letter on his bunk, which Fulbright read. We knew, from his pale face when he rejoined class, something of momentous occasion had happened. Woodley was clearly shaken and took the warning to heart, even going to the other extreme and 'toadying' to the officers, not that this passed without their noticing. I suspected his latest rocket went really deeply, especially after the police fiasco.

A couple of boys from our term were dismissed – one who proved the fallibility of college entrance exams by repeatedly failing weekly maths, physics and navigation tests – and another, who was caught stealing from a fellow cadet's personal locker by an unexpected chance appearance of his Divisional Officer. The first was quietly but firmly sent home (although offered a place on the next one-year course), whilst the latter was named and so used by the authorities as an example deterring others. Our training conditions flag certainly failed to see the light of that particular dawn.

Evenings were taken up with written tests and, for variety, a number of films on navigation and seamanship. One topic remembered particularly vividly was entitled: *Interaction between Ships*. It was presented by an old Scots pilot and showed a range of deep-sea craft, illustrating dramatically the effects of tankers surging at their moorings, and dangers inherent when overtaking (or being overtaken by) other vessels too quickly and closely. We amused ourselves for weeks afterwards imitating his broad accents and comments, so that our huts rebounded with mock Celtic cries, interspersed with the Goons' *Ying Tong* song which we had adopted as our Watch anthem. I gained considerable kudos from my colleagues by inventing a series of magnificently obscene words to the tune aimed at 'our Fred'.

Night antics were interesting, to put things mildly, once the duty officer had completed rounds. I often thought that perhaps the college should have reversed the day's shower routine. Often Dathan and I looked and listened to an amazing repertoire of crude jokes, stories, banter and, as the term progressed, quite unrestrained activity. Coming from sheltered backgrounds (Peter had been at a cathedral choir school) we were both fairly unworldly and comparatively innocent amidst this male sexual aggression.

Woodley was as randy as anything (but so were Peter and I – even if considerably more subtle). It was inevitable that he was well to the fore, as he exuded a fervour that possibly boded ill for the Merchant Navy and doubtless proved an unlamented loss to the Liverpool constabulary, for which he had been bound. Many a time we lay there as Woodley and Fulbright, in particular, outdid each other regaling the rest of us with tales of girl-friends and what passed for 'a good evening's fun'. Few details were spared and, indeed, no stone left unturned in the cess-pits which constituted their minds. I wondered periodically what my mother would have made of it all. Luckily Dathan and I were largely left out of things, and our thoughts remained very much our own. It was certainly an aspect of my education that had not appeared in the college prospectus.

I often wondered if the authorities might have been somewhere to blame. I recognised ours was a very intensive course, needing tuition on most evenings, and understood, by virtue of our ages, they had a measure of responsibility for us. It was possibly better for boys attending Keddleston over the whole academic year; they were allowed out to meet girls on occasional evenings – and have weekend parental visits. We were granted occasional leave for shopping during the last two instructional periods on a Saturday morning. Our weekends were a mixture of events, sometimes consisting of games during the afternoon, with instruction in the evenings, and other times on maintenance duties around the college. We tidied gardens, creosoted fences, painted anything and everything that stood still, and frequently climbed onto the roof of Nissen huts applying pitch and tarpaulin to countless leaks. For variety, we also took out sailing cutters and rowing boats.

Waterproofing a Nissen hut – regular Saturday afternoon employment
(courtesy Southampton Institute Warsash Maritime Centre).

Learning to row on the lake (courtesy Southampton Institute Warsash Maritime Centre).

Every third weekend we went with other Watches to follow 'double field days'. Peter told me the origin of the expression lay in public school Combined Cadet Force activities when, for one day each term, the various Sections had a day off lessons to follow military pursuits. According to him the RN went up mountains; the Army took to the water, whilst the RAF went pot-holing. Becoming more accustomed to his dry sense of humour by this time, I merely grinned, but did wonder. We spent Saturday night in a couple of Nissen huts, about twenty or so miles from college, with two or three divisional officers, depending on the number of Watches away. These proved quite strenuous, but fun weekends (notwithstanding Fred), following what the College euphemistically termed 'adventure training'. We climbed extremely steep hills that, to my mind, bordered on small mountains. Groups also went route marching using map and compass. These proved quite hilarious as we trainee navigators managed to get ourselves hopelessly lost in and around the jungles and lakes of Keddleston's outlying district. Fred really laboured on these activities, much to our delight and more than *sotto voce* comments. This was the only chance open to us of getting our own back on him; his unpopularity being universal. He was clearly well out of condition – needing what Fulton described as 'a pack of Bob Martin's conditioner every day, mixed with his booze'. On a couple of occasions we actually managed to lose him (unfortunately not permanently) enjoying his eventual return; sweaty, angry and completely tired. It was a matter of conjecture just how the College, and his colleagues for that matter, managed to put up with him – 'ours not to reason why', but that did not prevent us having our own opinions.

Rock climbing weekend, in theory preparation for the climbing of ships' masts
(courtesy Shell IT&S).

Of course, the glory of weekends away meant that we missed Sunday Divisions and Church Parade. This was the College's 'Big Moment' when our officers really went to town with inspections and drills. Everything was inspected – from the heads adjoining our huts, through a minute examination of the hut itself, to our good selves on the parade ground. The Boss led his entourage, consisting of the Deputy Superintendent and respective Divisional Officer, into the huts where we were called to attention by our senior cadet. Anything arousing the ire of these august personages was written in a log book carried by the deputy, and followed by a blistering delivered to us from Fred, sometimes through the senior cadet. As 'shorties' we got away with things considerably easier than our colleagues on the one year course. They were blessed (or cursed) with a course cadet captain, two deputies, and the whole paraphernalia of what Woodley (and for once we were in universal agreement) adroitly called 'bull-dust'. It was not too bad, but I questioned quietly the necessity of a system reminding me vaguely of school prefects. The college Chaplain came in to conduct a short service. The whole procedure took most of the morning but, once we had changed into unfamiliar civvies, the remainder of our day was free.

There was not a great deal for us to do during these afternoons and evenings. Cinema and a meal 'ashore' proved customary, with occasional parental visits – not that my Mum and Dad could travel the distance involved – but I was invited out with parents of other cadets, making an enjoyable change in routine. Some boys, who had fallen foul of the system during the week, found themselves 'turned-to' for extra duties which consisted mainly of 'litter and tidy-up squads' under the supervision of the Bosun. I received a two-hour stint for 'slovenly attitude' – having been a little slow on the up-take during a parade – not exactly the worlds' eighth deadly sin.

I did however experience one 'occasion of monumental achievement' that came quite out of the blue and proved both exciting and un-nerving. It certainly raised me to elevated heights with my fellow cadets – especially after lights-out. I was in the boat-shed loft looking for a box of Inglefield clips that were 'up there somewhere' and needed next day for splicing onto halyards facilitating the attachment of signal flags. Returning to college after afternoon boating was always a frantic time. The coach was hired and the driver invariably in a rush to make the twenty minute college journey and return to his base before setting out to collect children from local schools and take them to outlying district villages.

With fifty-plus cadets piling into the bus it was very easy for one to be missed as, indeed, had periodically happened before. The staff packed themselves into one car. Anyway, engrossed in my task amongst the shackles, blocks, varnish and wires; drinking in the tarred-oily-rope smell, (and most certainly not 'day-dreaming', as later accused by Fred), I heard the coach engine start. By the time the ladder had been negotiated and I was outside, it had pulled away. I sought out the seamanship instructor who lived with his family on site and looked after security. Receiving his mild rocket, a lengthy walk from boat-yard to college appeared my lot. Unwisely, I decided to take a short cut through the 'red-light' district – very much a 'prohibited zone' – thus enabling me to make it back to College in time for supper.

I was nearly out of danger when the voice of a woman called to me from a nearby house and asked the time. Fatally stopping and telling her, using our customary twenty-four hour clock, led her to question if I were from the Navigation school. Approaching her, I answered in the affirmative and noticed she was looking at me a bit oddly. Being over made-up, which did not do much for me, and wearing a tight skirt and blouse, her figure was dramatised as much as emphasised. Frankly, she looked revolting.

The discourse continued with her comment that I seemed very young to be going away in the Merchant Navy, which led me to tell (yes, somewhat proudly) of my training to be a navigating officer cadet. This information was quickly absorbed, but I suspected her mind was on other things. These were soon discovered, for she paused and enquired directly if I had ever been with a woman. My astonishment was absolute and my mouth suddenly went very dry. Her sally was a far cry from conversations usually enjoyed with older ladies, during social evenings at home, or at the vicarage tea party. The shock left my mind totally blank with not the slightest idea how to react or what to say.

Reaching out her hand she stroked my face, admiring what was described as 'my lovely smooth cheeks and slender body', and telling me what a 'nice looking lad I was' – one very obviously 'ready for action', as it was termed. I stood there aghast, unclear whether her strong Northern accent had been understood correctly. In my experience, women simply did not know the words she used. Involuntarily, I started to shake like a leaf and wondered how to escape this situation.

Suddenly, she took my hand and put it on her breasts, at the same time placing her hand in between my legs, fondling me gently. Nobody had ever touched there before and my knees buckled in excitable shock. I almost heard my heart pounding wildly and shot back in horror.

"I've gooott tttoo-oo get bacc-cck for supp-pper", I finally managed to stammer out of a dry mouth and, pulling myself away from her grasp, ran with bated breath down the street, to the sound of her raucous laugh echoing in my ears.

Racing back to the college, I reported to the office, and explained my late arrival to Fred, deciding it might be wise to leave interim events unrelated. I blessed the guardian angel that led me to keep my mouth firmly shut. Any officer, other than him, might have been sufficiently perceptive to tell by my demeanour that something of a shock had happened to me, but Fred was Fred.

I was not so reluctant in telling Peter what had happened. Of course, without suspecting his presence, Woodley just had to be listening behind his open locker door. Needless to say, he wasted no time in telling the others so, after lights out that night, I was forced to relate events repeatedly and accept the ensuing barrage. Strangely enough, no-one actually blamed me for running away which led me to think they were perhaps not as worldly as they liked to give the impression. I was popular in a quiet sort of way, but this incident gave me enhanced status in the eyes of my fellow cadets. Peter was full of admiration and unbridled envy, whilst Fulbright asserted (with total conviction) that he also might miss the bus the following day.

Four weeks into the course all cadets were summoned individually for an interview with their respective watch officer. We had many important issues to discuss including progress, future career and, more specifically, decisions made about joining the Royal Naval Reserve and selecting and applying to a shipping company. The college had an excellent reputation within the marine industry and, in recent years, no cadets who still wanted to go away to sea had been unsuccessful in finding a berth.

My interview was not with Fred, as he was 'indisposed' for a reason that was never fully explained by the college. We cadets, of course, retained our own speculations – ones that probably came near the truth. As it happened, I was interviewed by Second Mate Dearnley, the Watch Officer of Beresford. He had accompanied us on some expedition weekends and, unlike Fred, was by nature friendly and supportive. He had often chatted with me as we hiked or were in the boats, and I suspected knew something of the attitude which my esteemed DO held towards me. Anyway, he complimented me on the solid progress being made with my studies, adding that my practical boat work also was very commendable, whilst my behaviour had led to few complaints from any source.

His unreserved enthusiasm led me to wonder just how much the staff really knew about what went on outside classroom and instruction times. I was called back to reality by hearing him asking if I was still listening to him: 'appearing lost in a world of my own'. I assured him – as convincingly as possible – of my undivided attention, pointing out that I knew a number of important decisions had to be made at this interview. He shot me a look that was a little suspicious, and picked up his thread of exploring my problems in practical rope work – emphasising especially that my splicing and knots were really quite weak, and that too many staff had complained of my inattention on occasions.

Assuming the best method of defence to be attack, I plunged into an explanation which focused on the weak rope work; telling about my efforts during spare moments to improve things, and how Dathan had been assisting. I explained that whilst the theory was known, putting this into practice caused things to 'go a bit wonky'; I then requested his suggestions as to how the situation might be improved.

Faced with such a frantically breathless barrage, the officer plunged into ideas and suggestions intended to guide my 'two right hands and left feet'. In doing so he lost track momentarily of the other issue which was, of course, my intention. I quickly rushed into the conversation, before that rather more delicate strand could be retrieved for extra airing by thanking him for his advice, and telling him of my intention to apply to the Ellerton Lines as a deck cadet.

His response was one of amazement. He pointed out this Company was a really top British shipping line and, faltering a bit, stated he did not wish to discourage me, but it would not be worth my while even contacting Ellertons as their cadets were recruited only from public schools. They insisted additionally on at least six subjects with 'B' grades, including mathematics, English, physics, geography, a foreign language and any other one, as absolute minimum. In fact, he assured me, most of their cadets possessed around eight or nine passes, whilst some held 'A' levels.

Mr Dearnley paused for breath and looked at me pensively, before pointing out my own background of an incomplete grammar school course with, as a result, no formal educational qualifications. Noticing this was being taken quite well, the suggestion followed that applying to some general trading companies, who were more open to considering cadets not so highly qualified, might be more realistic. I agreed that what he said was true but, with all the stubborn perversity of persistent youth, stated my wish to have a stab at applying anyway, allowing them to tell me if I was not up to standard. Thus it was my completed college application form was despatched to the Ellerton Lines' Steamship Group and, to everyone's astonishment (not the least my own), I was called for interview.

In view of the exceptional circumstances a now safely returned and rejuvenated Fred (euphemism for 'dried-out', we wondered) called me into his office. He was really quite offensive and explained that if he had conducted my interview I most definitely would not have applied to Ellertons. He told me how he had sailed with them as a Chief Officer, and in his opinion, they were not really my sort of Company.

I maintained a very strong silence. There was no point in telling him that, under those circumstances, my approach would have been 'over his head' directly to the Boss. I did wonder, if they had employed him, whether I wanted to sail with them after all. He called me back to reality by telling me this was hardly the time to 'wander-off into space', causing me a simultaneous sense of *deja-vu*. I assured him (without a great deal of mutual conviction) how much he had my undivided attention. Gradually, as Fred rambled on, the thread emerged that Captain Mobbs wanted to see me 0900 next day.

My initial reaction was to wonder if the Boss had picked up vibrations regarding my red light district encounter (amongst a random selection of other rich possibilities) which I then dismissed as unlikely. My mind totally missed the main reason as, in answer to an obviously mystified query, Fred explained rather vindictively this interview had arisen from Ellerton's status and my application to them.

The next day, at the appointed time, I saw Captain Mobbs who, without preamble told me to be seated. He explained how, the previous day, a phone discussion with the Chief Marine Superintendent of Ellertons had confirmed that his personnel department wished me to go for interview in London the following Wednesday. He stated six cadets in all had been selected from Keddleston for interviews: three were going that same week, but Dathan, Gortley and I had been called the following

Wednesday, although that was 'by the by', as he said. It had been mentioned to ensure both parties travelled together under the same rail warrant. He smiled briefly before continuing with the main reason for asking me to see him. Although my application was unusual, he assured me that the College supported me and, indeed, had already had their say, but none of the staff – himself included – considered I could hold much hope of acceptance and should be prepared for disappointment. Placing both arms across his desk-top blotter, he mentioned the Chief Superintendent would chair my interview panel, and my ultimate acceptance would rely purely on the manner I performed before them.

His brows lightened and features softened as he offered an unexpected note of hope. He stressed that if the criterion of 'potential' was high amongst their selection procedures, then my application might just be in with a chance and advised me simply 'to be myself'. Then, in customary firm but pleasant tones, he stated how I took his best wishes with me. Noticing a somewhat longer than normal pause led me to assume he had finished with me, so I moved my chair as a preliminary to leaving, before being signalled to remain seated.

My naive view of interview procedures received an interesting input when the subject of joining the Royal Naval Reserve was mentioned. The Boss explained how Ellertons strongly supported Reserve training amongst their officers and would certainly applaud my enthusiasm by joining *before* I came to the college. This had been mentioned at my initial interview, so clearly my enterprising action had, for some reason, gone quite deeply with Captain Mobbs, leading him to temporise encouragement with a healthily reinforced side-swipe.

It was true I had submitted papers for the RNR. My motives however were not as enthusiastic as he assumed. I knew very little (and frankly cared even less) about Naval Reserves and my early application had been motivated more by material than training benefits. Each Cadet RNR was issued with a complete naval outfit from safety pin to weathered jacket. It included everything a well dressed (and some would say over dressed) mariner would be likely to need in the course of his seagoing career, plus a few optional extras rarely seen in the Merchant Navy, such as gaiters and a detachable starched wing collar. Coming from a quite poor background, the kit provision was a veritable wind-fall – a cornucopia even – which more than compensated for the modest training requirement of an initial two week course at the Britannia Royal Naval College, Dartmouth (which I eagerly anticipated) and fortnightly annual periods of sea-training aboard varied units of the Fleet. My provisional appearance before an Admiralty Interview Board, with the college's letter of acceptance behind me, was relatively straightforward. In fact, I had received my uniform just prior to joining navigation school, which had proved a very timely arrangement. I had still to complete the Dartmouth course, planned to take place later in the year following consultation with my eventual seagoing employers, and had to finish college fairly high on the pass list – having obtained their leaving certificates.

At Ellertons, I followed Gortley and then Dathan who were in for about twenty minutes each and I came out, my shirt soaked by nervous sweat, after almost three-quarters of an hour.

All six members of the panel 'had their go' as a number of extremely penetrating questions were posed. I was really put on the spot, following a number of gentle 'warmers' designed to put me at ease. Almost before taking my seat at the bottom of a T-shaped set of tables, the first probe enquired why I had selected Ellerton Lines as my first choice, in the face of so many other (strongly emphasised, but not too much) good companies offering deck officer cadetships. That one was easy. It seemed a pretty obvious question so I had thought constructively about my answer beforehand. Having also heard the other two discussing their responses, I had a rough idea of their answers (or, at least what they said they would say) and had carefully prepared my own version which, hopefully, would take a different slant.

I paused very slightly, giving the impression of considered thought – nothing like the psychological approach, I hoped (even before understanding remotely what that was) – and explained how the variety of shipping trades covered by the Group and number of ships in their fleet, would give me a better chance of learning a range of cargo loading, care and discharging procedures. Such experience would otherwise be unavailable to me and the enhanced knowledge would stand me in good stead for my Second Mate examinations.

That seemed to go well, after which the process became progressively more direct. A small bearded man at the end of the table, whom I found out later was a serving Master aboard one of Ellerton's passenger-cargo liners, asked me to explain which aspects of my course had been found most difficult. This had been put, after the easiest had been dealt with in quite a prolonged discussion on navigational theory. I had not been expecting that version to follow and it made me pause, genuinely this time, to think more deeply. From my two more major weaknesses, knots and splices seemed the obvious choice. After all, there had to be one 'most difficult' and truth seemed to be least threatening. It led to an exchange on the importance of such manual tasks to a deck officer.

The Chairman of the Board, the dreaded chief marine superintendent, then took up the cudgel by asking me to go over to a chart on the adjacent wall and give them the latitude and longitude of the light on the eastern mole of Keddleston harbour. Once I had found the thing, I swiftly read these off and he asked me then to explain the description of the light.

That was no problem, so I replied, "It has a characteristic of 'Iso.W.R.2 sec', which means a white sector and a red sector light: both on for two seconds, then off for two seconds. The 'W.9M.R.8M' indicates, on a clear dark night, the white is visible 9 miles and red visible for 8 miles. The height of the lantern is 37 feet above High Water Springs, with ranges of Red sector 242º to 285º; white sector 285º to 073º; red sector 073º to 113º."

"Is that white sector through north or south?"

"South, Sir," came my confident announcement. There was a pause, and I identified some mysteriously blank expressions facing me. Thinking quickly back over my quite complex answer, there appeared little fundamentally wrong.

"Caridia", came measured tones from the Chief Superintendent, looking at me sternly. "That's incorrect. Bearings of lights are true from seaward, you know."

The panel also looked at me, but with barely concealed smiles of interest, obviously wondering how I would extricate myself from this predicament.

"Clang, Sir," was my spontaneous reaction. The panel smiled indulgently and I detected some warmth coming in my direction.

"Yes. Clang, indeed," smiled the Super.

He rapidly followed his remark by asking how I thought my stay at Keddleston had influenced my development as a person – distinct from my professional studies.

I gulped as thoughts of 'extra-curricular activities' raced through my mind, and began very lamely whilst possible answers flew rapidly across my mind. In the end I plunged in by telling the Board that although still very young with many areas in which I had to develop, the Navigation School had helped me mature in a number of unexpected ways. I paused for breath, wondering what these were and how the hell to continue.

The panel stared – expectantly this time – watching me very obviously grabbing for straws. Inspiration finally came in the form of Fred so, with increasing confidence, I asserted that the greatest area in which I had developed was tolerance – tolerance of other cadets and some officers – by learning to accept views and opinions, and even actions previously different to my own.

The panel smiled benevolently, and looked at each other, clearly approving of the quickness of response I had managed. However, they had not finished with me yet as the Chief Super again caught my eye, glaringly it seemed, along the extended table.

"Tell us Caridia ..."

(By now, I had come to hate that approach.)

"... what do you consider your greatest weakness?"

'Hell', was my immediate reaction. 'That is one big, difficult and totally unexpected onslaught.'

"Crumbs, sir," I verbalised, again fighting for thinking time, "th-that's a real stinker of a question, sir."

"Yes, young man, I know it is." He paused. "But I STILL want an answer to it – like NOW, please," he added, glowering slightly.

The panel hugged themselves gleefully. They clearly loved selection interviews, but I was not sure of the extent to which they were seeking entirely enterprising candidates amongst their cadets. Anyway, once more into the breech went my shell and I pressed the firing pin.

"Well, sir. I recognise that like all humans I have weaknesses, but do not believe any of mine would stop me eventually, after training, from being a good navigating officer, sir."

"Do you mean training at developing your weaknesses, Caridia?" The super thrust quickly.

"Well, not that, sir. No. I mean after my training as a navigating officer, sir."

"Hmmm, young man. Depends on the weakness, I suppose. After all, your training as a navigator might well 'kill two birds with one stone', as the expression goes."

The super glanced at the rest of his colleagues as they all erupted in open laughter.

I sat in silence, wondering if we were all thinking along the same lines – suspecting possibly not – but unsure why.

The super glanced understanding at my mystified expression. He then gathered his composure and suggested to the other members that, unless there were further questions, he saw no reason why they could not let me go. The panel nodded its affirmation and my dismissal, without any indication or feed-back concerning progress. I felt, on the whole, that things had not gone too badly. I relived my discomfiture, regarding the *faux pas* over the light before dismissing this incident from my mind. Overall I did not think my performance had been too disastrous and found myself pleasantly surprised that the experience had been vaguely enjoyable.

In some respects I was not really over bothered. Of course, Ellertons appealed to me as a company, but Captain Mobbs words had been taken to heart. It was the latter interview in fact which enabled me to be quite relaxed there. I had after all little to lose, with possibly much to gain, and had already selected in my mind an alternative line upon whom to press my dubious services.

Peter, inevitably, was totally self-composed during the train journey home (as we by now thought of the navigation school). His mind was clearly on the slap-up lunch they had given us. We both felt that it was worth going to the interview for that alone. Gortley however was very subdued. He was from a different Watch and we did not really know him, but he was certainly not as chirpy as on the outward journey.

None of us were told the result of the interview on the day, so it was with an uneasy mixture of thoughts and feelings that we returned to the school. It came as no surprise to learn Gortley had been rejected for reasons he never declared, but Peter was advised four days later of his acceptance. Of the other three, only two were accepted, which did little to enhance my confidence. It was a further three days before I was handed a letter by Peter that he had collected from the cadet pigeon holes.

A definite buzz was experienced as I glanced at the official envelope embossed with the Company house-flag in the top left-hand corner. We both looked at each other pensively as the all-important missive was opened. I experienced an even greater thrill, casting an eye over its contents, and then handed it to Peter for him to read.

His face mirrored my own pleasure as he offered me his heartiest congratulations and I believed they were genuinely meant. It was true. Ellerton's had accepted me, subject to satisfactorily completing my present course – including gaining my Ordinary Seaman and Lifeboat certificates – and would forward joining instructions for a ship soon after I left college. So, in such an unemotional way, I had the distinction of being accepted by my first choice company – who had never previously accepted a non public-secondary school cadet.

Every cadet left with a Lifeboat Certificate as well as Efficient Deck Hand qualification (courtesy London Nautical School).

Mum and Dad, as well as most of the college staff, shared my pleasure and delight. Another interview with Fred and Captain Mobbs followed. Nothing was said or even hinted, but I came away from the latter with the distinct impression I owed almost as much to the Boss as my own performance before the panel. The Captain-Superintendent said he was particularly pleased with this result, not only for me, but because it encouraged the college to send 'similarly qualified applicants' in future – a remark I regarded as a delightful hyperbole. He further confided my successful interview (combined with other factors) would probably lead to Ellertons looking more closely at non public-school boys.

Other cadets were also warm in their congratulations. Like Fred, a reassuring silence (rather than a vitriolic side-swipe) came from Woodley, whose popularity was waning with many – a fact he was sufficiently intelligent to perceive. But I was certainly not perturbed about their views.

Chapter 2

PRE-SEA TRIALS

———

At some stage, all cadets on our short course had to go for a week's cruise aboard the College training vessel. Anson Watch was last to go and we left immediately after breakfast on the penultimate Monday morning. Following the inevitable rush, collecting belongings and cadets more or less efficiently at departure point in the Quad, we boarded one transport of delight destined to take us to another. I think we were all slightly apprehensive of what might be in store.

Entering Keddleston docks, the minibus swerved violently to avoid a pothole, throwing me from my seat onto the floor, although my curses became lost in muttered oaths from the other cadets. The driver laughed his apologies, adding that the jolt we had received was nothing compared to that which we had coming our way. He added, mysteriously we thought, that this would not only be from the sea as he directed our glances towards the vessel upon which we were to embark. She was lying low in the water below us alongside a redundant fish berth in a dock basin.

I remember glancing at Peter and feeling relieved that our driver's sadistically gleeful remark mirrored, in my fellow cadet's expression, something of my own concerns. As the first two cadets into the minibus we were last to leave and, collecting our gear from a still smirking driver, joined the remainder of our Watch waiting at the shore end of the gangway wondering what to do, while the suddenly friendly bus drove back to College.

My main thought was concerned with the ghastly colour of the water, as I glanced into the oily-sheen blackness below me, waiting patiently for the others to sort themselves out at the end of the gangway. I conjectured that to fall into the mess before me would most certainly entail a stomach pump job in a local hospital. The stench seemed equally uninviting, due no doubt to the lock gates not being opened all that frequently.

My day-dreams were interrupted by a booming voice, in the broadest of Scots tones, advising the futility of our merely standing 'looking gorrmless', as it said, and urging us to get on board as there was much to be done prior to sailing.

Fulbright led us onto the gangway under a dense cloud of uncharacteristic silence. I noticed Peter and me were not the only ones under some pressure. Even Woodley seemed subdued leading me to ponder how much substance might exist in those horror tales we had heard from each Watch preceding us. Resignedly, I guessed we should soon find out and reflected upon the varied stories covering their sea experiences to which we had been treated – and, indeed, disregarded so lightly – whilst snuggled protectively within the safe cocoon of College confines.

Suddenly, a further shout came from this pint-sized bearded figure that I estimated, inconsequentially, to be in his mid-forties. He was standing with my fellow cadets on deck and, it suddenly struck me, was speaking specifically to me this time, demanding to know if it was my intention to embark. Nervousness had clearly made me a little slow off the mark and I realised that, whilst meditating and waiting for the other cadets to clear the gangway, they had in fact done so with sufficient speed to leave me stranded lonesome on the jetty. Sarcastically this time, he shouted at me again, asking if my expectations were for him to come ashore and carry my gear on board for me. Grabbing my holdall I rapidly boarded the boat to join the 'smugly smiling eleven' already safely ensconced aft of the large wheelhouse. Even Peter, my presupposed friend, was (not surprisingly, I thought ruefully) grinning with the rest.

Wisely, I bit back any verbal response and, as our eyes met, offered this potential fire-ball an apologetic and, what was intended to be a genuinely warm, welcoming smile.

"We'll soon have that bloody grrin knocked off yourr face, you cheeky dozy little Crretin," was the only response to this friendly overture. I began to realise there might be unexpected problems with this part of my training – especially as the remark was accompanied by a look of such distasteful disdain.

He looked us over dismissively and continued to address us authoritatively and in the same sarcastic tone. Looking directly at me this time, he stated how pleased he was that we were now finally assembled, ready to start our voyage training. Introducing himself as Captain MacNab, skipper of the *Stenwood Navigator,* he pointed in the direction of another officer who suddenly appeared behind him out of the wheelhouse, whom he called Captain Henshaw. He told us that this officer was Mate of the vessel and would be in charge of us administratively, as our Divisional Officer, and would assist in our training.

My thoughts plummeted beyond the blackest depths as I realised the position held on board by this Little Bearded Buffer – or 'LBB' as he became (far from affectionately) known. I ruminated, with some fearful trepidation that he could, and probably would, make life extremely difficult for our Watch – especially me. In an effort to look anxiously for a bright side, I glanced at the Mate, thinking he at least seemed reasonably affable. Looking for further straws of nautical reassurance, my certainties were there was nothing personal in our welcome, and the skipper's reaction was probably just a spark of what psychologists term a warped personality. Already, however, I was beginning to appreciate that it was us on the dirty end of the stick – and not some 'bloudy' psychologist.

Becoming aware of the skipper again looking very closely at me, I chased rapidly after the others as they disappeared forward in the Mate's wake, towards our midships accommodation. This was the area previously used as a fish hold when this ex-middle sea trawler was operating commercially. It had been cleverly converted, with hinged double-tiered bunks down each side, and a large mess table running down the centre. There was a battery of small lockers below the bunks for the cadets' personal effects, but the overall effect generally was one of a bleakness far more spartan than our shore accommodation.

The effect was not enhanced by the steel-based bunks with their singularly uninviting, wafer-thin mattresses. A heavy-duty plastic curtain separated a double-cabin into self-contained accommodation, complete with washbasins, and 'heads' as I had learnt toilets aboard ships are called. The ante-cabin originally had been intended for two petty officers, but was used now by senior Watch cadets. Forward of this cabin, separated by a watertight bulkhead, was the chain locker for the anchor, and space for deck stores.

Fulbright, as sole senior cadet, looked smugly at his comparatively lavish quarters. We glanced in with unrestrained awe at the luxury that was his. Our washing and toilet facilities were right down aft on the main deck next to the paint locker and abaft the wheelhouse which, as we were soon to find, meant a very long trek to wash our hands or whatever. I wondered if he would allow us use of his senior 'heads' during the dark hours of the night – although with little expectation. On the lower deck, aft of the engine-room space, was situated the self-contained two-berthed officers' accommodation.

Lunch, like all meals, was cooked by a permanent rating and, akin to food ashore, was surprisingly tasty and plentiful. This AB, or able-bodied Seaman, lived in splendid isolation abaft the engine-room (which also fell within his domain), and was assisted – for want of a better word – in his various tasks by a duty cadet. Immediately after stowing away our gear we were to store ship for the seven-day voyage. The plan was to proceed down the English coast and spend a night in Ramsgate before setting course for Calais the following day, thence onwards to Boulogne – and possibly further south – depending on tidal timings. Storing entailed working what the Mate called a 'chain gang' appropriately enough, which was extremely effective, even if painfully back-breaking.

A slight mishap occurred just before we broke for mid-morning stand easy; a short break for biscuits and cup of strong sweet tea. I remain convinced to this day, knowing how strained already relations between LBB and myself were becoming, that Woodley (that unmitigated little dung-heap) continued his college practice of setting people up and selected me as a natural target. Perhaps if circumstances are explained then truth will speak for itself.

Standing on the after deck during a brief lull, waiting for additional stores to be lugged from the lorry, Woodley suddenly called my name attracting my attention, and simultaneously threw a heavy two-gallon can of paint. Obviously, not expecting this, the action caught me off-balance. I managed awkwardly to grab it, but the weight proved too much for me. The tin slipped out of my hands and, before I or anyone else could control events, it dropped onto the sky-light leading to the officers' quarters below. The shock of hitting the steel edge knocked it out of shape and directed its trajectory through the glass. Notwithstanding a double-tight fitting, the lid came off as the can began its descent, and the paint – a delicately restful shade of pastel green, I recall – gushed out, liberally covering the entire cabin including the officers' bunks.

Momentarily, we all stood there transfixed and utterly speechless. Even the face of Captain Henshaw, supervising storing from the jetty above, went slightly pale at the enormity of what had happened.

LBB however was not so restrained. It was obvious he was angry with me. In fact, he went ape and totally ballistic. He actually accused me (quite falsely as it happened) of 'going orrf in a bloody trrance', but that was very mild compared to his following remarks. In fact he blistered me for what seemed like hours – from apex to breakfast time – pausing only a few seconds before returning hungrily for the crumbs. One thing was quite certain. The vaguest hint of a smile – however nervously – would have led him to throw me off the ship (or worse) so, inevitably, I would have failed the course. In actual fact, being far too awed by what had happened, I could only stand there petrified, not knowing what to do.

LBB advanced even closer towards me as his tirade began to lose impetus. I noticed traces of spittle at the corners of his mouth as he urged me to 'get oot of his ------- sight', advising it would be best for me to join the other cadets, whilst Captain Henshaw and he decided what they should do 'about this bloudy mess'. I thought for one moment he was going to clout me, so needed little further encouragement to scamper thankfully along the deck to our accommodation hatch, for'ard of the wheelhouse.

I joined my supportive colleagues. Already recovered from their stupefied shock, they had long since made themselves scarce and disappeared to the mess-deck. Once there, led of course by Woodley, all eleven rolled around the cabin creased hysterically with uncontrollable shrieks of laughter; the condition in which, sadly, I found them.

Still shaking considerably, I heard their luridly expressed verdicts, on what they conjectured was likely to happen. These comments can well be imagined and are best left unrecorded. In retrospect, it is still impossible for me to recall all they said – even though their tones and hilarious laughter remain scored indelibly on my memory. It can be understood I was still very much in a state of shock.

Eventually, the Mate entered our mess deck and addressed us carefully, for some reason, avoiding my eye. Apparently, the skipper and he had discussed the incident and decided it should be referred to Captain Mobbs at college. In view of LBB's explosive temper, I felt to have been a secret eavesdropper at this electrifying conversation could have been quite revealing. Our shipboard officers were all for cancelling the cruise, but things were not quite that straightforward. Unwittingly, I had involved them in a more serious problem. We knew ours was booked as the last course for the current academic year and it was essential for practical sea-training to be completed before we could qualify and pass out. All of us were fixed up with shipping companies, by this late stage, subject to our completing this cruise successfully. If it did have to be cancelled, then our Watch alone would have to return to college early the following term, in a couple of months' time, with all the inconvenience to staff this would imply, not withstanding the chaos eight weeks' delay would cause our shipping companies. Solely because of this major consideration, the two officers had really been forced to agree with the Boss's suggestion that, notwithstanding anything other than a complete engine or vessel breakdown, this voyage had to be completed. Captain Henshaw's brows thickened as he explained there was no time for their own cabin to be cleaned and the sky-light repaired so, consequently, the voyage would be cut short by a few days and the officers would move into the senior cadets' cabin for'ard of our accommodation.

Not surprisingly perhaps, Fulbright shot Woodley and me a look of unmitigated malevolence across the cabin. He was (understandably) not a very happy senior cadet and, perversely, I was glad that Woodley was also involved. Fulbright seemed to hold him in considerably more respect than he did me, doubtless more for Woodley's physical prowess with his fists, than his personality. Glancing around the surrounding faces, I saw a wave of smothered delight begin its surge as other cadets (with varying degrees of comprehension) began to realise the import of what was said, and how envied privileges of rank so rapidly acquired could, equally as fast, disappear before the recipient's eyes.

Captain Henshaw had a few words of his own to add to those from the skipper, which were primarily addressed to me, although initially in far milder tones.

"You, Caridia, really have proved to be walking disaster area already. I can't believe that you have done so much damage in just a couple of hours. Bloody Hell," his patience snapped. "We've not even had lunch yet. Let me tell you, the skipper is only taking you along because of the direct intervention of Captain-Superintendent Mobbs and is far from happy with this decision. Consequently, I would suggest that you keep a really low profile for the remainder of your time aboard, and do your best to reinstate yourself into the Captain's esteem. Basically, you've got to wake your bloody ideas up and stop being so gormless. We will, you don't need to be reminded, have to compile an end of voyage report on each one of you before you can leave us to go to sea."

The final broadside was glared around the cabin in a vaguely threatening manner. Only too well aware of my narrow escape, I stammered grateful thanks and promised fervently to be the paragon of all known (and unknown) nautical virtues for the remainder of the cruise. And I actually meant it.

Having completed the storing in silence, apart from surreptitious muffled giggles from Woodley, which set off the others, we were split into bridge watches, each of three cadets. The evening, after supper (a singularly subdued meal), was taken up either with resting or duties. High tide was at twenty-two hundred hours, allowing the deck watch to open the lock gates in preparation for our departure. Peter, Felsted and I were placed on sea duties so we were told-off to turn in immediately after finishing our meal. A team was already preparing charts for the passage to Ramsgate in readiness for the first duty, as helmsmen-cum-navigators-cum lookouts, once we had cleared the river. As the navigators were supervised by the skipper in the roomy wheelhouse, LBB and I were kept safely apart.

For obvious reasons, I had made a point of sitting at the other end of the mess table to LLB during both luncheon and the evening meal. I believed that discretion might well be the key to my survival which, after all, I genuinely desired. Losing my coveted cadetship with Ellertons, after all the work put into gaining it (and not just by me); having to return the kit to the Royal Naval Reserve, and possibly go back to the shipping line's offices, brought me out in quite a sweat. I was extremely anxious not to drop further clangers.

Being in a shallow sleep when we sailed, I was only vaguely aware of changes not only of watch-keepers, but the smooth motion of our vessel, as she rolled easily in a north-easterly breeze. The night was dry and clear when our team turned-to and took watch in the wheelhouse. Already, the craft was well on passage and easing into the coastal shipping lanes to head round North Foreland and drop into Ramsgate Harbour. We were beckoned in by the Mate. I was told to come over to the chart-table and work with him, whilst Felsted did look-out and Dathan relieved the wheel.

I breathed a sigh of relief that Captain Henshaw was on watch and not the skipper. I was sufficiently aware that we would have to meet soon, but was equally appreciative that this precise moment was perhaps not quite the appropriate time. In my naïve innocence, I thought it best for a longer interval to elapse in the hope he might even have forgotten about the incident by then.

Hearing the slightly exasperated tones of the Mate call me, I realised that already the helm had been relieved and the other cadets were scampering swiftly to their bunks. My prominence by the wheelhouse door was therefore even more conspicuous. I somewhat apprehensively went over to look at the charts.

The reason for my concern was not so much to do with translating navigational theory into practice, but views already being exchanged between us cadets regarding the Mate. We were seriously beginning to wonder if he had what was euphemistically known as 'a bit of a problem'. Something we supposed the Americans referred to as not quite being 'a regular guy'. In fact, we were rapidly starting to believe he fancied us.

There was not a great deal which cadets of our age could do about it practically. We supposed safety lay in numbers and, anyway, did not think he was particularly dangerous; but certainly the signs were there. Gortley had remarked casually over afternoon stand easy how the Chief Officer had accidentally allowed his hand to brush against the cadet's apparently enticingly young nubile bottom, whilst correcting his chart-work for the first leg of our trip. Pickerstaff also definitely thought the Mate stood just a little too close for comfort when he bent over the compass binnacle whilst taking practice bearings shortly before leaving port.

Even I had experienced a warm, friendly, reassuring gentle hand caressing my skinny shoulder blades whilst I was being directed to the forward store locker earlier. Not expecting anything even remotely amiss from a member of staff I had not at the time registered anything odd. In fact, after the paint incident and with my report in mind, I was actually reassured that at least someone in authority had a soft spot (as it were) for me. I began to comprehend however, with enhanced understanding, some of the meaningful comments from cadets on previous trips.

Practical coastal navigation during training cruises
(courtesy Southampton Institute Warsash Maritime Centre).

As it happened, my practical work passed without incident and I thoroughly enjoyed the couple of one-hour navigational stints. These were sandwiched between relieving Peter for a steering trick at the helm, and Felsted at lookout. I found considerable pleasure accurately identifying distant shore lights shining brightly in the dark clear night, taking visual bearings and then radar ranges, and plotting our position onto the chart. We were encouraged to use the ship's Decca Mark Twelve 'Navigator' as an additional position check. "You have probably painted with numbers in your earlier days, well, Decca is navigating with numbers," our shore-based instructor gleefully, if not very originally told us, whilst explaining theories upon which the system was based, so we could apply these practically and accurately at sea. Little difficulty was found applying tidal set and drift to my courses and passing these to Peter or Felsted for them to steer. Apart from keeping a close professional eye on what I was doing, the Mate left me to it. Look-out duties were responsible, but merely carried the onus of looking for shipping and any visible dangers to navigation, reporting these to the Mate, and recognising the characteristics of occasional buoys or lighthouses and passing these to the navigators. Subsequently, lookout proved an enjoyable respite demanding little intellectually or over much concentration.

Using the Decca Navigator
(courtesy Southampton Institute Warsash Maritime Centre).

My most profound recollection during tricks at the wheel was of the sea. I actually relished, wallowed almost, in the peculiarly heavy salty tang which assailed my nostrils as unique sea smells permeated through open windows whilst, in turn, steering the courses given me by other cadets.

Once we recognised basic signs of the Mate's inclinations, we became increasingly alert to what were interpreted as covert glances in our direction at meals from where the Mate sat (appropriately enough we thought) at the bottom of the mess table, opposite LBB. We had seen already his inclination to be kindly in his manner towards us – itself a demeanour very much in opposition to the skipper's temperament.

Earlier in the course two cadets in Frobisher Watch had been caught 'red-handed', in *flagrante delicto* (or, perhaps, in*delicto),* which had made a significant contribution towards the social aspects of weaknesses in human nature within my nautical education. I was really quite repulsed by the imagined implications about what the Mate might wish to do to our various persons but, at the same time, felt rather sorry for him – considering he must live a very lonely and extremely frustrated life.

Anyway, these more charitable aspects of my thoughts did not stop me, as the trip continued, from joining other cadets in leading the Mate on in subtle ways – and it is surprising just how subtle teenage boys can be when they make a concerted effort. After all, we reasoned, it might be as well to have an ally in the enemy camp. The other consideration, of course, was that he helped structure our end of voyage reports and even if he had to wait to get his reward in heaven, because there was unlikely to be much on account with us lot, then we did not really mind him having a few compensatory thrills at our expense. Even if one of us had felt responsive towards him, there was not much opportunity of anything happening on a crowded mess-deck, with just a curtained partition separating the officers and ourselves. So, under the truly inspired leadership of Fulbright, using that considerable resilience which exists with youth – if not always with age – we found ways to turn the accommodation difficulties to our advantage.

Apart from two cadets, chosen from a watch bill to be on duty overnight when alongside, the rest turned into smelly little pits and (from amongst a number of instances) a few *sotto voce* strongly homoerotic comments between the group could probably be guaranteed to raise the Mate's blood pressure. And, as randy lusty teenagers totally obsessed by sex, the pleasant process of a number of exaggerated simulated 'not so quiet night exercises' possibly helped drive him demented. We could only agree with Fulbright's conjecture that, whilst never completely sure of the results, if the black looks received from LBB on subsequent mornings were any kind of yard stick, then much of our psychological warfare must have penetrated curtained defences into the next cabin. "If he can hear, then so can the Mate," Fulbright surmised with unaccustomed logic. Had a philosophical sage uttered, 'Every positive action has a negative one', then we believed our behaviour led LBB to think this entire watch of twelve cadets was queer – probably leading him all the more positively to despise us.

I was in the fo'c'sle mooring party of the ketch, under the direction of Captain Henshaw, when the craft came alongside the jetty on the eastern pier of Ramsgate Harbour. LBB took the helm himself for the intricate ship handling involved approaching and laying our rather plump fishing vessel onto the berth. He simultaneously kept an eye on the AB in charge of the after mooring party, just within view of the wheelhouse windows.

The skipper's true thoughts about our watch were never really discovered. His impressions, however, were hardly influenced favourably by an incident shortly after we arrived alongside.

Peter, realising that the Mate was glancing at him from behind the wheelhouse started to mince down the jetty; waggling his hips most provocatively, flapping his hands aimlessly, and generally 'poofing things up' in a delightfully exaggerated effeminate manner. What Peter had not noticed was Kelly watching from inside the wheelhouse where he was working with Woodley and LBB on the next batch of charts, surreptitiously and quickly nudge his fellow cadet.

"Ooooooh! Cruumbs! Gooodness me! Just look at Dathan!" exclaimed the accursed Woodley, never losing an opportunity, as he pointed out Peter – ostensibly to Kelly but more importantly, by implication, to LBB:

"Do you think he is suffering from an attack of something, Sir?" he asked LBB directly, with innocent guile. Our esteemed skipper apparently did not say anything, but gave the rapidly vanishing cadet on the quayside a decidedly jaundiced look.

Peter had also failed to spot the small group of tourists who, as luck would have it, were passing the stern of the vessel just as he set off along the jetty. Cheesing mooring ropes on the fore-deck I was an interested listener and observer. Little time was lost during our next stand easy of my reporting the variegated thoughts obviously evoked in their minds, and clearly expressed in bemused and amazed faces, at the sight of this uniformed gangly youth camping his way around the harbour. Their thoughts, looks and comments presented an enchanting cameo.

"Eeee ther', Fred," exclaimed one of the ladies, in a voice of total disbelief: "Take a look at that ther' boy. What on earth's the matter with 'im? Is he having a fit or sommink?"

Fred was clearly far worldlier than his better half: "Dunno about a fit – looks like a proper little poofter to me!" followed his exclamation. "He's from this little ship 'ere", he added looking at our vessel (and me) with some amazement.

"Nice to see the Navy's keeping up the old traditions then," sung a supporting voice.

"What's them, then?" the other lady asked, in tones of interested speculation.

"Rum, Bum and Baccy", chorused Fred and his mate simultaneously. They were clearly 'old salts'.

"I thought that sort of thing had died out by now," stated the better half. "He looks such a nice boy as well."

"Yeah! I bet that's what all the men say!" Fred interrupted jocularly.

The two then fell about laughing whilst their long-suffering wives gave somewhat whimsical smiles, probably more at the antics of their men-folk than the incident.

Mindful of LBB, I continued looking busy but, surreptitiously glancing at the wheelhouse, saw his face presented another picture as he overheard this conversation passing our vessel. Apparently though, he refrained from any comment whatsoever, but merely directed the cadets' thoughts back to the job in hand.

Peter and I had an overnight two-hour deck stint before we sailed. Our duties were not exactly onerous. We had to keep an eye on the moorings and general security of the vessel, as well as making endless cups of cocoa. Our main job however was to keep very quiet so we would not disturb the others, especially our esteemed officers and of course, Fulbright, who was not averse to clumping junior cadets who upset him. Time passed slowly with so little to do. The weather produced one of those cold, slightly windy and occasionally damp nights, making near-distance lights of the town glare brightly in the clear air.

We amused ourselves eventually by taking post in the wheelhouse and glancing through ship's copies of *Brown's Nautical Almanac* and the blue-covered *Channel Pilot Volume 1*. Both books shone with assorted nuggets of nautical knowledge and provided a veritable harvest for any potential mariner. We revelled in such gems as the 'Specific Gravities of Dock or Harbour Water Throughout the World', which was proudly exhibited in the former (devoid alas of Keddleston), whilst the latter offered such mouth-watering temptations as:

> 'Ramsgate road, at the northern end of Ramsgate channel, affords good anchorage, with winds between west-north-west and north-north-east; but with southerly or easterly winds a cross sea gets up, making it an uneasy anchorage with a strong tidal stream. A vessel can anchor, about 5 cables southward of the entrance to Ramsgate harbour, in a depth of about 12 feet.'

The best gift I felt any potential cadet might receive, from doting parents, adoring sister or benign uncle, would be a copy of either of these publications for birthday or Christmas.

It was 1400 hours when Peter, Felsted and I went to the wheelhouse for our turn on watch once the vessel had cleared harbour. By this time, the tide and the strong north-easterly wind had worked against each other sufficiently effectively to produce an extremely steep sea as we entered the centre of the Dover Strait. Gorton from the previous team was still on duty, completing some aspect of chart-work with LLB. Peter went to help them and Felsted was put to look-out duty, whilst LBB, giving me a very savage look, told me to take a trick at the helm.

After steering for about twenty minutes, just prior to being relieved by Peter, I became aware of LBB standing to one side watching me. Preparing myself for I did not know what, I heard that broad familiar voice, asking in mocking sarcastic tones, if my name was Carridia. His enquiry was made all the more threatening and sinister by the conversational way in which it was uttered sibilantly into my right ear. I tensed myself quietly, wondering what was going to happen next. LBB had spoken sufficiently clearly so the other two cadets in the wheelhouse were bound to hear it.

Taking a deep breath and using a neutral tone of voice I confirmed he was correct. The sentiment of course which really ran through my mind was: by now, he ought to know my name only too well. Struggling to keep the vessel on something remotely resembling its course line, I considered myself in sufficient trouble already, so trod very carefully. There was a pause whilst he looked aft and then, like a snapping shark, came in again for the attack.

"I thought so," he said, "because you have just written it in the bloudy waterr."

I kept a very tight silence, but my thoughts were electric. I realised he had just 'cracked a funny' so, in the name of self-preservation smiled thinly, even though his comment was far from original. My uncle 'Wag' had told me that story from his deck boy days thirty years previously. I wondered also just what he expected from a cadet who had never steered before and was trying to make the best of his trick at the helm in a Storm Force 10 wind.

In actual fact, the sea was only surging around Force 6, but it certainly seemed like more than a moderate gale to me, especially when viewed from such a low angle. It was a very different view from the previous evening and, this time, the compass fought me every degree of the way. In fact, I had to struggle really hard with the wheel in an attempt to gain some sort of control. Each time I glanced out of the window, from the miniature binnacle, a vicious spread of mountainous grey-green spume-topped waves met my gaze. It seemed that each one was surging at me personally, only to change its mind at the very last moment. Vindictively, the swell pushed up the bows to pound the keel of this now very small boat, allowing it to fall into the next trough with hammering effect. Of course it not only knocked the hell from any semblance of accurate steering, but also hammered my stomach. It was really quite scary, without the added distraction of what LBB might do or say next.

Peter and Felsted, fighting to keep sea-sickness at bay and anxious in their own interests to keep on the good side of the Skipper, gave each other a by now familiarly knowing look, and dutifully sniggered with just the right amount of enthusiasm at his ponderous wit.

He has really got off lightly, I considered, as LBB rejoined the others at the chart-table. After all, there were only twelve of us cadets instead of the eighteen usually constituting a Watch due no doubt to his reputation having resounded in careers offices throughout the nation. The true reason though, I suspected, was a gradual lack of enthusiasm from young people choosing the sea and going to other more alluring professions which had led to this inevitable shortage of trainees.

Still, I reasoned further, working myself up into ever increasing heat, there was no excuse to take it out on us who had elected to become potential navigating officers in the Merchant Navy. We were at least helping to keep him in a job – and, being realistic, I could see no-one else shore-side employing this little runt.

"Carridia." croaked a familiarly frantic voice, shouting with exasperation now into my ear, even more frantically: "Just wherrre the --------- Hell arre you going? Wake your bloudy self up, you gorrrmless, uselesss little sperrrm spot."

I realised that such profound meditations had distracted my steering to an extent we were 100° off course, and putting tenfold fear of the gods up the officer-of-the-watch on what had previously been a safely passing tanker. Even if an ex-student from the same college, hence full of compassionate understanding, he was probably wondering (with some justification) just where we were heading, and what was going on in our happy and cosy little nautical domain.

LBB apparently, discussing a further point of navigational interest with his intrepid navigators, suddenly felt the difference in movement and sensed rather than saw a shadow forward of the wheelhouse, where previously a shadow had not been. Glancing up he had seen the large tanker, which had been passing clear and open on our port side, appear almost magically and very closely, fine off the starboard bow. Carried away by my thoughts I had not heard Peter, who was lookout, attempting to attract surreptitiously my attention.

I'm not a 'sperrrm spot', at all I thought rather hurt, as I struggled to regain the course-line. I thought of getting Dad to see a solicitor and sue him – but then thought again. Incidentally, came my quiet reflection, it was interesting to think once more how, in moments of stress, LBB's Scots accent became increasingly pronounced. He was difficult enough for me to understand at the best of times.

My supportive colleagues by this time were quietly creased with laughter and dare not look at each other directly. Oh well, I hummed quietly to myself, might as well spread a little happiness. At least their minds had been taken off sea-sickness for awhile.

I have still never learnt the name of the shore-based intellectual Pellmanist reputed to have said: 'Thought is innovator of action'. Whoever, he had a lot to answer for in the next sequence of events, as my thought became precisely that. I spewed all over the deck. I covered effectively the steering wheel, compass binnacle, and front of my working uniform and – horror of blessed horrors – the entire left-hand side, below the shoulder, of LBB himself. Judging that this cadet needed perhaps a tighter eye on his steering, he unwisely stood just a little too closely. Everything came up and out – breakfast, lunch and a generous handful of chocolates Peter had shared, stolen from the store-cubby when the AB's back was turned.

LBB was – OK fair enough, this time – angry with me. To be quite honest he was slightly more so and rose to the occasion admirably. Even after the blistering of our previous contretemps, LBB never repeated himself once in five minutes of atomic blistering. He called me all the 'so-and-so's' he could lay his tongue to – and a number of others besides I had never heard before. It was poetry in nautical harmony.

I found myself, even in the depths of illness, admiring the Skipper for yet another extra-curricular contribution to my maritime education. Even as 'a second time round' as it were, feeling really ill was virtually worthwhile for the honour of listening to this virtuoso past-master of nautical expression.

The other cadets by this time were frenetic almost to the point of paralysis. They were bursting to laugh out loud, but had to restrain themselves because LBB's temper was white hot. With just a little more goading, he would have killed the three of us, and willingly faced the consequences ashore.

Anyway I was stood down, told to change, and get a bucket of water and some swabs to clean up the mess. Peter was made to take the wheel. Inevitably, the psychological effect of my actions – and the lovely residual smell of vomit – got him going as well. Felsted was sent to get the Mate enabling LBB, still bellowing furiously, to go below to change his clothes – and presumably recover something of his normal sweet-natured temper. Felsted, needless to say, made the most of an opportunity to relieve pent-up humour by regaling his fellow cadets with the latest 'Caridia cock-up'.

"I really don't believe this. What the bloody Hell have you done now?" enquired the Mate as he entered the wheelhouse with, perhaps, an acceptable level of exasperation. "I warned you, Caridia, about keeping a low profile. According to my book, you seem to have a bloody funny way of doing it," he added.

Of course, amidst the confused sequence of events, no-one luckily ever thought to enquire why I had not turned my head in the other direction.

Considering what we supposed LBB heard of our nocturnal antics, and bearing in mind he was quite 'switched-on', I have no idea (and definitely lacked the courage to enquire) how he managed to resolve our actions with those regarding the local girls when finally our joyful crew arrived in Calais.

The vessel berthed astern of an unmanned dredger on the working jetty of the harbour and the cadets were granted shore-leave. I, for some reason, was exempt. My entire French stay was to be spent making a kind of effort to tidy-up the officers' official quarters.

This particular harbour section was generally closed to the public, but one of the cadets managed to bring his girl friend into the comparatively secluded area. I was too scared, naive, and not worldly enough to try the local talent, even if given the opportunity, so could only watch both aghast and with a strongly excited interest, as Fulbright (it had to be) snogged extremely heavily with his *femme fatale* so they were soon having it off on the after-deck of the dredger, of all places.

Dathan and I watched this, with dry mouths and shaking hands, through binoculars from the wheelhouse. Peter had called me there as soon as he determined what was going on. It was quite safe with both officers ashore. He commented, with an appallingly appropriate choice of words, that my eyes were protruding 'like -------- telegraph handles', proving how he had clearly benefited from the classical emphasis contributed to his expensive education by a minor public school. Frankly, the sight of naked female legs and bursting little boobies was all too much for me and I had to excuse myself rapidly. It came as no surprise, following my return to the wheelhouse; Peter himself had to shoot down below, as it were. We found ourselves reflecting, like Congreve: such was 'the Way of the World'.

The remainder of our short stay was without major incident, apart from a minor *debacle* whilst ordering stores in a French language uttered by cadets hard pressed even to speak Fowler's English. The vessel ended up festooned with sufficient loaves of French stick bread to feed the entire college, but hardly enough milk to see us clear of the harbour. Perhaps it had been unwise of our officers to have entrusted us with the task in the first place as, despairingly, they took the stores back to arrange a more proportional balance.

The return home was comparatively uneventful in terms of maritime passages, but one that had me biting my nails a little. I was cleaning paint from a certain cabin or, at least, going through the motions of doing so. Frankly, the job was formidable; my enthusiasm, the handful of swabs and ironically empty paint tin making little constructive impression. Suddenly, my rambling thoughts concerning the pointlessness of my task were interrupted from a voice above my head – as if from Heaven – calling my name. Glad of any excuse to cease this labour of love, I glanced up, only to look directly into the eyes of LBB. He did not appear any more endearing from this aspect but then, probably, neither did I to him. Anyway, he told me to come on deck, adding – totally unnecessarily – the reminder to 'scrrew back the top of the paint rremover.' I did so and joined my esteemed Skipper on deck.

He glanced at me dispassionately and told me he wanted me to act as navigator on the coming return trip: that our destination for the first leg back to Keddleston would be Tilbury landing stage in the River Thames, where we were to spend the night alongside. He added that no shore leave would be granted on this occasion, and looked at me so fixedly I wondered if he suspected what had happened on the dredger. Telling me to make an immediate start, I was to lay off the requisite courses and show him my passage plan once this had been completed.

I mused, making my way thoughtfully to the wheelhouse, that for me there was to be neither help from other cadets nor even the benefit of reassuring assistance from benevolent hierarchy. I was just left to get on with it. From an indeterminate sense, emanating from something in the Skipper's attitude and tone of voice, I was suddenly aware of confronting a moment of truth. One of those sudden revealing and all-embracing experiences which Old Harber, my lamented English master from school, called – racking my memory – yes; an epiphany. I realised that, epiphany or not, if a mess-up were made by me of this task, then LBB would undoubtedly fail me. So, if ever there was a time not to day-dream, as he rudely remarked (not that I could recall ever doing so) now was not the time to do it.

I sorted out the relevant charts and cleaned away the course lines from the outward passage. Then, consulting very carefully both tidal atlas and tables, I worked out it would be more favourable, once outside Calais approaches, to cross the world's busiest water way at right-angles heading for the South Foreland light. I could then follow the dredged channel to North Foreland and, passing Tongue Light Vessel on our port hand side, proceed through the Edinburgh Channel to the Thames and up to Tilbury. Luckily, the winds and seas had abated during our stay in Calais.

Carefully and neatly, I wrote out the passage plan from my rough notes, with time of departure, variation and deviation for the various courses, tidal details, waypoints and our ETA at the landing stage. Double-checking this carefully, I took it to LBB in the PO's cabin. He glanced up on hearing my knock and, in a surprisingly friendly tone, questioned if my task had been finished. I merely confirmed this and passed my plan to him. He received it without comment. The scene was vaguely reminiscent of Bligh receiving a mouldy breadfruit from one of his midshipmen. Not even bothering to check my calculations he simply glanced, grunted; accepted the timings, called the Mate and told him to make preparations for leaving Calais accordingly.

My mother used to say, in moments of stress, that she was on 'tenter-hooks' (whatever they may have been), and to suggest her offspring also was in that state would have been a cynical understatement. I watched our progress more closely and attentively than anything previously undertaken so far in my short life.

The other cadets soon cottoned-on to yet more non-verbal psychological entertainment permeating our training voyage and, as was their wont, made varying encouraging contributions to my welfare. Woodley of course took great delight telling me, after I returned to the wheelhouse from lunch, how dense fog had been forecast imminent in the Thames Estuary. I had to confess, even making allowances for Woodley-isms, his news did have me decidedly worried. Certainly, the English coast appeared in the distance as only a very indistinct shape, merging into heavy mist. I was far from reassured even after hearing the next shipping forecast myself. The interest aboard knew no bounds. Without much conviction, I tried to think positively about the contribution my task was making to raising shipboard morale. I then stopped abruptly upon recalling the mess-up which had followed the last time I had thought positively.

Once we had cleared the Dover Strait, after my giving numerous alterations of course for collision avoidance, life became easier as we passed the South Foreland Light and headed up past Deal Pier and Ramsgate. Soon after passing the Tongue light vessel we entered the dredged channel into the Thames, from thence it was easy to check the passing of each fairway buoy against my plan. I think my sigh of relief was virtually tangible as LBB took the helm and brought our craft alongside the landing stage – within a couple of minutes of my estimate.

For a while I revelled in the praise of my fellow cadets (including what was regarded as a complimentary: "You jammy mucker", from Woodley). Captain Henshaw winked congratulations at me – or at least, that is how I interpreted his gesture – whilst LBB's contribution was delivered in acerbic tones as he said:

"Well, Carridia, you have been an unbelievably rright little sod for most of the time this trrip, but we may make a navigating officerr out of you, yet." This would have been accolade indeed, if he had not added: "Of course, I feel bloudy sorry for the poorr officers who end up with you on their ship. But maybe they'll have more time to sorrt you out than I've had. I notice you are RNR. Heaven help the Royal Navy when you join theirr rranks – I don't know who's likely to be in for the grreatest shock – but I should preparre yourrself for a rreal shake-up when you get to Darrtmouth. Taste of Naval discipline is just what you need, I'm inclined to think. The CPO's there'll soon sorrt you out, I've nae doubt." This lengthy and untimely addendum was uttered with considerable venom but, strangely, I did not think particularly less of him for that.

My final report on professional performance was extremely good and I scored nine out of ten points but, for some unaccountable reason, was really 'taken to the cleaners' by comments regarding behaviour, for which two points only were awarded. This diversity caused me to be called for interview with the Boss upon our arrival back at college. I was becoming quite accustomed to this particular venue but, on this occasion, entered full of trepidation.

My heart started to sink when he greeted me with a grim expression and heavily creased eyebrows. Motioning me to stand in front of his desk he began speaking quietly, yet firmly, in the voice of one who has lost all hope:

"Following uneventful progress here in College and success with your studies – as well of course your acceptance with Ellertons, you seem to have had an extremely unfortunate trip in a number of respects, Caridia." He commenced.

"Yes, sir." I replied. There seemed little point in saying or adding anything else. 'My fate's sealed anyway,' was my thought.

"Hmm … mm." The great man mused intelligently.

'He is clearly either at a loss to know what to say, or there's something he's trying to tell me,' was my deduction from this exclamation, whilst attempting to read anything at all concerning my future from his expression – with some pessimism and considerably sweating hands.

He continued: "Well, yes, Caridia. We've never had such a series of behavioural incidents arising from a trip on the *Stenwood Navigator* in all my years here."

'For God's sake, get on with it,' I almost blurted out, with increasing anxiety. 'Put me out of my misery.'

"It's just not good enough, is it?" He enquired, I assumed rhetorically, and therefore made no answer. He addressed me once more:

"You really must try to wake up your ideas you know, and curb your behaviour. Your attitude, I suppose it is, will not help you once you are away at sea," was his stern comment. "In fact, it will get you into really serious trouble with your officers and, at a last resort, could even lead to the termination of your cadetship. Your RN officers will not take too kindly to you either."

I waited to see what was next on this particular bill of fare.

"Yes, you were fortunate to be accepted by the Royal Naval Reserve and are going away with a top shipping company. You really do owe it to both, you know, to conform more closely."

"Yes, Sir. I really shall try, sir," was my soberly contrite contribution to this extremely mild rebuke.

I realised that he was still talking to me:

"Well, good luck, anyway, and don't forget to keep in touch with us," were his farewell words, after what I thought was going to be (yet another) real shocker of an interview.

He got up from his chair and offered his hand across the desk. Putting my sweaty, nervous little mitt into it we went through the ritual. Still in a state of shock, it did not seem possible such a calm dismissal was being offered. Leaving his office, the secretary, for some reason, gave me a deeply warm smile.

'Boozy' Fred must have been a particular friend of LBB because he was not quite so understanding. In fact, he gave me a vicious right royal rocket which, in an odd sort of way, left me strangely reassured. After the Boss's interview I could not take anything he had to say seriously, but felt it might have been a different story if the interviews had been reversed. My shaking continued whilst leaving his office and diminished only on entering the safety of Anson hut.

I had to admit, following this unfortunate character building and sea experience trip, I had been messing myself in case adverse reports were sent to both the RNR and Ellertons that could have had disastrous results on my future. Luckily, as Captain Mobbs had confirmed, my time studying the academic stuff ashore had been extremely successful. In fact, Mr. Dearnley told me just before leaving nautical college, as he wished me good fortune for my future; I had missed by just five marks, the much coveted navigational prize of a sextant, awarded by The Honourable Company of Master Mariners to the cadet achieving highest marks for theoretical navigation. I knew this prize had gone to an older cadet in another Watch who had 'A' level passes in mathematics and physics, but had not guessed I was even in the running for such a singular honour. It was definitely some aptitude in this direction that had saved me.

I was surprised to discover how my previous wafer thin feelings towards LBB, however, had changed. Perhaps, even at my age, I had the prescience to realise that our officers aboard the vessel had not experienced a particularly easy trip. But then, came my rueful reflection, neither had we – or, more accurately, my good self. Still, my supposition ran, it does help to see the humour which exists in most things. And, after all, the trip has proved it is not only ships that undergo pre-sea trials.

With fond farewells and exchanges of addresses with my fellow cadets, but most decidedly not Woodley – of whom I was glad to see the back as he wended his way to a leading tanker company – I went home to my virginal, chaste little bed. And, of course, a proud Mum and Dad who rightly, never completely discovered even one fifth of the events which had happened to beloved 'son and heir'. Peter and I wondered if we might serve together on the same ship.

My leave time had also its own unique series of ups and downs. A distant cousin of Mum's and her husband were very strict and particular Plymouth Brethren. Cousin Alfred and his wife lived in a large country house from where he farmed a massive estate. They belted around Winchester in the latest Rolls Royce and did not believe in newspapers, radio, television, or any communications – other than with family and 'members of the faith'. What on earth possessed them to invite me to stay for a weekend was (and remains) totally beyond my comprehension. I could only assume it was the result of an infrequent visit that had coincided with my arrival home from nautical college fresh-faced, debonair, uniformed, and superficially innocent. They had probably taken a fancy to me and decided to invite me back and so get to know me better. The outcome, even beforehand, was guaranteed to smash completely their illusions and widen even more the generation gap.

It must be understood that I was full of *joie de vivre*. Having recently survived both nautical college and especially LBB, I had not only been accepted as a navigating officer cadet, but had received a train and ferry travel warrant through the morning post on the day of my arrival home. This was accompanied by instructions to join Ellerton Shipping Company's *Earl of Bath* fourteen days hence in Amsterdam. A phone chat with Peter confirmed he also had received joining instructions but his voice broke with excited enthusiasm – he was flying the following week to join his ship, the *Earl of Auckland*, in Keppel Harbour at Singapore. Needless to say he hoped to spend some time, even if only a few hours, with his parents.

The relationships with aunt and uncle during my holiday were cordial enough, but I dropped a veritable multitude of clangers in my strivings to be a social success. The family had never had children and regarded teenagers as a breed totally alien to their sombre life-style – which of course they were. Unfortunately, because I had become so accustomed to referring to LBB as precisely that, explanations were required explaining the what's and why's of this trip so, most unwisely perhaps, I recounted some of my adventures at the nautical college and training ship – including some instructors' comments. Exercising sophisticated tact was never one of my strong points. All parties breathed a sigh of relief as I was finally deposited on Winchester railway station for the journey home.

The family, shortly afterwards, wrote breaking off all relationships with 'those who are not of the faith' – a matter of some puzzlement to Mum and Dad. I suspected however that Dad, although not saying anything at least to me, probably put more than a dubious two and two together connecting their action and his son's visit.

My next official duty was to call at Ellerton's head office, meet the cadet-training officer and collect a letter authorising issue of an Identity Card and Discharge Book. I recall my immense pleasure examining these documents closely on the train home – revelling momentarily in the pride of being a deck cadet in my chosen service.

The remainder of my leave was spent being shown off in uniform, wearing those much coveted, two shining cadet's gorgets, as Mum shunted me around to visit relatives.

One of my distant second cousins (many times 'removed' – a term which I loved) was a delicately-faced and shapely seventeen-year old, with a figure that was the very epitome of my adolescent dreams – a typical English rose, in fact. The effect of my uniform obviously stirred something deep within her bosom. She was very friendly and showed me around the garden whilst our mothers embarked on the inevitable exchange of family gossip and chit-chat. Sue was wearing an open-necked blouse that displayed her exciting curves and my eyes were drawn magnetically in that direction. We wandered among the flower beds.

"These are hydrangeas", she said absently and slightly breathlessly.

'Gosh. I thought they are called breasts,' was my immediate response, whilst at the same time cursing that devilish sense of humour with which I had been blessed.

"Oh, right," came my unconvincing reply.

We drifted into the potting shed and she – obviously overcome by the momentum of events – sidled up closely alongside me. I certainly found her extremely attractive and discovered a dry sensation in my throat which made breathing difficult. My hands started to sweat and there was a distinctly familiar prickling sensation within my pleasurable regions. It was so totally different to that encounter with the whore. Sue kissed me gently on the cheek with electric effect. This was my first kiss, other than by my mother and elderly female relatives and, frankly, I did not know what to do. Breathlessly, she urged me not to say anything, although all I could do was to stutter incomprehensible words, placing my hands gently on her shoulders and kissing her on her cheek. This was dangerous stuff. Her skin felt silky smooth to my dry lips and her slightly trembling body vulnerable to my touch. I moved my left hand and gently drew a loose slip of hair away from her eyes to the side of her head, wondering if a cuddle would be appropriate.

No – I couldn't. What now?

We both stood there and looked at each other. It was with a feeling of frustrated relief – probably to us both – when we heard my aunt call us in for tea. I quickly gave

Sue the name of my ship and the Company's address and we agreed to write to each other.

My metabolism was definitely affected and it was with considerable effort that I managed to keep my mind on the ensuing conversation. I was decidedly and uncharacteristically quiet on the way home and could not wait to go to bed. Mum seemed a little worried about my silence so, thinking quickly – in an effort to reassure her – simply blamed my apparent condition on apprehension over joining my ship the following Friday in Amsterdam. She seemed satisfied with this explanation but, somehow, I did not think either of us was totally convinced.

But I certainly experienced some delightfully disturbing thoughts over Sue; waking next morning feeling empty and shattered. Memories of recent class teaching came to my mind during which we had been told that any 'over-indulgence' was equivalent to playing consecutively three or four games of soccer. I experienced another Joycean epiphany – a revelation making me a kindred spirit with at least part of my education. I suddenly knew exactly what that master was talking about.

I acquired also some thoughts of Sue that were to contribute towards my downfall on the long hauls between ports during my first voyage to sea.

Chapter 3

MAIDEN VOYAGE

——

Nervous tension was probably responsible for lack of sleep that previous night. I was awoken in the early hours by a myriad of images floating across my mind which were difficult to understand. I had experienced no problems sleeping the night prior to departing for nautical college, which was quite remarkable considering that had been my first time away from home. Perhaps it was the realisation a foreign voyage would certainly prevent me coming home if things went awry. My mind was full of concerns: what the ship would be like, the countries and ports we would visit, for how long we would be away. How would I react to officers and crew – whether or not there might be officers like Fred and LBB and then what I should do; could I handle the work expected; would I be seasick as on the *Stenwood Navigator* – a crop of minor worries that were in danger of becoming major concerns.

I caught sight of favourite posters covering bedroom walls, my books, things of childhood, my record player – all of which would have to be left at home. I became aware of warm cosy smells in the house. Somehow everything suddenly seemed to contribute towards an atmosphere – they reminded me, in an equally odd way, of the disinfectant stink at Anson.

With mind in overdrive, sleep was not to be so I popped down stairs to make a cup of tea. My continued thoughts were disrupted by a clamouring squawk from the boiling kettle and, reaching for teapot and mug, heard Mum moving towards the kitchen. There was a decidedly pensive tone in her voice as she enquired if all was well. Cheerfully, I hastened to re-assure her there were no problems: that I merely felt thirsty and my presence in the kitchen, at two o'clock in the morning, was perfectly natural. She did not seem convinced so, taking a second mug whilst speaking (knowing only too well her likely reaction), offered her tea. Her affirmation was on cue, possibly a little too enthusiastically. She said, rather hesitatingly, she had heard me moving and supposed, like herself, I was not sleeping very well. Asking if my father was awake, she replied with a trace of her familiar smile, that he was 'sleeping like a log – only not one being sawn'. At least we were both putting on a brave face.

There was a pause as we looked at each other over the tea-tray. It was peculiar – as if suddenly seeing each other for the first time; a paradoxically intimate moment, not a time for words, as we wanted to say so much. Inevitably, of course, the questions started to flow anyway: had I finished packing, got my passport and seaman's documents ready. I interrupted her, rather irritably, assuring her she should not worry and, although appreciating her concern, sorting out these things was now up to me. Regretting my outburst, especially when she looked downcast, I apologised and reminded her how within less than a year events had moved dramatically and conclusively. Mum mentioned they had thought (and hoped) I would be staying at school for 'A' levels, but my quick interruption emphasised a reluctance to walk again over such shifting sands. I explained patiently that, although appreciating where they were coming from, this was the way things had worked out and, if a slight attack of 'the panics' was being experienced, my certainty held regarding the future and I would write once on board ship.

This seemed to re-assure her, partially at least, for her face muscles relaxed, easing the worry lines across her forehead. Mum reiterated how Dad and their Church home group would be praying for me, and they would look forward to my letters as they had whilst I was at Keddleston. Defensively, she added it was only natural for all to be concerned at this stage. I concurred and, with tea finished, we returned to our rooms – each sensitively aware of mutual feelings, but knowing further expression was futile.

Mindful of my previous departure I strictly forbade them to see me off at the station. Dad could not anyway because of work, so the last glimpses Mum and I had, were looks on each other's face as we waved farewell through the taxi window.

At Liverpool Street railway station I met the Third Officer and Fourth Engineer who were also joining the ship. The office had given clear instructions how we should meet and, I found out later – in the way of a caring Company – had instructed these more experienced officers to make a point of looking for me. The situation was easy for them as all Company cadets joined and left ships wearing cap and No.1 doeskin uniform reefer and trousers. So, standing alone by the barrier to platform one, a convenient meeting point – I stood out prominently – like a lighthouse on a clear dark night.

My slight reverie, listening to shunting noises of steam engines and bustling concourse life, was broken by the sight of two smartly dressed, sun-tanned young men approaching, looking enquiringly in my direction. The taller one smiled and, in cultured tones, asked if I were Jonathan Caridia. He introduced himself as Julian Blandford, Third Officer of the *Earl of Bath* and humorously brought the other officer into the conversation by referring to 'this bearded apparition who goes by the name of Jim Hunter'. Julian's humour continued as he told me Jim was the Fourth 'ginger beer' or engineering officer and, because of this, deck officers did not normally speak to him. His warm smile was joined by an interested grin from the engineering officer who mildly protested his innocence. My instant reaction to this welcome was to feel at ease – and a few worries slipped quietly away.

Julian pointed out we had to change our travel warrants. I had been given mine separately just in case both officers were missed. Going to the ticket office he mentioned that because we were all early, there was plenty of time to look around station shops and enjoy a pre-travel coffee. He gave me a friendly glance and explained, having just qualified as Third Mate, he was on his first trip as an officer. In view of his junior status, and with only a few years difference in our ages, he suggested I call him by his Christian name.

I mumbled thanks and asked if he knew anything about our ship, voyage or cargo. Catching his quick intelligent glance I sensed, through tone and questions, he had instinctively perceived my concerns. Julian did not comment on this, but merely supplied the details. She was a general cargo ship, loading at one of Amsterdam's grain terminals and bound for a number of Red Sea ports. She was of 7,030 gross tons and had been built before the Second World War at Blythswood's Glasgow Yard. His explanations were interrupted by the Fourth Engineer expressing astonishment at an unusual charter for Ellertons. He asked if Julian knew which ports we would be calling at, bringing forth names which sounded almost like a foreign language to my ears. Our first discharge was to be Port Sudan, whence we would head for Massowah, Assab, Djibouti and Berbera. Following discharge, we would probably pop across to Aden for bunkers. Julian stressed he had no idea why the company had undertaken this run, but guessed it sounded like a 'good-will' cargo and we would probably revert to the company's traditional trading patterns afterwards, possibly by being sent India-bound (as we were so close) for loading to the United States, or Far East. That morning I learnt my first Merchant naval adage, 'life at sea is mainly uncertainty – so wait patiently'.

In my naivety, the Fourth's gloomy reaction was unexpected. He held the view that my romantically sounding places were, as he put it rather picturesquely, well up the 'rectum of the world', adding they were just slightly better than trading in the Persian Gulf. Either way he foresaw little chance for a good run ashore. I thought about all I had heard and felt a little perturbed concerning the possibility of no shore leave. Julian agreed they were pretty duff places and continued telling me more about our ship. She was had five hatches, served by eighteen derricks, with No. 2 – the largest hatch – fitted with heavy lift facilities. So far as he knew, there was one deck cadet already on board, who had been junior to Julian on a trip discharging a deep-sea cargo. They had relieved the regular officers and taken the vessel around United Kingdom and continental ports before calling into the Royal Group of docks in London to load for south and east Africa. With another touch of humour, he compared the ship's trading pattern to a British Road Services lorry. The cadet's name was Page, and he thought I would get along with him very well, especially if help were needed initially in finding my way around.

A train and then ferry trip to the Hook of Holland provided ample time for us to become better acquainted – and for me to feel increasingly relaxed in such friendly company. It was about three o'clock in the morning by the time we joined the ship. There were no mishaps over our local train journey or indeed the entire trip from London, although the taxi driver lost his way from Amsterdam railway station and took us to the wrong berth. A telephone call by Julian to the Agent soon sorted that out – although the latter (unlike the taxi driver) was not a happy Dutchman with his early morning shake.

Cargo was being worked when we arrived on board, and the Second Officer taking the watch, greeted Julian like a long lost brother. I wondered if they had sailed together but, listening to their exchange, found the ship was short of deck officers so, in finest Merchant Naval traditions, the Chief and Second Officers were each doing twelve hour shifts. The Fourth Engineer disappeared to his own accommodation. I sensed the Second Mate looking closely at me. He asked Julian, with a whisper of a smile, who this new specimen of cadet standing innocently before him might be, leading Julian to introduce us. Instinctively, I knew that there would be no christian names in my relationship with Mr. Eyres who stood, from my point of view, very much in senior officer territory. I was happy enough with this state of affairs (which was just as well – seeing that they were unalterable). I then realised the Second was telling me about my fellow cadet. Catching sight of him at the end of the accommodation block, he called over a tall, fresh faced lad, very 'public school' looking, and clearly older than me. These features were taken in as he crossed the deck from starboard to where we stood by the gangway on the port side.

Mr. Eyres introduced both me and the Third Mate telling Page, for his sins, he had a new cadet to look after. He would be relieved from deck duties for a while to take me to our accommodation, see me settled and then was to report back to the Second on deck.

The cadet greeted Julian with enthusiasm, simultaneously giving me a look of calm appraisal before shaking my hand warmly – a contribution that added considerably to my reassurance. The mates stood on for a few moments whilst we exchanged pleasantries, until interrupted by Mr. Eyres who enquired, in a gentle Cornish burr, if I would like something to eat and drink. He explained Page would be 'knocking up' supper for the Third Officer and himself shortly and that it was easy to add an extra sausage or something for me. I liked his easy yet firm manner and suddenly became aware of feeling very hungry, so replied strongly in the affirmative, mentioning we had a meal on the ferry, but that had been hours previously. The Second laughed, explaining it might be a bit premature to sound too enthusiastic, as I had not yet sampled what my fellow minion had the effrontery to call cooking. He suggested my judgment should be saved, presumably while munching my way through a 'ton of indigestion tablets' for afters.

With relaxed smiles all round, Page led the way to the officers' deck and our cadet quarters making small-time yet informative conversation. He introduced himself again as Victor or Vic for preference, confirming he and the Third had sailed as cadets for six weeks round the coast on the *Earl of Pretoria,* in between that ship's deep-sea African voyages, early the previous year. From the enthusiasm in his voice, I gathered Vic held Julian in considerable respect, admiring the way he had acted as senior cadet. He changed tack by enquiring if this was my first voyage and where I had been pre-sea trained.

I told him about Keddleston, but Vic's blank look indicated he had not met any cadets from my nautical college or even heard of it. This led me to explain, a little diffidently, something of my background and the circumstances of my application to Ellertons. His lead encouraged me to ask similar questions.

Vic answered indirectly, asserting I must have made an extremely solid impact with the Chief Marine Super and he also was suitably impressed. Casually, his own background unfolded for, after attending Harrow School, a couple of years had been spent at Pangbourne Nautical College. He had left over three years previously and was soon to take Second Mates' certificate. With what was to prove typical modesty, Vic added neither school had proved too unnerving. I was very impressed, and blanched a bit, as they stood firmly in the First division. He showed me around the cadets' self-contained accommodation block and left me to settle in whilst he reported again to the Second Officer.

In the process of unpacking and sorting my gear into the locker and under-bunk drawer pointed out as my own, I mused delightedly how friendly towards me everyone had been. My relieved excitement was perhaps understandable and, almost hugging myself, I thought perhaps my parents' prayers were working after all.

Having stowed everything neatly, I went out the starboard side door onto the boat deck momentarily relishing the atmosphere and view confronting me. My ears were assailed by a swishing sound, as hundreds of tons of grain shot into the after of two ship's holds, abaft the accommodation block, from an elevator on the port side. Everything, for the distance I could see, was bathed in an eerie series of lights from ashore and onboard, creating massive shadows along the deck immediately below me. Through the lattice of derricks, swung to starboard to keep them out of the way, the raised poop accommodation house stood starkly white in the mixtures of light. To my inexperienced eye, it seemed an endless way along the after deck.

On the other side of the river three tugs hooted stridently, in varying tones, as they edged a large cargo ship from her berth. The mournful siren of a motor barge taking the river bend added its anxious voice and I watched, with newly found professional interest, as it gave way to the burdened tugs. A series of hitherto unknown smells wafted across my nostrils: agitated grain dust and indistinguishable shipboard aromas, mixed with a heady smell from the river and an oily tarry taint from cargo handling gear. The latter made me think reminiscently of the boat yard at college. I felt slight dampness from the wooden rail beneath my elbow through my uniform sleeve and shivered slightly. There was no doubt I was profoundly grateful things were going so well and appreciated the start Keddleston had given me – but I had absolutely no regrets about leaving.

After a few moments, I made my way down a series of brass-edged ladders to the main deck and looked for the Second Officer by the gangway. Not surprisingly, he was nowhere to be seen, causing me to pause hesitatingly unsure what to do next or where to go. Suddenly, from the entrance into the accommodation block behind me, a voice spoke into my ear in a kind of Welsh-accented English, asking if assistance was needed. It made me jump slightly. Turning, my glance caught sight of a dark skinned man in a black uniform patrol jacket smiling his query. Explaining I was looking for the Second Officer, he informed me that "Secondee-officer Sahib" had gone to the galley, and asked if this was my first ship. I smiled affirmatively and paused again, uncertainly. He grinned once more and, in confidently lilting tones, told me he was the duty *Secunny* and Watchman. He suggested I should go with him to the galley. Without further ado, he led the way aft of the accommodation block and entered a large thickly built varnished door, slightly spattered by weathering. Speaking to somebody inside and simultaneously standing aside, the *Secunny* allowed me to enter. Vic's friendly tones thanked him and invited me in. A large steel range extended across the entire after part of the galley, with sinks and working tables across the other two sides and centre. I was unable to identify any of the large cookers and pots, but noted how clean and shiny everything looked, aside from the area where Vic had been performing his arts. This part was a confused mess of peelings, skins and rinds.

As I glanced around, a large plate heaped with sausages, bacon, mushrooms, beans, two eggs and a pile of chips was thrust into one hand, and a mug of steaming tea into the other. I was then directed to the duty mess across an alleyway, from which came the sound of laughter and chat, as both deck officers joked and discussed colleagues and ships across the fleet. They caught sight of me, standing hesitatingly outside, and the Second Officer invited me to join them, moving along to make room for me at the polished wooden table. Julian pushed a heaped plate of bread and butter in my direction, as Vic joined us with his own plateful, taking the place directly opposite me.

The senior cadet suggested that, following this meal, it might be best for me to get my head down. He would call in our cabin at 0700, in about three hours time to wake me, pointing out I would not have long to kip, but at least it would enable me to have a shower before meeting the Chief Officer at 0730 when we would both receive our day's instructions. Concerning his own plans he hoped that, having completed a twelve hour cargo watch, he would be allowed to turn in – unless the Mate wanted him for anything else.

A ship's galley of the period (courtesy Shell IT&S).

Munching away happily and nodding agreement, I found it quite a struggle to put away 'my extra sausage or something'. As a contribution towards the generally relaxed conversation, I commented that it seemed unlikely that we would starve on this particular ship. Vic's spontaneous response confirmed that feeding on all Ellerton Indian-crewed ships was invariably excellent and I could eagerly anticipate the chief cook's curries and puddings. Before he could proceed further the Third Officer interrupted, jocularly complaining Page was a typical cadet – always thinking of his stomach and food. Quick off the mark, Vic in turn interrupted the third by asserting sex was also a major priority. This brought Mr. Eyres into the conversation. He dramatically raised his eyes heavenwards in mock solemnity and, half turning to the third mate, stated he wondered how long it would be before 'the topic of the moment' raised its never weary head. The despairing tones however were belied by the smile in his eyes as he stated the younger generation never seemed to change and how their one-track minds left him wondering if there was any hope at all for the human race. Vic retorted that there would be even less hope for humanity if his generation never changed their views. I was impressed by the quick-witted exchange, and realised suddenly Julian was bringing me into the melee by shooting a quick glance across the table and questioning whether or not I was any different. Rapidly gathering my wits, I confirmed that in both areas there was certainly no difference at all, my mouth being far too full for further amplification. The cross banter continued for a while before Mr. Eyres, offering a shrewd look over the table which included Vic and myself, stated categorically that I would probably 'be all right, after a little time to settle-in', a comment that spoke volumes. It had never dawned on me, until that moment, that my officers and fellow cadet might also have experienced a few reservations regarding a new arrival in their ranks.

Back in our cabin I undressed quickly and, in just my pyjama bottoms, turned- in to the narrow bunk on the starboard side of the cabin, below a curtain covering a small port-hole. Vic's bunk was against the opposite bulkhead, whilst a desk and settee flanked the other parts. The door next to our table led to a cross alleyway, from which branched our study and washroom. Our cabin was carpeted, small, but adequate; with the furniture a darkly stained, highly polished teak. Frankly, I was too excited and so relieved by the friendliness encountered, that initially sleep seemed impossible. My thoughts were accompanied by a slight vibration along my back from the ship's generator. There was also a mixture of constant external noises; deep-toned muffled hoots from nearby ships wrestled with the lighter – almost neurotic – squeaks from smaller river craft; whirling machinery struggled with anonymous shipboard crashes, and a myriad of other unidentifiably intriguing sounds. Cosily, I wrapped the sheet around my neck and, as sleep finally wafted in, felt contentedly that I could probably cope with whatever the future held.

It was a little after 0700 when I was rudely awakened by Vic barging into the cabin like a neurotic banshee in a whirlwind. He was running a bit late and called his instructions to me even before clearing the door. Apologising for the delay, due to a problem on deck, he urged me to get a move on. By the time this information had been taken-in, he had vanished. It took a few minutes to gather together my thoughts and realise where I was and what was going on. Rubbing sleep from my eyes, and allowing Vic's words to penetrate, I staggered from my bunk into the shower. The mechanics of the thing were finally mastered, without giving myself a third degree scald, and I was completing dressing into my uniform, when Vic came back to take me to meet the Chief Officer. Leaving the cabin and, locking the door as we were in port, he explained that as cadets we were not allowed the services of a steward, but Mr. Gaskell had no objections if we *baksheeshed* the *Topaz*, an Asian equivalent to a galley boy, to look after personal laundry and bed linen changes. We had to keep the cabin, showers and study clean ourselves though; it all sounded a very reasonable arrangement to me.

The Chief Officer was of medium height and, like my father, had dark hair turning slightly grey at the temples. His uniform was immaculate and I caught sight of two rows of medal ribbons above the handkerchief in his top pocket, indicating service in the last war – now some years past. He greeted me with a quick smile and welcomed me on board with pleasantries about my joining and our forthcoming trip. I replied, aware all the time that he was watching me closely, and explained how, with the Third Officer and Fourth Engineer, we had joined in the early hours of the morning; that I had just left nautical college and was pleased to be on board. Nervousness doubtless ensured I offered information the Mate knew anyway.

He took this in politely, confirmed Page was responsible for my progress and would look after me, and suggested any problems experienced should initially be 'aimed in that direction'. Mr. Gaskell assured me that all officers would help me settle as much as they could. All I had to do was to ask, but his features hardened as he urged me to make sure it was at the right time. Before dismissing us both to go for breakfast, he added there were two sittings for all meals and junior officers, including cadets, used the first, as normally the second was reserved for senior officers. They however were coming in early on this occasion, but this was not to worry me. After eating, I was to change from uniform into working gear and collect my Discharge Book, following which we would go to the Captain's cabin for 'signing-on', where the Ship's Articles would be dealt with. He turned to Vic, telling him once he had eaten he could 'get his head down' until further duties at 1800, thus giving opportunity for a good rest. We acknowledged our respective instructions and left.

The cadet's table in the main-deck saloon was the after one of two, on the port side near the swing doors, next to a window overlooking the quay. I noticed immediately the crisp white tablecloths, napkins, and jackets of the two stewards; the polished cutlery and china neatly arrayed on our table. It reminded me of a top class London hotel and was equally as impressive. My view outside consisted of the weathered black and grey paint-smeared bulk of our grain elevator, surmounted by a maze of rusty dank pipes, streaked with bird droppings. The Goanese steward came over and showed the menu to Vic, afterwards offering it to me. This neatly typed card advertised a variety of five courses, including a fish kedgeree – something I had never even associated with breakfast – although my father occasionally enjoyed a kipper or two first thing in the morning. In my newness, unlike Vic, I missed out the fruit juice and cereal and merely gave an order for the main course. He returned shortly with my second heaped plate of food in less than four hours. I caught one or two glances coming my way from senior navigating and engineering officers seated around the centre table. As my eyes crossed to the two small tables on the starboard side, overlooking the still busy river, Jim Hunter the Fourth Engineer, in animated conversation with his colleagues, threw me a quick smile of welcome.

An authoritative voice disrupted our casual talk as a smartly uniformed figure passed our table on his way out of the saloon. I noted the four gold rings surmounted by a diamond on the sleeve of the hand resting on our table and, even whilst Vic answered, guessed this was the ship's Captain. Rapidly, I joined Vic in getting up from the chair and raised my eyes to look directly into the piercing glance from a determined, but kindly, weather beaten face confronting me. So I met the Master – Captain Henderson-Smyth. He stated it was good to have me serving on board his ship and he was looking forward to us meeting more formally later, with Mr. Gaskell the Chief Officer, but there was no harm in being introduced now. I responded, acknowledging the man who would influence considerably my immediate future and who, for some reason, reminded me very strongly of Captain Mobbs from my navigational school. The Captain smiled slightly before passing out of the saloon without further comment, leaving us to finish our meal.

Vic enthused about the Captain as 'a really good skipper both professionally and as a person', pointing out that nearly all of the masters and officers in Ellertons were from a similar mould. He stressed conditions with the Group were certainly different from many other companies where cadets could sometimes experience a very rough time indeed. With some Lines, for example, they were not allowed in the saloon, but had to eat all meals in the duty mess. He added we were both pretty fortunate to be with this company, an assertion which – in my innocence – I could only agree. It soon became obvious that such emphasis on mutual loyalty, with Company Contract officers being the accepted method of employment, was common currency within Ellertons.

Before I could change into my blue working gear and report to the Mate's office, he called to me along the alleyway as he left the saloon, simultaneously sharing a joke with the Chief and Second engineering officers. Confirming I had with me my Discharge Book (which had luckily been slipped into my pocket) he took me up the green-carpeted companionway two decks to the captain's cabin. Here, I again met the Master and signed an impressive looking ship's copy of The Articles of Agreement. Being formally welcomed on board by Captain Henderson-Smyth, he advised me that the British Consul would be notified of my presence legally on the ship, thus complying with current legislation. Glancing in a blur at the small print as I signed, my eye caught a sentence advising, 'the voyage could be prolonged for up to two years duration', but 'had to be between the limits of 70º N and 60º S'. It seemed a suddenly sobering thought.

Back in the ship's office, I was told to go on deck and report to the Third Officer who would be 'out there somewhere'. Vic was fast asleep when I returned to our quarters and quietly changed. Glancing at his face, relaxed in repose, he seemed very much younger. I did not feel my anticipated tiredness, after just a couple hours' sleep and, closing the door gently, went down external ladders to the main deck. There was no sign of the Third Officer aft, so I walked forward along the starboard outboard side, hence keeping clear of cargo workings to port. Suddenly, I caught glimpses of a white peaked capped and boiler-suited figure, looking down into No. 3 hatch and went over to join him.

Julian glanced up, recognised me and smiled a welcome, asking if I had slept well and if everything was all right. I grinned and thanked him for asking, adding a 'Sir' to my response. I had not forgotten the invitation to refer to him by his Christian name, but the mark of respect simply came naturally. He gave me a slightly surprised look, but offered no further comment, merely telling me I should turn to with the *Serang* for the day. He was the senior rating in charge of the deck crowd and would look after me for much of my deck periods on board during the trip.

We stood watching grain cascading into the upper tween-decks from three 'giant vacuum cleaner tubes', operating in reverse, as it were. The lower hold had been filled, but not yet boarded over. There was a gang of men sweeping loose grain into piles, from the port corners of the hatch, where a couple of small bulldozers collected it, pushing it into the lower hold. Another gang was preparing to fit timber partitions at the mouth of the hatch coming. These, Julian told me, were shifting boards, necessary to contain the upper part of the cargo so that it did not move around too much and so interfere with the stability of the ship. Three men on top of the cargo were using large scrapers to shift the loading flow into the starboard corners of the hatch. It seemed to me a lot of men were required. Julian said grain was an easy cargo to load, from the duty mates' point of view, for all that was required was to make certain it was evenly distributed. I asked him the rate at which we were loading and was told 'about 450 tons per hour' which, to my inexperienced ear, seemed very fast. Julian agreed and said, as the bagged grain had already been taken, we would soon complete the bulk and then be away. We paused watching for a few moments longer until he told me to accompany him so the *Serang* and I could be introduced.

The Deck *Serang* was the equivalent to the Bosun on a European-crewed ship and was a very imposing figure. With grey hair, and dressed in dark blue working uniform and black turban with red facings, he wore silver chains around his neck as his badge of office. He greeted us warmly. Used to working cadets, he handed over his duties to the *Tindal*, or second-in-command, and showed me around the ship. I felt a distinct thrill climbing the ladder leading to the fo'c'sle head and, impressed by the height, tried to make sense of the machinery and moorings. Certainly, from seamanship lessons, the head and breast ropes were easily identified, along with the for'ard backspring wire. I found considerable confidence in recalling their functions. The *Serang* pointed out things of interest (which to me was everything) in clear, only slightly accented English, and allowed me to climb onto the contactor house top, serving No. 2 hatch, pointing out winch controls and explaining their workings. I was really much too excited and apprehensive however to take in much of what he said.

The morning passed rapidly. I popped into the duty mess, remembered from the previous night, for a mid-morning cup of tea and some biscuits before rejoining the *Serang* forward. Later Julian dismissed me to change into uniform and go into the saloon for lunch. Afterwards, I was to report back to the *Serang* and join in whatever deck work the crew were doing. The Mate, at the end of the day, asked me how I thought things had gone and listened carefully, obviously allowing me to ramble on enthusiastically, although I suspected he was assessing my interest and observations.

Clearly aware of my unusual background and, without being condescending, he said my past was of only vague interest to the officers on board; that the Captain and he were concerned purely with the way I settled into the Company, mainly because they had a responsibility – taken very seriously – for my training. He stressed I would find things quite easy sailing with Asian crew and the lifestyle for me, 'by the very nature of things,' would be far more relaxed with Ellertons than many contemporary British shipping companies. So far, initial reports about me from officers and *Serang* had been extremely favourable, even though it was still very early days. Urging me to keep up the good work, he then explained some routines which would come my way during the passage. I would be on day work with the *Serang* for the time being, normally on deck from 0800 until 1700, except when the ship was on a stand by for harbour stations, or any other circumstance, when I would work in with the rest of the officers and crew, regardless of hours.

I liked the way he explained the reasons for what would take place instead of merely relating what would happen. He continued to elaborate, explaining that being used this way would free up Page, enabling him to be put on watches, in order to gain bridge experience prior to taking his 2nd Mates' ticket, next time we were in the UK. He urged me to take in as much as possible and my training could start next day by drawing rough sketches of gear, deck layouts, etc. and writing these up neatly into my journal, or record book, 'whatever it was called'. I was to show this to him every Saturday as convenient, but probably directly after breakfast. Mr. Eyres would also keep an eye on my correspondence course and professional, technical and academic progress. The Mate would additionally expect me to learn one Collision Regulation every week and repeat this to him without error when we talked through my book. Such specific instructions were very re-assuring; the workload sounded formidable, but at least, I thought to myself, one had been given me 'to formid about'.

> '… so let me put your minds at rest, immediately. I am very happy and everyone is so kind to me. They really take an interest. The Chief Officer is my direct boss on board, not the Captain as I thought, whilst Vic the senior cadet, is a great chap. His father is a very senior Royal Naval officer – an Admiral of all things, but Vic is a genuine and really quite humble person who had no desire to follow the family career-line, preferring the informality of the Merchant Navy instead. The food is excellent as well, whilst the Asian crew are fun to work with …'

So ran parts of my first letter home. I wrote also my first rather guarded one to Sue; my very first letter to a girl friend.

I was not able to go ashore, as the ship completed loading the day after reporting on board, so went into the smoke room after dinner and mixed with the officers. Whilst names remained something of a blur, certain personalities immediately made a strong impression. 'Sparks', the radio officer, and 'Lecky', as the electrical officer was called, figured prominently amongst the characters encountered. They bought me a beer and I was invited to join a cribbage school. This was a game my father had taught me which enabled me to make a fair impression. The Mate came in later, saw us playing and joined in, making a two partnered game. I was with Sparks against the other two. Initially, it felt quite awkward playing cards with the man who earlier had been so very much in charge of my affairs, but the atmosphere was so relaxed I soon became likewise, joining in the laughter which accompanied the more serious undertones of the game, and contributing occasional quips – which seemed well received. Sparks and I lost a couple of games, but won the overall set – a matter of some teasing to me from the Chief Officer who threatened a work-load the next day which would 'kill a whole crew of first-trip cadets'.

The Officer's smoke room (courtesy BP plc).

I was awakened just after three o'clock in the morning, told by Vic that stand-by had been called and the Mate wanted me on the bridge. I must turn-to, in serge battle-dress with uniform cap, as quickly as possible. Tugs had been ordered and were closing the ship, whilst the Pilot was already in the Captain's cabin. We were to sail very shortly. Vic was 'going forward' with the Chief Officer, but I would be with Mr. Blandford in the wheelhouse, who would give me instructions. I soon made my way there and was told by Julian to keep the Movement Book. This, he explained, was a legal document into which were entered the times (synchronized with the duty engineering officer) of all telegraph movements and courses to steer. The name of the Pilot was always recorded, as well as that of the tugs taken fore and aft, and whether or not these were made fast or merely in attendance. He had already tested the steering gear and telegraphs. Shortly afterwards the Captain came onto the bridge, chatting casually to the Pilot. Julian was keeping an eye on the quartermaster or *Secunny* – as well, of course, on me.

Manoeuvring with cadet keeping the Movement Book (courtesy BP plc).

My first impressions were of the business-like atmosphere on the bridge. It also appeared extraordinarily high up. The Captain smiled at Julian and me, without saying anything, and the Pilot gave initial orders necessary for us to leave the berth. Although I understood little of what was happening, it seemed a reasonably straightforward operation to my eyes, but one full of interest. I listened and tried to take in as much as possible, whilst writing instructions called to me by the Third Officer. As both Pilot and Master went out onto the port bridge wing, Julian positioned himself at the entrance to the wheelhouse, stationing me by the large telegraph explaining that my job, additional to keeping the Movement Book, was to work the telegraph as he relayed commands from Pilot or Master to me. I enquired, a little diffidently, how officers on the bridge wing could know the state of manoeuvring controls whilst outside, only to be informed that repeaters of engine room revolutions and position of helm indicators were fitted above the wheelhouse door.

"Half Ahead", Julian suddenly called out. I felt a distinct thrill as I moved the brass telegraph handle from Slow and, gaining confidence amidst the stentorian ringing response from the engine-room, automatically noted this movement and time. At what looked like a considerable distance, I could make out the Chief Officer and Vic on the fo'c'sle head. It looked as if the cadet was directing operations. I mentioned this to Julian, during a quiet period, who told me that it was good experience for him. He broke off the conversation suddenly to shout, "Full Ahead, Jon."

I repeated the order, complied and then moved swiftly out of the way as Julian shot across to a battery of telephones on the forward part of the control panel – one of which was ringing stridently.

"Half Ahead on the engines please," called the Pilot.

I felt a slight panic and then pleasure, as I yelled back the command indicating I had understood it, and then yanked the telegraphs once again. Julian, still speaking into the phone, smiled his approval to me. Below my peaked cap, I suddenly felt ten feet tall.

It was daylight by the time we cleared the thirteen-mile long North Sea Canal and the Pilot left our ship. As Julian escorted him to the gangway, the Master ordered me onto the monkey island above the wheelhouse, to take down the 'H' flag and Dutch courtesy ensign. Whilst undoing the Inglefield clips, I blessed my pre-sea training, shuddering as I thought back over memories of my encounter with that 'ghastly woman' (as I still thought of her), and went back to the wheelhouse. Upon my return, I was told by the Captain to go below.

So my very first stand-by ended. It was a never to be forgotten experience – even as familiarity eventually overcame uniqueness.

The next few days soon settled into a thoroughly enjoyable routine. I was working on deck as we passed Dover and Folkestone, watching these familiar holiday landmarks sliding swiftly away off our starboard quarter – and, yes, thinking back with a shiver to the last time these waters had been navigated. The weather and sea were kind and I relished the slight pitching and rolling as *my* ship moved easily to a slight head swell into the English Channel. The sea seemed deep azure blue, topped with a gentle white spume, and I could again almost taste its saltiness. I worked agreeably enough with the *Serang* and deck crew, liking the ready smiles accompanying the antics of the ratings as they hosed away residual grain from beneath hatches and scuppers. My job was to help sweep this milchy stink from under ladders and out of bulwark obstructions as the *Tindal* operated a large hose-pipe. It was a pretty casual routine.

The weather took a distinct turn for the worse as we entered the Bay of Biscay. I felt decidedly ill but was not actually sea-sick, but came very close to it. Little more than dry toast and a cup of coffee could be taken in the saloon. Vic stressed the importance for me to go for all meals and at least have something to eat; whether I felt like it or not and whether or not it stayed there, pointing out it was better for me to have taken some food. My job that morning was to clean out cabin, study and 'heads'. It was good to have something to do, but I felt really ghastly and could not wait to turn in immediately after what passed for dinner.

Whilst lying part-dozing in my bunk, my mind attempted to rationalise this illness. I appreciated the sensation experienced was only minor compared to what it could have been. It was plainly associated with unfamiliar and unexpected motions of the ship – sudden violent rolling and pitching movements in apparently diverse directions: after all, earthquakes never happened where I lived in south-east London. It could also have something to do with fear – of being frightened by the immense powerful expanses of the sea – and was probably linked with possibilities that she might founder (a word learnt comparatively recently by reading Conrad at school). My newness to the sea and way of seafaring life might also have made a contribution – activating a sense of wider apprehension. There was almost certainly a medical explanation – though what precisely that might be, I had no idea. Trying to understand possible causes proved little compensation for the effects, as my tightened stomach muscles and unnatural taste of bile in the mouth, bore witness.

Vic had his own theory about the weather, which he expounded next morning as I moved around the cabin on one leg trying to dry off after my shower. His theories were interspersed between mortifying comments on my actions – which I tried to ignore. Apparently, one could generalise that smooth water before and after the Bay of Biscay often indicated roughness inside it, and vice versa. All I could do was lurch to an unexpected roll of the ship, as I struggled into my underwear, and then dressed into working gear. Vic was on the 0400 to 0800 bridge watch with the Chief Officer, but had been stood down early. Before turning-in, he was going to have breakfast and wanted to pass on orders for my day's work. There was little that could be done on deck in the weather we were still experiencing, so the Mate wanted me to clean brass and put a broom round bridge wings, wheelhouse and chartroom.

I went up, just as Mr. Gaskell was handing over the watch to Julian, and listened to their exchange. It sounded very impressive as they went through routines which included courses, shipping movements, radar targets and compass checks. The Mate smiled a greeting at me as he went below, whilst Julian showed me the working area, pointing out the after house locker where all cleaning gear was kept.

In the fresh air, my sea-sickness and I decided to call a marginal truce so I grabbed broom, dustpan and brush and returned with my haul. Julian showed me how to lift bridge wing gratings and, even more importantly, how to replace them in the correct order afterwards. It was a pleasant venue for working. I could not see much coastline, but noticed a few ships around whilst taking sneak previews each time the radar was passed. Afterwards, Brasso was applied enthusiastically to window clasps and steering binnacle. I found the latter particularly pleasing. Once the liquid dried, and had been given a good hard polish, the king-pin and boss shone effectively. They looked smart against the dark oiled oak of the wheel. In between working and chatting to Julian, my loaded thoughts centred on keeping my own watch there one day.

It was about ten when the Captain popped up for a chat with the Third Mate, and to share a cup of coffee brought in on a tray by the officers' steward. I was sent below to the duty mess for my 'smoke-oh' – as the Mate called both morning and afternoon breaks. It was quite a handy place for meals and snacks obviating the need to change into uniform and go into the saloon. On this occasion, duty engineering officers were in the mess, taking their 'stand-easy', as they called the same thing, and I was soon included in the general chat and humour.

The Old Man was still in the wheelhouse upon my return and had quite a long talk with me, exchanging comments about how seafaring and I were getting on. With his authoritative air and firm jaw, he had a habit of looking at you whilst speaking, and sometimes directly into your eyes. It was neither threatening nor intimidating, but initially seemed rather unnerving. It was me that had to get used to it, though. I suddenly deduced why a similarity between him and Captain Mobbs had been detected – it was nothing physical after all, but something of a presence – an aura of authority almost, for they both had 'the same stamp'. Afterwards, Julian called me 'a right little creep', but the smile accompanying his remark confirmed he was only jokingly pulling my leg.

The wheelhouse had its own unique atmosphere. It was generally a quiet place, apart from the swishing of the sea some fifty feet below, and the constant click of the gyro-repeater compensating for slight deviations from the ship's course caused by fluctuations in wind and tidal effects. It had a number of oak and teak panels with a chartroom behind separated by a curtained partition. This excluded any light that might interfere with night-time lookout duties. A battery of telephones, light switches and other controls was on the wheelhouse side, behind a centre-line steering binnacle. On the other side, a large chart table was surrounded by various electronic navigational instruments. I was quick to recognise the Decca Navigator from sea-training days (now seemingly so distant), but the remainder meant very little to me. There was also a rack for parallel rules, protractors, erasers and 2B pencils.

I took a quick preview at a chart of the distant Spanish coast and noticed the position fixes, each neatly timed, indicating our progress. It seemed much more interesting than my manual tasks. Later, Sparks came along with a routine weather report – nothing serious – and stopped for a chat and joke. I liked the way he and Julian included me in a wider teasing, and his comments about the drubbing we had again given the Mate at cribbage the previous evening.

After lunch in the saloon, I changed back into working gear and turned to with the *Serang* and crew on deck. My task was to clean the fo'c'sle head of grain debris which had become lodged there and which the recent motion had brought to light. Being so far forward, I felt decidedly ill but stuck at it, even though I was violently sick after a while. I was sent by the *Serang* to rinse my mouth with water from the duty mess, and came back slightly refreshed, although feeling 'like death warmed up', as my mother used to say. I stayed in the fo'c'sle, until stood down around 1700 to change for dinner. Needless to say, the saloon and I did not meet for very long on that occasion, but my bunk made me feel very welcome.

Two days later we passed Gibraltar and I caught my first glimpse of the famous rock. Working with Vic, we hoisted the ship's signal letters, so notifying the signal station on Europa Point. They, in turn, would let Lloyd's of London know of our passing for eventual insertion into their famous *Lloyd's List and Shipping Gazette*. It was fascinating to see ships of all types and nationalities seemingly closing us from every direction.

As we approached Port Said, the increasing temperatures meant officers changed daily uniform from blue reefers into whites for saloon meals and off-duty time in the smoke room. I had to take the order book round for every officer to sign, indicating they had been advised, so all would appear in correct rig the next day. Blue shorts with black socks and shoes soon became my working gear – though I kept on my long-sleeved shirt and trousers for a few extra days, until my skin tanned gently, so preventing burning. Both Mr. Gaskell and Vic strongly recommended my adopting a sensible approach to this. It was still great to swim in the pool and mix socially.

My deck duties were varied. I quite liked going into the Cassab's domain where he kept the deck working stores. This was in the fo'c'sle-head and possessed a distinct 'painty-tarry' smell of its own. There was a thick wooden bench, stained and tainted with paint splashes of virtually every recognisable colour – and a few indistinguishable shades, caused by merging of countless painting expeditions. Numerous old encrusted paint tins served as receptacles for oddments, with racks containing small sized ropes and cordage; wooden and metal marlin spikes, crowbars, gigantic metal levers, blocks and tackles, broom handles without heads, complete brooms and just broom heads. There was also, partially hidden under the biggest pile of cotton-waste and swabs I had ever seen, an enormous vice. The store was a veritable Aladdin's Cave, reminding me inevitably once more of Keddleston boatyard. My foraging there was not spectator-sport. Work emanated from this little cubby-hole as much as from the engine-room (where, apart from an occasional stand-by to see what went on, I rarely ventured). My duties included soogee-ing paintwork, using one of the empty paint-tins filled with a generous mixture of liquid washing soap and soda, and applying this to numerous external bulkheads as a prelude to endless smartening and tidying-up, thus keeping the ship in a spotless condition. I joined the crew throughout the voyage on a run of deck scaling, chipping and scraping paint on rails and the funnel base. I became more familiar with a chipping hammer than I did with a parallel rule – using the latter only during my study periods while working exercises from that Navigators' Bible, *Nicholls's Concise Guide – Volume One.*

Cadets working with the Serang and the crew
(courtesy Southampton Institute Warsash Maritime Centre).

My evenings varied. I had to keep quiet in our accommodation because Vic was turned-in. He was now regularly on watch with the Second Officer from midnight until 0400 and, after a seven-bell lunch, from noon. Often I used the pool or went into the smoke room to share whatever was taking place. There were frequent deck games such as quoits and cricket (until the ball went over the side, that is). Invariably, someone was off-watch with whom I could relax and share conversation. Sometimes we played chess, crib or darts, and occasionally watched a film, after going through the performance of rigging the projector with its massive spools. The films, and a large library of varied books, were supplied by the Seafarers' Education Service in London and changed every voyage. If the ship was away from UK for any length of time, the Service granted permission for us to exchange with another ship. The Captain or Chief Engineer often joined us for the film and would sometimes remain behind afterwards to join in our chat before leaving and going to the Old Man's cabin "for a wet" as Sparks referred to it.

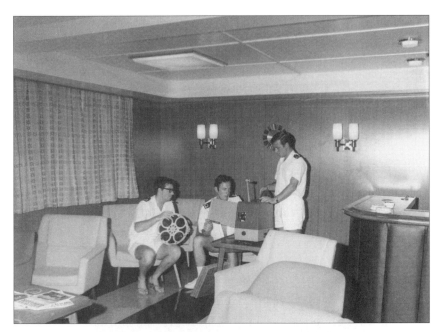

Officers preparing a cinema projector (courtesy BP plc).

Servicing emergency 'Not Under Command' lamps (courtesy BP plc).

Although given every Tuesday and Thursday afternoon for academic work whilst we were at sea, I spent some time each evening working quietly in our study on my Second Mates' correspondence course. My studies were shared between seamanship theory, ship construction, navigation and mathematics. I had also to learn my weekly Collision Regulation for repeating to the Mate and currently was working on the lights and shapes for ships Not-Under-Command. This occurs not when the Captain drops dead, but in instances of engine or steering failure, indicating that our ship would be unable to get out of the way of another. It was quite interesting to imagine situations when the Rules could be applied and, so far, I had experienced no real problems learning or repeating them accurately to the Mate during our hour-long weekly meetings. These were conducted in his large and spacious day-room, but there the social aspects of the occasion ended abruptly. He was kind and helpful, but *very* firm.

Private study on the correspondence course (courtesy BP plc).

Weekly meetings with the Chief Officer during which the deck cadet had to produce evidence of the week's work (courtesy BP plc).

My first impressions of the Suez Canal were captured as I awoke before breakfast a few days after clearing Gibraltar. I could see a row of distant white buildings of uneven height, through which the Canal entrance was just visible, as we rode sluggishly to anchor in the swell. I counted at least forty other ships lying quietly around us, whilst making my way towards the bridge to receive orders for my day's work from the Chief Officer. Vic was there on his own keeping the anchor watch and greeted me warmly. He explained the Canal queuing system and pointed out various types of ships and possible Lines to which they belonged. I was immediately impressed by what seemed to me the sleek lines of tankers as they also wallowed to their anchors and was reminded of the photograph in Captain Mobbs cabin at Keddleston. I thought they might be good ships upon which to serve without, of course, having any real idea what was meant by a good ship. I mentioned this to Vic, receiving his reply that he had never served on them, but had heard they spent little time in port and therefore offered limited opportunity for shore leave. He did say that a fleet of tankers was under the Ellerton umbrella, as a separate company within the Group, and officers had sometimes inter-changed, even though he had felt no desire to apply. Having met a couple of engineering officers who had 'come over' to gain different main engine experience, he said they seemed very good types. He terminated this conversation by telling me about the Canal and how ships navigated it. The 108-mile transit could take between twelve and fifteen hours, but the time was often extended to include an overnight anchorage. The speed of convoys was normally around 8 knots, with ships keeping roughly ¼ mile apart. After telling me this, he sent me below for breakfast, following which I was to report to the Mate for daily orders.

During our transit, I worked again with the *Serang* and learned how to rig the canal searchlight, which was required to pick up fairway buoys during our night passage. I also looked after the Quarantine flag 'Q', Pilot flags and courtesy ensigns during our arrival. It was fascinating to watch dry sandy banks passing so closely, with a road snaking alongside, and diverse antics of local natives. For much of our transit, a strong dry warm wind blew across our faces out of Jordan and Saudi Arabia. Much of my work was spent with the *Tindal*, oiling and generally servicing derricks and their attendant wires, in preparation for eventual loading once we had discharged our grain cargo and received orders. Already some sense of both order and purpose was being made out of an apparent cat's cradle presented initially by topping lift gear, guy, runner, bull rope, and preventers controlling each derrick. Even so, I missed very little of what was happening around me and, in the evening, went onto the bridge with the watch officer and Pilot taking in sights, sounds and atmosphere.

Once we cleared Port Tewfiq, at the southern exit, and entered the Red Sea, the heat became really oppressive and my clothes stuck uncomfortably closely to my skin. Working on deck chipping and painting, I changed into just shorts and strong shoes and socks, which had been bartered at Suez from numerous 'bum boats' alongside as we waited for the Pilot boat to close us. Ever reliable, Vic had guided these transactions, pointing out the dangers of being 'ripped off'. He had given me some out-dated tins of condensed milk, obtained from the English Purser/chief steward – the catering officer in charge of the department responsible for victualling and doing the numerous crew-lists and sundry forms required each time we came into port. Vic often popped-in and helped him out with typing, receiving in return a 'few extra goodies'.

Suez harbour (courtesy Kruger Photo's).

It was not long before we again anchored and waited for the Pilot to bring us alongside our first port of call, Port Sudan. This took all of two days, during which officers and crew passed their leisure time by fishing from our main deck. I found it quietly amusing, amidst mild feelings of guilt, watching my fellow officers using expensive fishing gear and pulling in their modest catches whilst, further along the deck, our Asian crew with hand-lines and bent pins hauled in considerable quantities of assorted fish, almost without effort, which they then took to their *Bhandary* in his galley aft to dry and cook for later curries. A number of small sharks were caught and I gazed with fascinated horror at their vicious rows of sharp triangular teeth. Larger specimens were often seen sliding beneath the surface of the water, dorsal fins just visible whilst they patrolled, scavenging for any scraps that might be thrown over the side. The Mate told me, whilst engaged in casual conversation, that he had been large shark fishing on previous ships using a cargo hook and runner, baited with a rotten cabbage or other seemingly tempting morsel. He promised that we also would try the same, but this failed to materialise. I often passed the Asian crew galleys on the poop-deck and was intrigued by the mixture of curry smells and the sheer indescribable mess and noise which emanated from there. The *Bhandary's* themselves were immensely friendly and frequently offered me tit-bits of a delicious spicy current bread, as well as pickings from bowls of rice and meat which they were preparing for their respective crews meals.

True to other forecasts made when I first met the two officers at Liverpool Street railway station, seemingly light years ago, all Red Sea ports were disappointedly uninteresting. There was simply nothing to do, and my first step ashore with Vic in foreign parts, was to walk only from our berth along a hot dusty road leading into the town. It had not even proved worthwhile for the purser to draw local currency because there was nothing to buy. Swimming from any beach was too dangerous so Vic and I, in the manner of all other officers, cut our losses and provided our own on-board entertainment. Thus I was introduced to that familiar way of passing many long evenings – known throughout the Merchant Navy as the Ships' Officers Dramatic Society – or more colloquially, 'having a Sod's Opera'. This consisted of sing-songs, whilst lubricated with ample quantities of beer or spirits, making up verses to popular songs or, even more satisfying, to hymn tunes. Whilst never over-fond of beer, I still used to take the modest limit of ale allowed us cadets by the Mate, but at providing obscene words to tunes, my ingenuity knew few bounds. I found myself elevated to unimaginable heights in the eyes of my fellow officers, which helped confirm my acceptance aboard. I was glad to see even Vic admired my ingenuity at scanning tunes for metre and rhyming words. The procedure generally adopted was the singing of a few familiar favourites – which ashore would be called Rugby songs – followed by a round to a fixed chorus when verses were sung by each officer following his neighbour. One well-known chorus was:

> *"Sing us another one – just like the other one,*
> *Sing us another one do..do..bloody well do.*
> *Sing us another one do".*

A round of long-remembered verses followed in limerick form and if, during the interval awaiting one's turn, an officer could invent new words, 'great was the rejoicing'. Usually, these were unbelievably obscene, hence quite unprintable, but often extremely funny and, in some cases, very subtle. A slightly 'cleaned-up version' of a verse which soon became one of my favourites went as follows:

> *"There was a young man of Bengal,*
> *Who had a mathematical ball,*
> *The sum of its weight*
> *was pi-cubed over eight,*
> *Plus three times the square root of frig all."*

The way words blended with tune to make a distinctive flowing harmony appealed to me immensely. I felt my maths master at school, and choir master of the parish church in which I had sung prior to entering Keddleston, would have approved – even if each had to 'put tongue firmly in cheek' to do so. Amongst other popular musical gems were the traditional *Eskimo Nell* and *The Ball of Kirriemuir.*

Mr. Gaskell confirmed, during casual conversation in the smoke room, that this trip was an unusual one and was part of a wider United Nations Food and Agricultural Organisation's charter of a range of ships necessary to deliver parcels of 'goodwill' grain. Of other ports we were destined to call at: Massowah, Assab, Djibouti and Berbera, there is little to add. They were interesting to 'clock up' as having been visited, but even more interesting to leave. The sacks were discharged by slings, but the bulk was by a number of grab cranes, each of which held a load of about two tons per lift, creating a process tediously slow. We were all nearly driven to distraction with boredom. It was good to turn-to with the crew working on deck, even in the often stifling heat, just for something constructive to do. The only saving grace in each port was the Ellerton Lines' agent who visited the ship upon arrival, regularly during our stay and prior to departure. He was the 'man of the moment', as the Mate described him to me, with the ability to obtain whatever happened to be the local commodity – plus 'a few other services besides', he had added cryptically. More important to me was the mail brought aboard and that which he took ashore to post on our behalf. I received letters from my parents and Sue and made it a point to send at least a postcard, if a letter was inappropriate, from every port. It was really good to receive news from home – already though, "it appeared a distant place in which things were done differently," as L.P.Hartley wrote. As I settled into my new way of life, home became very much a place of my past. I also began to receive back, from Keddleston, work despatched on the 2nd Mates' correspondence course upon which I had enrolled prior to leaving. Progress seemed to be promising apart from, I was soon to discover, a propensity of mine to make silly errors – adding 24 to 35, for example, and calling the result 69. The Chief Officer, when I discussed my returns with him, put his finger on this problem. He described my computations as 'being executed too hastily' – a fate, he went on with dry humour, that would be mine unless more time was taken to re-check my work. I took the message on board (appropriately enough), but it proved a fault which took me a long time to eliminate.

Just prior to leaving the final port of discharge, Berbera, we received our long awaited and much speculated orders. Vic and I had spent the morning in swimming trunks, up to our knees in really stinking water following hatch washing, trying to clean grain from the strum boxes at the bottom of a couple of holds; 'bilge diving', Vic called it – a delightfully unpleasant job. We had cleaned-up ready for lunch and, in the smoke room afterwards where everyone adjourned for coffee, learned our ship was to bunker across the Gulf in Aden, afterwards proceeding to Lourenço Marques to load raw sugar, ivory and copra in all five lower holds. Upon completion, we were to head for Durban and complete with general cargo for Perth, Fremantle, Melbourne and Sydney. There was great rejoicing at this news from all the officers who clearly anticipated good runs ashore in these far more attractive ports.

The 'Red Sea haul' as Vic called it had been very slow, with the time spent there approaching four months. Aden, Vic told me, was good for shopping and, assuming the Mate would allow us shore leave, we made plans for various things to buy. I wanted even more working gear and perhaps to look around for a few presents for Mum, Dad and Sue.

On passage towards Aden, I learnt the intricacies of the goose-neck fittings and topping lifts thus adding to my knowledge of the working parts of derricks. The *Serang* showed me how to use the winch controls and I thoroughly enjoyed myself raising and lowering the long arms of our five ton standard derricks, in between the inevitable oiling and greasing of all moving parts and, of course, the ubiquitous chipping and painting of various deck areas.

True to Vic's forecast, the Mate indeed allowed us both ashore in Aden, and we left with the Agent in his launch. Sparks, of course, was foremost to be ready as his radio station was always closed down in port. We went also with some off duty engineering officers and Mr. Eyres, parting to go our separate ways once we reached the jetty. It was good having Vic around because everything was so strange to me; sights, smells, sounds and the general hustle of the bazaar stall attendants – shouting and gesticulating as we passed, urging us to buy their wares. He again helped with the noble art of barter and I was easily able to obtain the extra working gear so desperately needed. At his suggestion, I bought very cheaply three sets of khaki coloured shorts, shirts and long trousers – purchases never to be regretted. I treated myself also to a Parker '51 pen, propelling pencil and biro set, along with trinkets for the people at home. When we met the Second Officer in the Missions to Seamen bar, awaiting the launch to return on board, he was enthusiastic about the working gear and writing set, but clearly regarded my presents as 'so much junk'. He was, of course, far too polite to say this, but already I was sufficiently perceptive to pick up vibrations from his non-verbal communication – not that it bothered me overmuch.

On passage to LM, as everyone called Lourenço Marques, the *Serang* took me off derrick work and put me with the *Cassab* checking deck stores to see what was required in Durban. It was easier for me to take notes than the *Cassab* whose English was rudimentary at the best of times. I had problems understanding him on numerous occasions, but we managed to communicate with smiles and what developed into a bizarre arrangement of hand signals and signs. He was a strange chap with a serious cast in his left eye; I found this a little disconcerting and had to make determined efforts not to stare at him too much whilst in conversation. It often seemed as if he were looking around corners. The next day I continued this work, but on my own, going around various paint stores and winch contactor houses compiling a complete on-board paint tally. Later, Mr. Gaskell showed me how to begin making forecasts for future requirements and introduced me to various indent forms and procedures for replenishing stocks. These included various types of oils, greases and varnishes carried. It was very interesting widening my knowledge and seeing these hitherto unknown areas of a deck officer's job. Later, Vic and I worked together filling in requisitions which, once the Mate had signed, were radioed in advance, along with indents from the engineers and purser. I was also told off to do some of the Purser's paper work in readiness for LM. These included crew lists, for port health, customs and immigration authorities; stores lists, assorted cargo manifests and crew personal effects lists, amongst other sundry documents and certificates. I was taken off deckwork, given a wad of scrap paper by the Mate, put in front of the typewriter in his ship's office and then told to learn how to use the thing. Life never ceased to be full of surprises. I thoroughly enjoyed this new task – even more so when he loaned me his battered Olivetti Lettera portable, enabling me to continue practising (and working) in our study.

Deck cadets enjoying shore leave (courtesy BP plc).

I was on stand-by once again in the wheelhouse for approaching and berthing of the vessel at LM, as for arrival and departure in all ports, so was gradually becoming very familiar with routines involved. It was even more interesting on this occasion as, for the first time, I was sent with a *Secunny* to meet the Pilot from our gangway and escort him to the wheelhouse. Led by the latter's example, we exchanged common place pleasantries on the way back to the bridge. I had found all Pilots encountered so far extremely friendly and helpful. Navigating around dangerous sandbanks from the Canal do Sul, through LM Bay to our loading jetty near the Custom House, was fascinating. I soon learnt, when a Pilot boarded, the ship would be entered 'VTMOPA' in my Movement Book for 'Vessel put To Master's Orders and Pilot's Advice.' Julian continued navigating the ship along the channel and supervised me in taking visual bearings, checking these with the radar for more accurate ranges, and then double checking these with a Decca reading, subsequently laying these off on the chart to provide a succession of accurate position fixes. The Captain actively encouraged my participation and this stand-by was thoroughly enjoyed. I was interested to watch Vic put on the helm and admired his obvious competence – and confidence. Steering, even with Julian keeping an eye on him, seemed a very responsible duty.

Taking visual bearings became almost second nature to most deck cadets (Crown copyright/MOD).

We commenced loading as soon as the hatch covers were off and I was put on overnight cargo watch with Mr. Eyres. An eye had to be kept on moorings and gangway under his supervision. Clearly, as cargo was loaded our ship lowered gradually in the water. All lines had to be kept taut, keeping the vessel alongside and preventing gangway and safety net from swinging too far from the jetty. I went round occasionally with the duty *Secunny* and, as we saw fore and aft ropes and back springs becoming slack, reported to the Second Mate who joined us by operating winches, whilst we put on stoppers and tightened lines as appropriate. I felt my knowledge of these everyday shipboard operations was increasing and made plenty of notes and rough sketches in my Journal to discuss with the Mate every Saturday morning. Similarly, the bilges had to be kept at an optimum level, but this was something Mr. Eyres did in consultation with the duty engineering officer.

Later it was with a considerable enthusiasm that I was stood down to make our supper. This gave a distinct sense of *déjà vu* as *I* prepared potatoes and other 'goodies' for, after all, this was my point of entry. It was with considerably more enthusiasm that I was relieved by Vic at 0600 the next day and allowed to go for breakfast and to turn-in. Notwithstanding continuous crashes and bangs accompanying the loading, which assaulted my ears initially once settled into my bunk, I had little difficulty sleeping. These noises were so completely alien following the more subdued discharge of grain.

On the second day after morning stand easy, Vic and I were granted shore leave and went into the city for a few hours. We wandered about intently observing everything around us and buying occasional souvenirs until Vic, tiring of sight-seeing, suggested that we had a drink in one of the local bars. He ordered a bottle of Lagosta wine which, he said reassuringly, was a lightly alcoholic local brew made apparently from lobsters. It certainly seemed pleasant enough to the palette, and very smooth – sliding easily down our parched throats. The level lowered surprisingly rapidly, so what could be more natural than to call for a second bottle. After all, I was now a fully recognised sailor, sitting in a bar (of all places) far from home and consuming wine. I was aware we had both become very animated as Vic regaled me with hilarious stories of his voyages to date and I related some college mishaps. He seemed to have lived a very full and exciting life, but the connection could never quite be made between this somewhat raucous youth sitting opposite me at the table and the same, obviously very English, ex-public schoolboy. It seemed a kind of contradiction. After a further bottle and a few hours passed we prepared to leave. I suddenly realised my head was spinning slightly, and my legs were refusing to obey commands from my brain. Vic looked at me with amusement and told me he thought I was 'somewhat squiffy', thus concentrating awareness to my befuddled senses of a third problem. Something odd had occurred to my speech. It had suddenly become defective, my words emerging only very slowly – almost having to be considered – then again deliberated, and only after following this laborious process – tentatively uttered. My senses felt sluggish in response to this immediate situation and, alas, had to agree I was, more than slightly, "squiffy".

Slowly, we left the bar and made our way into the blazing heat of an African early afternoon sun, heading slowly towards dock and ship. I have little recollection of returning to the quay: certainly, we walked along the railway line, taking what Vic called a short cut, and hearing the whistle of an engine coming rapidly behind us. It seemed sensible to intimate that perhaps it might be advisable for us to leave the track and *very* shortly afterwards a freight train thundered past. We finally reached the ship and, to my horror, Vic pointed out the Chief and Second Officers leaning over the rail on the boat deck chatting casually. In uncustomary agitated mood, he told me not to concentrate on walking in a straight line and I would be all right. Coming from an Ellerton senior cadet, this seemed extremely good advice to follow – so obediently, I did as instructed. The next thing I realised was leaning directly against the vessel's side, feeling the cold plates against my sweating forehead. Thus was learnt another, eminently more practical and less seaworthy reason why moorings had to be kept taut. My next problem was to go aboard the ship. In itself, this was obviously quite straightforward: the only difficulty was there were three gangways ahead of me. "Logic, Caridia, always works," I could almost hear our General Studies master informing us during those interesting lessons at school. So logically I headed for the centre gangway – and found myself walking alongside the thing. Turning back to my starting point, I wondered how this could have occurred, and mused that a few words to my school next time home, might not be amiss. I then remembered circumstances under which we had parted, and decided perhaps to think again.

By this time, I felt a strong hand on my arm and realised Mr. Eyres was leading me onto our offending gangway, along alleyways up through the internal companion-way towards our cadet quarters. It was astounding for me to see Mr. Gaskell likewise assisting Vic. We were led to our bunks and told to remain there; sleep off our indiscretions, and report together at the Mate's office 0800 next day.

I was violently sick twice during the night whilst Vic was ill once. At one stage, we met each other coming and going to the cadets' heads in our accommodation block, looked, then merely groaned, before returning again to a dreamless sleep. Vic, with the resilience of a hardened campaigner, soon recovered next morning, but it took a considerable time for my stomach to settle before I could face solid food. Before then, however, we had to meet the Chief Officer. Sheepishly, we knocked on his office door and, upon demand, ventured in cautiously. Our reprimand was short and sweet, but not too severe – in fact, as we left, he told us he would prefer to have two cadets 'of your ilk' rather than 'two mincing opera-loving pansies'. We felt we had got off quite lightly.

The other officers teased us both unmercifully, with me, as 'innocent first-tripper' receiving most flak. Comments suggesting a supply of 'matchsticks to keep open your eyes' were amongst the more printable offerings, but I felt too ill to respond, managing only wan smiles between one slice of dry toast and a cup of black coffee. Cargo watch that day was very heavy-going. I have no idea what happened, what I did or how I survived. Immediately upon being stood-down in the evening, it was not merely a matter of turning-in, but more collapsing onto my bunk. Happily, I felt a little better the next day.

LM saw the celebration of my seventeenth birthday. Loading had gone according to plan and we were ready for departure to Durban. We had missed the evening tide, so we cadets were invited to join the two mates, Sparky and most of the engineers to visit a bar called the 'Green Door Club'. I was treated to birthday drinks of rather soapy tasting beer, probably a local brew, but I drank extremely cautiously following my previous adventures ashore. The Green Door was a rowdy kind of place that my vicar would have referred to as a house of ill repute. Some quite pretty girls soon attached themselves to our party in a very determined sort of way. My interest was captured by the sight of a rather attractive woman across the bar – not the dusky maiden of my original African dreams, but more coffee coloured, with large eyes and, yes – what seemed to be a well-filled blouse. I had already noticed, to my chagrin (for after all that was why I had originally joined the Merchant Navy) that African breasts seen to date had been disappointedly covered. The girl intended for me, having said with a total lack of conviction that she loved me, had disappeared once she read an obvious lack of interest in my face. I was never very good at hiding my feelings and would have made an appalling poker player. Whilst the others were chatting intently to their respective females, I wandered over 'accidentally on purpose' to chat with my prospective paramour. My throat was dry with nervousness and whilst approaching her table all sorts of anticipatory sensations flooded my body. She gave me a funny kind of glance and invited me to sit down, commenting on my young looks – a remark, I supposed, which seemed true enough. Close-up, she seemed over made-up, reminding me (as did her initial comment) of a juvenile version of that ghastly woman encountered at Keddleston – a still far from pleasant memory. Anyway, I found chatting away easy enough for she led the conversation using our ship and voyage as subjects. It had never previously occurred to me that I might have looked a professional mariner so her interest was found secretly flattering.

Suddenly, our conversation was interrupted by the Second Mate who apologised to her and called me to re-join the others. It was certainly with mixed feelings that I followed him to our table, and was quite horrified when he explained that my 'she was a he'. Sparks led the others in giving me a heck of a lot of stick and hilarious teasing. 'She' obviously heard the commotion our table was making across the bar and, as I glanced in her direction seemed not at all upset, but waved, smiled and then blew me a kiss. I did not know what to do so sat there feeling uncomfortable, wondering how my birthday would have been spent at home. This led me to think of my parents and what they might have made of my situation now but my meanderings were interrupted by Mr. Eyres bringing across a whisky. Looking carefully at me he explained that, when I joined in Amsterdam, he had no idea his lot would be to act as my guardian angel for the voyage. He told me also about dangers lurking in 'some of these places', as he put things. I did reflect – perhaps ungratefully – it was a pity he had not mentioned these beforehand.

We finally arrived back on board at 0330, after some of the others had returned from visiting 'a certain upstairs room'. I was surprised that Vic had 'indulged', as he euphemistically put it, but not surprised that the Second Officer (as a family man) had not. I felt terrible; both tired and a little ill, but not so bad as after the Lagosta wine incident, yet managed to report to the wheelhouse for stand-by. After ringing 'Full Away' to the engine-room, indicating the start of our deep-sea passage as opposed to pilotage, my shattered personage was finally stood-down in time for breakfast. This proved an unnerving meal and, occurring so soon after the earlier incident, I was (again) teased unmercifully by Vic and other officers whilst fighting with cereal and coffee (all I could face). My vicar at home would hardly have appreciated the comments which wafted their way across the saloon. Luckily, the Old Man – as I now followed the other officers by calling him – came in early for his sitting, saving me further embarrassment. Vic told me afterwards that none of them thought I was 'queer' at all, but had found the intimacies of my involvement extremely amusing.

When I reported for duties to the Mate even he teased me about my 'midnight-cum-midday adventures in LM' – offering a play on words which appealed to my, by now, jaded sense of humour. But that was the only thing which did. He was duty officer on board the previous night, but the others had clearly wasted little time regaling him with my latest mishap. Although a bit uncomfortable, I felt flattered in a secret sort of way both by the attention and the fact that I seemed to be accepted fully by my fellow officers.

The passage en route to Durban was extremely interesting. I spent part of this cleaning out the wheelhouse (joy of joys) and part on deck. This time chipping and painting around the lower funnel area with a *Lascar* first-class seaman was my lot. Basically, he showed me what to do for I was not yet ready to go aloft in a chair with the other deck hands to paint the funnel itself. It was interesting to see how a bosun's chair was constructed and the way it was lowered and raised. The Chief Officer explained why it was necessary for me to do manual deck work as a first tripper – and throughout my cadetship. It seemed, by doing this myself, I would learn how long tasks took, the techniques involved, and how much paint and other materials were necessary. This was important, because on becoming a Mate – I liked that touch, it was *almost* as if he could see me in the rank – and working my own deck crew, I ought to know 'what is what', so if any 'smart ass decky' tried to 'pull a flanker on me', the situation could be dealt with based upon my own experience, and not merely on knowledge gained from books. My range of the English language expanded daily, although I was certain there were few expressions (and even fewer words) that I should be able to use when eventually the voyage ended and a period of leave came my way. As for becoming a Chief Officer – Wow! The thought of three gold rings and a diamond on my sleeve seemed simply light years away – even the Second Mate's rank appeared unattainable at present, whilst becoming Captain of a ship was totally unimaginable.

The Second Officer called me away from my painting job into the wheelhouse stating that it would be good to have the area clean for Durban. I was only too happy to be there however menial the task to be undertaken. After cleaning the place to his satisfaction, the time arrived for his change of watch with the Mate who, once the Second and Vic had gone, pointed out it was not worth my going back onto deckwork. He instructed me to have a shower, then return in white uniform shirt and shorts to share the watch with him until his meal relief. We spent time on coastal navigation and chart work and Vic showed me the radar, explaining in simple terms the basic controls and collision avoidance triangle. This was fundamentally precision geometry and, as such, appealed immensely. He read out a few targets and I used the RAS plotter to determine closest point of approach of a target, the time of this, and an estimation of its course and speed. This was great fun and became quite hectic as shipping built-up on our approaches to Durban Roads. I left off radar work then and he told me to stand lookout duties until the Third Officer came up for meal relief.

We arrived at Durban early in the morning and, to the surprise of all, took the Pilot immediately and entered, via the Bluff and Addington Point, to berth alongside Maydon Wharf. A highly excitable Vic told me, so far as the Nurses' Home in Addington was concerned, it was rarely necessary to use Bluff to get to the Point – a comment I appreciated fully for its play on words, but whose content remained rather hazy. Suspecting my leg was being well and truly pulled; it seemed very uncertain why or how – but he did little to enlighten me.

Durban, South Africa (courtesy Art Publishers Pty).

I was very impressed with the sight of the modern city and surrounding approaches as, escorted by tugs, we entered the Channel and approached our berth. After stand-by in the wheelhouse, I assisted the *Serang* and his crew to rig and lower our gangway. The Agent was soon aboard and proved particularly friendly. Meeting me on deck, he shoved an envelope into my shirt pocket, gently patted my cheek and, simultaneously urged me to go and 'have a good time ashore'. Remembering the Mate on our training vessel, reinforced by assorted stories overheard between officers during smoke room gossip, made me feel vaguely apprehensive. This increased even more so when, opening the envelope a considerable sum in local currency fell out – adding to my mystification. Vic had gone ashore on some ship's business or other for the Captain, so this apparent phenomenon could not be discussed, so I went and told the Mate what had happened. He looked closely at me without making any observation other than to suggest, if the Agent had told me to go ashore and have a good time, then that was precisely what should be done. He made no explanations regarding the windfall which had come my way, but merely told me to be back on board in time for the evening meal and to turn-to for work at 0800 the following day.

It was a strange sensation going down the gangway and setting foot on foreign soil alone for the first time. The dock gate was easily found; I simply followed the road and, showing my pass to the South African police officer on duty, made my way towards the city centre. Everything was new and exciting, particularly the ornately dressed Zulu rickshaw boys catering for passengers from an Italian liner in dock. I felt no desire to try a ride but it was fun just watching things happen around me, looking in shops and listening to nasal vowels of clipped South African English accents.

Eventually, I found the Merchant Navy Officers' Memorial Club and showing my identity card to the steward on duty, was duly enrolled, and given a pinkish-red membership card. After buying a lager and looking around the open bar I joined a fellow of similar age who was sitting idly at a table. He turned out to be one of Harrison Line's deck apprentices, of some two years' seniority, on a regular run between various African and Indian ports. Chatting with him and listening to his experiences made me appreciate just how fortunate I was sailing with Ellertons. Even with his sea experience, he spent most of his time on deck-work 'soogee-ing', chipping, painting and being used for numerous jobs which were considered by his Mate and Bosun as being too dirty for the regular deckhands, or too expensive to pay their overtime. He regarded himself not as a trainee navigating officer but, as he indelicately put it, with a disillusioned look, 'just another ------- deckhand'. I did not have to say much and merely listened, for he knew of Ellertons and had spoken to many Company cadets. He clearly envied considerably the life-style which, by comparison, we were fortunate to enjoy.

Eventually, I found my way back to the ship and, meeting Vic, was staggered to see all of his gear packed, with him preparing to sign-off Articles. Apparently, the Company's vessel *Earl of Cape Town* was loading for London and continental ports and he had been transferred on promotion to Fourth Officer, and was to enter nautical college for pre-2nd Mates' study leave immediately upon arrival at Liverpool. The Third Officer of *Cape Town* had been taken ashore with appendicitis and the Chief Marine Superintendent in London considered this a good opportunity for Vic to gain solid watch-keeping experience on the homeward trip. Vic suggested we miss the evening meal and eat ashore instead at the XL Restaurant – a place he had visited every trip on calling at Durban. He wanted to treat me to a farewell meal of T-bone steak with all trimmings. When this arrived it made a veritable mountain of food on a massive oval-shaped plate. Just as we sat down, the Mate walked in with the Second Engineer, saw us, and asked if they could join us. The Mates were working twelve hour cargo watches now we were in port, and I would be joining the Third next day to see what went on. We had an excellent time – the two senior officers proving relaxed and hilarious company, yet still managing to maintain conventions of discipline. It was quite late by the time we returned on board and, with Vic leaving next morning and both of us gently intoxicated, each settled to a quiet night's sleep.

I was out on deck with Julian just before the required time, having missed both breakfast (not feeling quite myself somehow) and saying goodbye to Vic. Such casual farewells were to prove a prominent feature of seafaring life. It was interesting to watch stevedores loading maize products, sugar, jam and canned fruit, together with other assorted African 'odds and sods' into the tween decks of our holds. To me, the idea of taking fruit to Australian ports seemed rather like taking coals to Newcastle, although I realised these cans were probably different types.

Anyway, our job was to look out for broken cases and tally the printed code on any boxes so broached or damaged. Needless to say, a few of the remains found their way into what was now my study for later consumption between us. Again, I found myself thinking about the number of men required to work cargo throughout the ship and, at a rough count, reckoned there must have been not far short of seventy dockers aboard. Mentioning this to Julian, he expressed only casual interest and the hope that the rest of me worked as actively as my mind. To this response, I had no comment.

It was during this watch I was told why the agent had slipped money to me and solved what I regarded as the Mate's 'Red Sea mystery' comment. Apparently, a little illicit bartering had taken place over the ship's deck stores, of which I was blissfully unaware, but the envelope had contained my automatic 'cut' of the proceedings. This was common practice concerning desirable commodities such as lead-based ship's paint and other stores like spare ropes, oils and varnishes and, whether I liked the system or not, was one which had operated through generations of seafarers and showed no signs of being discovered or stopped. On low wages, and not so conscience stricken as I thought might have been the case, it seemed there was no way of avoiding involvement and thus, only partially reluctantly, went along for the ride, accepting whatever portion came my way. Julian explained how the system worked. The idea of sides of bacon disappearing down the gangway (although sometimes happening, as a popular film about the Merchant Navy portrayed), rarely occurred, as the stores often failed to come on board in the first place. They were ordered, as I knew full well, but the demanded quantities were not delivered in full. This universal practice occurred with every department on board virtually every ship in the world. The catering departments were involved the most. This was because their orders were regularly similar at all ports at which ships called, when they re-stocked vegetable and meat rooms with local produce.

A more legitimate bonus was regular appearances of mail. I heard from my parents and felt re-assured that Mum was coming to terms with my choice of career as she, in turn, was happy treating the enthusiastic contentment expressed in my letters home as sound progress. Sue wrote and sent me a photograph in which she was wearing a two-piece bikini bathing costume. This left very little to the imagination – even one as innocently naïve as mine. As Adam said when first he caught sight of Eve – Wow! I pinned it to the side of my bunk so it could be gazed upon regularly – a move which led to the first of a series of shipboard disasters which happened to me – once Vic had left.

Turning in after cargo watch that day, enjoying the privacy of a cabin on my own for the first time, my eye fell upon Sue's photo and I realised my biology lessons from school actually worked. A series of pleasant sensations beguiled my body that increased with intensity the more I looked. All sorts of thoughts rushed into my mind as I could visualise myself gently 'exploring them there hills', as an old song described the process. Of course, it would have to be my luck that the Mate came into my cabin, to mention something he had forgotten to tell me during the day, thus catching me in *flagrante delicto*. Apologising briefly he left but, to my chagrin, I heard him roaring to himself with laughter as he disappeared towards the officers' accommodation. I lay there on top of my bunk, both naked and petrified, flushing with embarrassment and shame – praying he would have the decency to keep his mouth shut – 'after all,' ran my reasoning, 'had we not the previous evening shared a meal together, thus creating a bond for life?' Oh dear! No such luck for, entering the saloon next morning, I was attacked (there could be no other word) by a barrage of ribald comments floating their way in my direction. Such utterances highlighting my apparently haggard appearance, and mockingly wondering what the cause could be, came fast and furious. It was one of the few times I could not wait to eat my meal and leave 'sort of pronto-like', as Sparks was wont to say. I remained only long enough for the main course, and so missed the addition of fruit juice, cereals and umpteen rounds of toast and marmalade which normally made-up my breakfast. Even that caused additional attacks, as comments about needing 'to keep-up your strength' shot their way towards the cadets' table.

Going out onto deck to join Julian, brought little relief as even he added a contribution to my shame. Clearly accepted by my fellow officers, I was not so sure now this was always essentially for the good. It took a few days before I was able to live down that little lot, and only then because my embarrassment became overshadowed by tales related across the smoke room of experiences from other officers in that accursed city. The allusion Vic had made to the local nursing home gradually became understood. Apparently many of our officers had attended what were euphemistically described as 'dances', although their conversations left little to even an innocent imagination as my own.

Eventually, with some sighs of relief, we completed loading and set course for Australia.

It felt strange being the only cadet on board and certainly I missed Vic's company and friendship. In a way though I was glad he was not present, being certain that he would have been well to the fore in the far from gentle teasing which followed my previous misfortunes. Frankly, my frustration with 'that aspect of life common to all men' knew no bounds. It led me to wonder despairingly if I would ever 'know a woman' as the Bible so euphemistically stated things. Admittedly, I was still young, but felt my life was being wasted away. Many officers had been as active as rabbits during our sojourn in both ports, whilst my only achievement was to make a complete idiot of myself.

My self-esteem was at an all time low. The ebullient, effervescence of youth however soon assisted my personality to bounce back and, as a positive result, I resolved to have nothing further to do with girls.

The concrete determination of this decision was, of course, assisted by circum-stances. We were bound across the Indian Ocean towards Perth and the prospect of a number of lengthy day's sea-time, bronzing on deck in swimming trunks with total absence of females, helped concentrate my mind towards professional studies and deck duties with the crew. I relegated Sue's photograph to my writing case in the bureau permanently – apart, that is, from a few surreptitious glances occasionally (on a pretty regular basis) behind a locked cabin door.

My progress with learning the Collision Regulations was good and I was able to imagine a variety of situations between ships in which this knowledge could be applied. Part of each evening was spent on the bridge with Julian and he appeared to welcome these visits. It probably broke the monotony of a four-hour watch in open waters and he seemed to enjoy teaching aspects of navigation and seamanship within, of course, the limitations of my ability to learn. I could not yet understand, for example, the mathematical theories of spherical trigonometry behind the taking of sights mandatory for my examinations, but could at least learn how to use a sextant.

The Indian Ocean was like a millpond. There was scarcely a ripple. Out on deck, the sun was very hot, creating those kind of idealistic conditions normally associated with blue seas and skies so beloved of travel brochures. Only the now familiar gentle swishing sound was to be heard as the ship smoothed aside easily pliant waters.

A few days out, I was working with the crew on deck during the morning, learning more about my trade and continuing to get on extremely well with the *Serang* and his crew. I had showered immediately after being stood down and dressed in a set of clean white shirt and shorts. Great satisfaction was still found when attaching cadet shoulder straps to the eyelets in my shirt. The sight of the vertical gold stripe, surmounted by its shiny brass button gave tremendous secret pleasure.

Today was the birthday of a junior engineering officer so, along with everybody off watch, I had been invited to pre-luncheon drinks in the officers' smoke room. I had been spared treating the officers similarly, upon attaining seventeen, because cadets were never expected to push the boat out for birthdays. This occasion was certainly one of great joviality. Richard welcomed me like a long-lost brother (he had clearly been celebrating prematurely), and summoned the Asian steward to bring me a gin and lime. The drink came, packed with welcome ice and a slice of lemon.

The Old Man and senior officers were full of appropriate bonhomie as they drank enthusiastically – at someone else's expense. They even had time jovially to joke, chat and help me feel part of the proceedings. Although mixing with senior officers in the smoke room was still something of a novelty for me – my social life was usually built around the junior ranks – I felt quite relaxed.

"Hullo, Caridia," said the Captain. "How's the trip going? Mr. Gaskell gives me some very encouraging reports and, from what I see myself, you appear to be settling down very well."

"Things are fine, thank you sir," was my automatic response, as I added, "so far as I know." Bearing in mind I did not know how much he actually knew of my more recent antics to date.

"Yes." There was a pause. "You were at Keddleston Navigation School before you joined the Company, I believe?"

"Yes. Sir."

"And before that?" he queried.

"I went to a local grammar school in London, sir," I replied.

"So, why join the Merchant Navy?"

"An interest in navigation and shipping, generally, sir," I countered.

"Hmm, not much to know about navigation, I should have thought, once you've mastered the PZX triangle", he said. "Still, I can understand your fascination with the sea. That's something I think we all experience. How did you get on at Keddleston?" he asked suddenly.

Visions of college life and my training cruise with LBB came immediately to my mind.

"Fine actually, sir. I found it a very useful experience." I replied stolidly, skating carefully around any possibly sensitive areas, and restricting my answers to a purely neutral relating of facts. It was rather a pleasant experience, like talking to the Vicar after a Sunday morning service at home.

As the gong sounded, we took our drinks into the saloon for lunch. Even though the temperature was in the upper nineties, no culinary concessions were made to heat, and I sat down fully appreciating being on my own on this occasion. Setting to work with a will, following the worthy example of my superiors, vegetable soup was followed by two gargantuan helpings of magnificent curry with all the trimmings. The meal was finished with a really healthy dollop of treacle pudding and custard. Afterwards, our engineer officers invited me to re-join them in the smoke room for coffee, before I returned to my accommodation to change back into working rig.

The Master and all other off-duty officers went to their bunks for a traditional well earned afternoon 'zizz'. I, of course being merely the ship's minion, reported to Mr. Gaskell in his cabin at 1400 hours for three hours' deck work, just before he also turned in. He said, looking me sternly in the eye (clearly to observe whether or not his cadet was quite sober after unaccustomed gin), there was a very important job for me to do, before I continued spicing lights onto four of the new lifebuoys, upon which I had recently stencilled the ship's name and port of registry. He believed the buoys would be sufficiently dry by now for me to complete, and checked that I had seen the *Cassab* earlier, and collected a small fid and appropriately sized 'small stuff', as twine etc was customarily referred to. The lights, he informed me, had been unpacked and were in his office awaiting my collection. I confirmed everything necessary had been taken to my study during morning stand easy and, hesitating hopefully, asked if the splicing could be done there. This would save me working in the after contactor house or getting in the *Cassab's* way in his storeroom, and was a far more pleasant venue. Obviously impatient to be away to his bunk, he responded that he did not give a damn where I did them – so long as I made a really good job. I turned to leave, only to be called back as he remembered the important job which he wanted me to do before splicing.

Apparently, the chief steward had been agitating, 'and getting on his back recently', over the problem of cockroaches in his dry store below. I knew immediately what he meant. Ever since we had cleared Suez, and the weather had really warmed up, our entire accommodation block had been plagued by an ever-increasing infestation of cockroaches and other creepy crawlies. They were more of an irritant than anything else, but there could be more serious implications if they multiplied in too great numbers in the food stores.

I realised that he was still speaking to me and rallied my senses rapidly. There were some fumigation bombs in one of the lockers in his office, just alongside the buoys, and he wanted me to take a small one and pop-down to the store-room prior to doing the splicing. He gave me detailed instructions so 'there could be no room for error.' I was to make certain the punkah-louvres in the air conditioning trunkway were turned-off and put a sheet of paper over the uptakes. A sign would be required outside warning fumigation had taken place. A slight note of exasperation was detected in his voice as he added the admonition that I should not forget to lock the door.

Chief Steward's dry store (courtesy BP plc).

Keeping well quiet, and maintaining a neutral expression, my thoughts were very much my own. As if I would do such a silly thing as leave open the door. Actually, ninety per cent of my mind was more concerned with this blasted splicing job. As I knew from nautical college days, practical tasks such as splicing lights on securely was really quite fiddley, requiring a measure of patient dexterity of the type that usually escaped me. To be honest, my concern over this was far deeper than I let on; my relationship with the officers was going really well and, as I had learnt from the Harrison Line apprentice in Durban, the Mate was treating me very decently. As the only cadet on board, and certainly the youngest officer by some four years, mixing with the Asian ratings was out of the question, so somebody had to befriend me. But he had gone out of his way to make sure no-one intimidated me and had allowed me wide run of the social rooms. I continued to play cards, cribbage, chess and darts with the officers; used the pool frequently, participated in deck games – and, yes, life was good. So my intention was to make a 'proper job' of the splicing, as the Cornish second mate used to say.

I went to the cupboard in the office and collected an insecticide fumigation bomb. Then going below, unlocked the store, switched off the forced air outlet on the punkah-louvres, put paper over the uptakes, lit the bomb, lobbed it into the store, came sharply out turning the key firmly in its lock, and placed my previously prepared notice prominently on the door with sellotape. No problems. I then went up to the after end of the officers' deck to my study and apprehensively commenced the preparations for splicing.

After about ten or fifteen minutes, my concentration on the rope-work was disrupted by a vague sense of unease. There seemed to be a most peculiar tang in the air. Suddenly, my attention was riveted by noticing what appeared to be wisps of smoke coming out of the punkah-louvre situated directly over the study desk. I went quite cold for a moment, realising there might be a fire on board. 'After all', went my reasoning, 'how could smoke come out of an air-conditioning system?'

My mind went back to fire fighting courses at college and those lurid lectures, supporting the practical session, which had emphasised quite forcibly that fire was the worst and most dangerous hazard on board ships at sea. Then I came back to reality – pretty quickly. If my suspicions were correct and there *was* a fire then, with all off-duty officers asleep, I was the only person awake in the accommodation. The sober thought struck me that it was my responsibility to do something constructive about the situation. Visions of gratitude and profound thanks from our officers for possibly saving their lives flashed through my mind. It occurred to me also that seafarers could be awarded Lloyd's Medal for Gallantry in saving life at sea. I decided to act without further delay by alerting Mr. Eyres on the bridge.

By the time these tortuous thoughts had been completed, smoke had deepened considerably and was now being emitted in rapidly thickening clouds from every punka in the trunkway system inside the cadets' block.

Flying out of the entrance door with such haste, I tore open the pocket of my shorts on the heavy protruding latch; a small insignificant matter. Cursing, and frantic with concern, I mounted the ladder and ran along the after-end of the boat deck towards the bridge, my pocket flapping as agitatedly as myself. The sight that met my eyes was quite numbing. The fire was clearly situated in a deckhouse compartment as an increasing pall of black smoke was pouring from there in ever thickening clouds. It was obvious, by the sound of machinery, a motor had overheated and caught alight.

I hurried even faster towards the cloud. By this time smoke had virtually obscured the funnel base and everything forward. The boats in their reassuring davits stood out from this pall, their hulls wreathed in swirling billows. It was like a sight from Dante's *Inferno*. From the other side of the fog bank came frantic calls from the Second Mate on watch. I noticed mechanically how much broader had become his accent in the moment of excitement and, with a non-sequential association of ideas, thought of LBB.

As I became more immersed in the smoke, my nose was hit by a pungent smell never previously associated with fire. Certainly, smoke during practical demonstrations at college had not possessed such a tang. It was almost as if disinfectant was coming out of the system? I pulled up with a jerk. There was absolutely no sign of any flames that could be expected to accompany such thick dense smoke. The smell was also disconcerting, to say the least. I started to put two and two together and, although the logic of the situation completely escaped me, did begin to wonder if perhaps I was associated somehow with this event.

Mr. Eyres was calling out to Sparks as they ran towards the plant and I began to distinguish some of the words, far from delicate it might be added, wafting from the other side of the bank.

"It's in the air circulating plant. It's not a fire. I'm pretty certain of that – there are no flames."

'I was right on one score – and know now what compartment it is.' Came my detached thought.

"It stinks something awful – almost like DDT," squeaked the ever helpful Sparks.

DDT? Alarm bells rang in my mind. I felt it might just be prudent to make myself scarce for a while. So, without further ado, shot quickly out of my side of the smoke, taking strategic action by hiding behind the funnel casing, close to where previously carefree hours had been spent chipping, red-leading and painting.

A new duo of authoritative voices joined the ever-mounting clamour from the two officers.

"It's seems like fumigation smoke," exclaimed the Captain. "I recall a similar smell when the old *Earl of Derby* came back from the Far East with a massive infestation of copra bugs in all holds. She had to be thoroughly fumigated before even thinking about discharging; had to lay-off in the quarantine anchorage off Liverpool for a couple of days – we all lived in a hotel ashore."

'Great,' I thought. 'What a delightful time to go into reminiscent mode.'

"DDT?" questioned increasingly irate tones from the Chief Officer. "Where's that bloody cadet?" he asked, as I thought, rhetorically.

"The cadet? Why him?" came a duo of simultaneous questions from the Old Man.

"I set him the task of fumigating the chief hunk's dry store immediately after lunch. He's clearly messed things up with a vengeance – can be quite useless at times with anything practical – that blasted boy," came the Mate's totally unsympathetic retort.

I stood stock still; quite stunned. The realisation dawned that big trouble was heading my way this time – of such magnitude it might even engulf me. Almost traumatised, I backed carefully round the funnel to my side of the smoke bank and retreated swiftly to my quarters with absolutely no idea what to do. Even LBB from my training ship days suddenly seemed almost human and kindly.

'Lord, I wish I had not taken the Mickey out of those officers so much,' came my fervent prayer, in the vague hope that somehow atonement for that series of acts would compensate for this little lot, thus providentially offering me a way out of the tangle. The Lord however maintained an aggravating silence even though this was not, alas, extended to his subjects the other side of the smoke.

The voice of the Chief Officer, and other sundry tones of hate came wafting my way as surely as the smoke.

Something constructive had to be done. So, with short's pocket flapping as wildly as my thoughts, I returned to my quarters and went rapidly into the cadet's heads, entered the furthest bog, shut off both punkahs and opened my porthole – thus allowing most of the smoke to disperse. Locking the door firmly behind me, I seated myself on the pan, and waited: absolutely petrified.

"I've checked the store cupboard," the Mate's grim voice continued, coming alarmingly nearer. "One of the large hatch bombs is missing. That little piece of camel dung has used a fumigator for a hold of 150,000 cubic feet on a store-room of around four thousand. I told him specifically to take a small bomb. I know what happened – he was obviously bloody well day dreaming again, because he forgot to block-off the up-take properly."

Well, it was good to have my sin identified, even though I disagreed strongly with the day dreaming bit. Clearly, my fears of completing a first major solo job on the lifebuoys had overwhelmed what I thought was the more trivial job of fumigating the storeroom.

'I didn't know there *were* two kinds of bomb. I didn't see two different sizes.' I wailed to myself. 'Hell! Have some compassion, Lord. I can't learn everything after just a dog watch at sea,' was my confused prayer as I rapidly attempted to re-assure myself. This prayer also (not surprisingly, perhaps) was unanswered.

All right, it has to be admitted – I was almost close to tears.

"Where is the little bugger?" came the terse tones of the Chief Officer leaving my study, and asking anyone who would listen. "He must be somewhere around".

"Perhaps he has jumped over the side," suggested Julian, with what sounded suspiciously like a strong hint of veiled laughter in his voice.

'Hell!' I thought viciously. 'I hoped you could be relied on. I really need all the friends I can get now.'

"I'm sorely tempted to say good riddance to him," screamed the frantic Mate. "I've often thought twice about carrying cadets. Sometimes, they are more bloody trouble than they are worth."

"Yes," agreed the captain. "Do you remember young Stilwell?" he asked anyone who would listen.

"Yes, I recall the name," said Sparks. "Wasn't he the silly little devil who climbed up the lower arch of Sydney Harbour Bridge – and then got arrested as he came down the other side? Good heavens, he must be a Second Mate now, after all these years," he added inconsequentially.

"Never mind that," stated the Mate, rudely overriding the conversation originally initiated by his superior.

By now, other officers had joined the throng. They were engineers who had been sleeping below and then awoken, complete with hangovers, sore throats and running eyes, wondering what had occurred. I thought despondently that here was another lot after my blood.

Suddenly, thunderous footsteps were heard coming into my shower room, passing that cubicle and threateningly approaching the toilets. I heard a bang on the door and the Mate's voice asking: "Are you in there, Caridia?"

I managed to make what on stage would have been called a 'virginal squeak' and taking greater control of my voice, offered a dutiful: "Yes sir."

Before Mr Gaskell could deliver a broadside, sufficiently powerful to have demolished not only the door, but reduced the entire accommodation – including me – to liquid, the Captain spoke.

"Caridia. I think that you had better come out of there now, and report to me in my cabin. Understand?"

"Yess-s, sir," I replied. As no indications of forgiveness could be detected in his voice, whilst I comprehended extremely well, my resolve was most definitely not to come out.

"Come on," said the Mate. "Unlock this blasted door. Stop messing around and get yourself out of there."

At that moment, the bridge *Secunny* arrived with a note from Mr. Eyres, informing the Master that a passing ship had seen the smoke and kindly enquired if we needed assistance. Considering we had not even seen the glimpse of any ship, distant or otherwise for the past three days, I cursed the fates for bringing another vessel at that particular moment. I felt that was all I needed.

"Well, without an axe, we can't smash in the door," decided the Captain.

"Leave him be," said the Chief Officer. "He'll come out when he's hungry. And incidentally," he added, "why haven't you finished splicing the lights to those lifebuoys?"

With that final parting shot, as pungent as the smoke, everyone walked off and left me to ruminate upon my predicament. I wondered where on earth I stood now and what to do. Memories of salad days in school evoked my troubled soul, whilst strains of favourite English lessons flashed through my mind. My feelings were something akin to the unfortunate youth in Thomas Hardy's poem, *Midnight on the 'Great Eastern':*

'In the third-class seat sat the journeying boy
And the roof-lamp's oily flame
Played on his listless form and face,
Bewrapt, past knowing to where he was going,
Or whence he came.'

'O God,' I prayed, sitting on very much a fourth class seat: 'Why on earth did I leave school? All I have ever done since is to get into trouble. Why didn't you send some guardian angel to make me stay for 'A' levels – followed by a safe career in a bank somewhere? I really wish now I'd listened to Mum after all.'

After about an hour, more mournfully introspective daydreams were interrupted by Julian, coming to my cubicle door urging me to come out. He assured me, in persuasive tones, the seniors had calmed down and not only had the smoke disappeared, but tabnabs were available for tea. I remained silent and unconvinced, even in the face of my favourite mid-afternoon treat.

After a while, he went away – presumably to report to the Mate his cadet was not yet ready to budge. It was all of another two hours before the chief officer himself came to my refuge:

"Come on out now, Caridia," he said gently. "I must admit we were all extremely angry at the time. After all, nobody likes to be woken so dramatically from a deep afternoon sleep. And we did wonder initially what was happening. But we've all calmed down now, and it will be supper time shortly."

In the face of such unprecedented kindness, and after three hours of misery, I unlocked the door and glanced out fearfully. The Mate was standing to one side looking at me. My predicament must have stirred some deep paternal instinct within him. Perhaps it was tied up with the fact he had a son of his own, just slightly younger than me, also on his pre-determined way to nautical school deck cadet training. How I blessed the existence of that anonymous youngster, whose photo I had seen on the Mate's desk in a family group with his wife and two daughters. Once we reached his day cabin Mr. Gaskell took a piece of paper and, with an adroit sketch, explained the workings of the forced air system on a ship and how, by leaving just a corner of the uptake in the storeroom uncovered and by using such a powerful bomb, I had almost asphyxiated all the officers.

We then had to go and face the Captain. He looked at me directly and sternly told me to explain myself. All I could do was to stammer inadequately, explaining my apologies had already been made to the Mate, as if that was a sufficient (as well as necessary) condition. There was, after all, little else left to say. He then asked me, sensibly I thought, what had been learnt from the incident, giving me a chance to explain how perhaps more time should be taken over things when next given a job to do and, pausing, probably to let the Chief Officer know my mind was more pre-occupied with my inability to do a decent splicing job.

The Mate looked astonished at my astounding revelation of knowledge (or lack of it) but, before he could comment further, the Master suggested he take over from that point, upon which note we turned to leave his cabin. The Captain called me back just as we reached his day-room door and, as I turned, noticed the merest trace of a twinkle in his eye:

"You can re-assure yourself, Caridia, that you have done one thing exceptionally well. There are no signs of cockroaches or any thing else that creeps and crawls in the accommodation or store-rooms on my ship."

"No sir. Thank you, sir." I muttered, returning with the Mate to his quarters.

The officers however, whilst being forgiving, were very determined the incident should not be forgotten that easily. In the same way they had teased me previously, following those unfortunate incidents around the African coast, so my emotional system had to suffer more psychological abuse. I felt it was likely my nerves would be shot to pieces before signing-off this ship. When I returned to my cabin after deckwork the next day, some comedian had pasted – yes, pasted – a massive great sign across the entire door to my cabin proudly announcing in block letters:

"RENTOKIL Ltd. Knock Here".

It took me ages and a lot of really hard work to scrape it off before the Captain's inspection the following Saturday.

Entering the saloon for luncheon, they starting singing that old tune, *Smoke gets in your eyes,* at the tops of their voices. Additionally, all sorts of other caustic comments pursued my progress across the Indian Ocean until the heat (as it were) died out of the situation as other things occurred to replace it. They still called me 'The Rentokil Kid', however, for weeks afterwards.

The lights were eventually spliced onto the buoys, but they looked 'limp and soggy' as the Mate described my efforts, with an appropriately crude comparison. Eventually, he got the *Serang* to slap a coat of paint over my handiwork to 'hide that bloody abortion and tighten the things up.'

The other come-back, of course, was my being turned-to with the *Tindal* on a regular basis for instruction in splicing and ropework – evidence of which had to be produced to the chief officer during weekly meetings.

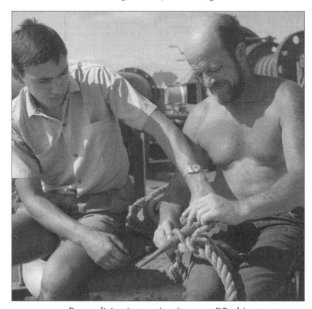

Rope splicing instruction (courtesy BP plc).

There were few further incidents affecting me directly prior to our arrival Perth and our only excitement was when the ship stopped dead a few days off the Australian coast and wallowed helplessly in a heavy swell. From what I could gather from the Third Officer, whilst preparing emergency 'Not Under Command' oil lamps for hoisting, something had gone temporarily amiss with the pistons of the main engine. Repairs were eventually rendered by engineering officers and our Asian carpenter, who shored the things up with timber, just a couple of hours' prior to the receipt of a severe gale warning in our sea area that would have necessitated calling for a tug and subsequent tow. The nearest Australian port with sufficiently large repair facilities to take our 430 x 56 foot vessel would probably have been Melbourne. This would have created a diversion making a delightful mess of the Mate's carefully calculated discharge programme.

We eventually arrived without further mishap at Perth and commenced discharging the tween deck and lower hold cargoes for that port.

Yet another surprise was in store for me when a new senior cadet was assigned to the ship, having been transferred by the company to gain additional sea-time. The ways of the sea and vagaries of shipping companies seemed to me a complete mystery but then, of course, nobody asked my opinion. Pete Dawson was well into his cadetship and had been pre-sea trained aboard HMS *Worcester*, on the River Thames. A character in very similar mould to Victor Page, he was even more devious in approaching his chosen profession; seeing everything happening to him from a dryly humorous jaundiced view. I found this particularly appealing and, as a result, we took to each other immediately. I, of course, took my customary back seat again – somewhat thankfully – following my disaster with that blasted fumigation bomb. Julian wasted little time relating this adventure to Pete in the smoke room over a pint of beer. Some gratification was found in Pete's reaction, but I had no idea at the time what would develop from his assessment of what he termed 'the obvious ingenuity of a Rentokill Kid'.

I was on stand-by in the wheelhouse again for arrival in Fremantle and, immediately we had berthed, was sent to help with rigging the gangway, and then to stand-by there doing quartermaster duties. Almost immediately after the ship had been cleared inwards, a telephone line had been connected and I was astounded when literally, within seconds, we received our first call. This was from the local Nurse's Home. The *Secunny* assigned with me, whilst admirable in every way, was not up to answering the phone, so this was my main task until a shore watchman could be appointed. The voice asked if she could speak to 'Mr. Brown, the fifth engineering officer'. I replied that our Fifth was called Mr. Samuels but, far from being perturbed, the caller merely asked to talk to him anyway.

The situation seemed a little odd, especially as we had just berthed, and my thoughts returned incomprehensibly to overheard comments in the smoke room at Durban. I went to fetch him anyway and was even more flummoxed by his knowing smile as he left his comfortable armchair and headed for the ship's office where the phone had been rigged. I remained an innocent party and followed the ensuing one-sided conversation. Apparently, the nurse was phoning on behalf of a friend who had never before been aboard a ship, and enquired if it might be possible for such a visit to be arranged. Our Fifth agreed enthusiastically and the next thing I knew was the party number had increased to ten, and arrangements were being made with a duty mate for a pass to be made out and deposited with the harbour gate police, for the girls' arrival at twenty-one hundred. It all seemed pretty quick work to me.

When Pete relieved me, so I could go for supper, his enthusiasm was unbounded as he listened to me relating what had occurred. He offered a simple explanation. It appeared this sort of call was received frequently in many ports and he was surprised it had not happened in either Perth or Durban. Frequently, when ships arrived, the local nurses recognised it as a heaven-sent opportunity for a party, and the call was their ruse to gain access to any ship. Equally as apparently, officers on board enthusiastically played their part in the charade. I saw the results when a minibus with its cargo of females was directed by one of the juniors, who hung precariously onto the front offside door by standing on the running board, head towards our gangway.

By midnight, the ship was almost like a floating bordello with officers and girls dancing away in poses that would have got them arrested back in the more sober UK. I was dancing (of sorts) clutched tightly to the bosom of a tall, lanky woman twice my age, who smiled at me benignly. Frankly, I was scared stiff and could only gyrate around the smoke room and think dispassionately of England, my home, and how escape could reasonably be made from this predicament. I finally managed to creep away unnoticed from the party before the action really began and had no idea what time Pete eventually turned-in. Whilst cleaning the study a couple of days later, I found an ear-ring at the back of our settee, which led me to put yet another two-and-two together determining how it might have got there and who could have been responsible.

My education so far this trip was being expanded in areas previously not even envisaged in the wildest of my dreams. It was a social skill for which my nautical college had offered no assistance, but I wondered dimly whether or not there might be a little more than truth in the gentle teasing received at my Ellerton selection board interview.

It was shortly after five o'clock on Thursday morning when Pete and I were called to stand-by for arrival Sydney. Needless to say, it was far too early for breakfast and fate had an additional laugh because it was pouring down with rain. And I mean pouring down. It was torrential. The black night sky was painted even more densely with sea level pitch-black clouds.

With more than a rueful glance at the literally bouncing rain Pete turned away from our cabin window and, reaching for his oilies, told me of my good fortune to be in the dry wheelhouse, doing the Movement Book, whilst he was with the Second Mate down aft, after supervising the gangway, getting drenched. Defensively, I explained getting wet going onto the monkey island hoisting flags was also going to be my lot and, going in for my own attack, said how preferable it must be for him to turn-to with Mr. Eyres, knowing he would probably allow Pete to take charge of the docking operation, standing by to step in only if the cadet showed signs of messing things up. My target merely smiled in response and throwing my uniform cap, urged me to get up on the bridge without further delay.

Captain Henderson-Smyth was already there when I arrived, standing by the Mate who had been on watch. I was closely followed by Julian who came in, yawning slightly, and looking decidedly jaundiced. Catching sight of him entering the wheelhouse, Mr. Gaskell told him and the Old Man of his intention to go forward.

I busied myself looking out the Red and Australian courtesy ensigns; 'G', 'H' and 'Q' flags, knowing that these would be required later. Then, I ruled up the Movement Book and synchronised times with the engine-room. After this, glowing in probably mistaken unspoken approval of the still half asleep Third Mate, I stood around trying to look intelligent until the Pilot boat, in the vicinity of Sydney Heads, closed us. We could see her lights coming in fast on the port bow. Checking the radar PPI she was found about half a mile away.

On reporting this distance to the Master, I received his expected order to pop down and meet the Pilot, so went onto the main deck, port side, where the wooden-slatted rope ladder with its spreader planks had already been rigged by the crew, under Pete's directions, on their way aft.

"Ah, Cadet sahib," said the *lascar* standing by in his oilskins, "plenty panni come."

I shot him a grin, but before I could say anything in response, the launch flowed powerfully alongside and he lowered a light rope to take the Pilot's bag.

"Good morning, young man," boomed the Pilot's strong Aussie tones, as he threw his leg over the bulwark of the ship. "You've certainly arrived with some good weather. Typical bloody Pom!" He said jovially.

"Good morning, sir." I said laughing. "I thought you had laid this on for us knowing, as we were a British ship, it would help make us feel at home." I took his bag from the *lascar* and led him to the accommodation, and inner companionway to the wheelhouse.

On catching sight of us entering, Julian mentioned quietly to the Captain that it looked as if we were going alongside immediately. The Pilot overhearing smiled at him and, turning to the Master, disillusioned us all by telling of an unexpected change in orders. Apparently, the ship on our berth had been delayed, owing to a dockers' strike, and we were therefore going to the main anchorage.

We received this news without comment and the Captain instructed the Third Mate to phone a stand down to the Second Officer's crew aft. He then told me to let the Chief Officer up for'ard know, as well as the engine-room and Chief Steward. There was not much else to say. The rain continued to deluge us as dawn started to brighten the leaden sky.

Without further comment, I put on my oilies and taking the offending flags, went onto the monkey island above the wheelhouse. Julian grinned as I passed him the Movement Book and watched the Pilot take the con from the Old Man. The three of them were chatting jovially as they turned our ship towards the mass of ships already awaiting berths in the anchorage off Shark Island.

Circular Quay, Sydney (courtesy Murfett).

Pete was already halfway through breakfast when, having been stood-down, I entered the saloon and joined him at our table. He greeted me with a moan that he had received his drenching aft for nothing, to which I replied something of this had been shared by my good self on the monkey island. Then, turning the conversation to more positive things, I asked if he had received orders for the day; only to learn the Mate had not yet been consulted and he would see him after breakfast and meet up with me in our cabin later.

Pete joined me in our study and, glancing out of the porthole, passed on the Mate's instructions. He was on anchor watch from noon – whilst I (predictably) would turn-to with the deck crew, but there was a variation. It seemed, Pete told me: 'promotion had come my way', because the Mate wanted us both to take the 8-12 *Secunny* and clean out the lifeboats. He queried if I knew what to do and explained as he would be there until seven bells – or 1130 hours – he would help. Initially, I had to see the purser and arrange to change existing condensed milk tins for fresh ones; then empty and refill both water tanks. Meanwhile, he would look at the oars and inside the boat, to see if any varnishing or painting was needed so he could start me on these jobs before going on watch. Until the rain stopped we could work in one of the contactor houses serving a winch and use the seaman to fetch whatever gear was needed before turning him to with the rest of the deck crowd.

We both looked idly out of our window at the rapidly moderating rain, putting off the moment when we would become galvanised into some sort of action. Pete drew my attention to one of the Japanese cargo ships, pondering why they invariably had names of operating companies painted across their hull, venturing this company was 'a crap outfit anyway,' as he elegantly termed it. Casually following his glance I saw, emblazoned in white letters against the black hull, the words YOMASHIATOBA LINE on the side of the nearest ship, swinging gently to her anchor off our starboard quarter. An idea grew in my mind and I asked him to repeat his comments. He did so, giving me in the process a decidedly quizzical look. Unusually for him, he seemed a little slow on the up-take – either that, or his expensive public school had not offered elements on lateral thinking as introduced by our forward thinking English master. He still looked rather blank so I spelled out thoughts crossing my mind, suggesting a visit be made that night in our larch dinghy, equipped with suitable painting materials. In response he shot me a warmly appraising grin.

It was midnight when he came off watch and we met in the cadets' study. During the day, under the legitimate guise of doing the lifeboats, I had visited the bosun's store and, although admittedly bemusing the *Cassab*, had drawn requisite items for our venture. He paused before we set off and, giving me a penetratingly direct look, enquired 'if I was feeling all right?' My reassurance satisfied him and we ventured onto the boat deck.

Quietly, our handy twenty-foot work boat was lowered into the water using its well oiled blocks. I had already loaded the gear required and, in our navy blue uniforms, we were virtually invisible in moonless confines of the night. Sculling over to the Japanese ship was hard and quite slow work and I reflected the last time we had used the dinghy was for sailing off Perth. Whilst on watch, Pete had checked tide tables and re-assured me our return journey would be much easier with a one-knot current astern of us, so long as we were reasonably quick in our task. Whilst he sculled, I lashed a roller brush to long bamboo poles, joining two of these together, and prepared our tray of Stockholm tar. This latter was Peter's idea. I had naturally considered the use of black paint, but inventive as ever, he suggested that were we to use tar, it might make a more permanent job. We brought up alongside the 'enemy' ship and, with Peter keeping the dinghy in place and moving along as necessary, I rapidly painted out the first three letters, the eighth and the last three of the name on the ship's side.

It was closer to 0200 hours when we finally came alongside our own vessel. I climbed up the rope ladder and secured the painter. Peter joined me and we winched the dinghy back onto its chocks. After de-rigging the rope ladder, and re-stowing it in-board of the ship's side we went to our cabins; hid the gear in our study, had a shower and, with all the innocence of youth, turned in.

During the first light of morning it was not possible to see the results of our labours. I returned the residue of equipment used discreetly to the stores, waiting until the *Cassab* and *Tindal* had shot off for their "smoke-oh". It was not until the tide turned, when the vessels swung to more convenient positions, we could witness a new advertisement on the Japanese ship. In blazing white letters was declared the proud boast of this esteemed company: ASHI T LINE.

Word soon spread amongst our officers and, as a boredom breaker, nothing more appealing to the Merchant Navy mind could have been provided. Cameras clicked, tongues wagged, and one enterprising mariner from another ship (we found out later), hawked his prints around local newspaper offices. The reactions, balanced delicately around unsubtle Australian humour, could easily be visualised and we could almost hear the ribald comments with which the snaps were greeted.

In the midday edition of the *Sydney Tribune* (let us call it) the *fait* was truly *accompli*. Under a suitable heavily sarcastic headline appeared the night's handiwork in all its glory.

Aboard *Earl of Bath*, the saloon talk was animated – to say the least. Hilarity reached its climax as officers discussed the incident and made varying conjectures concerning which ship (as undoubtedly it had to be) might have been responsible. Thinking of the strong tidal sets in the harbour, and the idea of taking a small boat into heavily shark-infested waters, much praise was bestowed upon the nerve and, indeed, professionalism of the perpetrators. Of one thing we were quite certain, no one even suspected our ship might have been responsible. Peter and I revelled in agonising anonymity, considering it more than prudent to maintain a very mean silence.

So life continued in a pattern of day-work and watches. The ship received orders to load a full cargo of wool and, initially, to ship this to unspecified Japanese ports. These orders were later changed and we were told to proceed with all due speed towards the United Kingdom, our discharge port to be specified whilst on passage. Loading being well towards completion, we would have got away with our adventure had it not been for a routine pre-sailing inspection of the boat deck by the Mate. Apparently, wandering around, he noticed what appeared to be black smudges on the work boat. Pete and I had done our best to remove the stuff, but it was difficult and we just could not, despite our best efforts, eradicate completely tar splashes from inside the boat.

The Mate knew that his crew had not used the larch dinghy for a while and was thus more than a little mystified at the extent and range of what, on closer inspection, appeared to be tar. Now, as a Company's senior Chief Officer aboard an ocean going ship, he was nobody's fool. He had noticed after the Japanese crew finally saw the condition of their hull, they had worked very hard in eradicating the gaps to restore the lettering. He had observed they had laboured long and hard for an inordinate amount of time, on what had first appeared to be paint, without making much impression.

His own professionalism clicked into place, but it was not until the state of the dinghy on his own ship was noticed, that he started a process of mental enquiry which led him to believe not only had a more adhesive substance than boot-topping black been used – like tar? – but perhaps (perish the thought) his ship might somehow be involved.

Voicing his views to the other mates, and drawing a reasonable enough blank whilst provoking considerable interest, he then went to the Captain. Immediately (for some reason) they thought of us cadets and Julian was sent to fetch Pete and me to the Old Man's cabin.

We received the summons without too much concern for, after all, the incident had been some time previously and, amidst some quiet chuckles, genuinely considered we had got away with it.

"Right, you two," began Captain Henderson-Smyth, as a blunt preamble. "Do you know anything at all about the incident with the Japanese ship, which resulted in her hull being defaced?"

"Yes, sir," Pete said. "We did it."

There was a pregnant pause whilst our Captain and Mate exchanged glances. They were clearly momentarily thrown by such an abruptly honest admission.

"I suppose it is pointless making much further comment," stated the Old Man, glowing beautifully. "You had better explain, in detail, exactly what happened."

They looked expectantly from one to the other of us.

I, as junior cadet, maintained an interested silence and listened as Pete, using all the guile which had clearly got him out of many a scrape in the past, explained the circumstances surrounding that fateful night. My only contribution was to look shamefaced, full of remorse, and add the occasionally confirming "yes, sir" at appropriate intervals.

The Old Man and Mate told us to wait outside the cabin whilst they went into a huddle to decide a course of action. Clearly, we could not be allowed to get away with it, but even we appreciated their quandary concerning our punishment. After all, informing the shore authorities was not really an option.

We were summoned again into their presence.

"This is a disgraceful thing you have done – the pair of you," commenced the Old Man. "We are a British ship and if ever this leaks out, there is no telling what the reactions of the Japanese will be – particularly in terms of reprisals. You will both be restricted to the ship for the remainder of our stay in Australian waters. No shore leave. You will each do extra day-work until we leave, so that you'll not have further time for such childish pranks. Now, away with you both – and report to the Mate immediately after supper. Your punishment starts from now."

We both left, with me at least reasonably subdued. On the bright side, we were both completely broke and knew, with cargo close to completion, our time in Aussie waters was limited. There was nothing we wanted ashore and could accept our punishment quite readily. Once we left the cabin, Pete's face lit up with a smile and he told me to follow him – to be both quick and silent. Mystified, I chased after him as he shot up to the boat deck and, crept on all fours towards the Old Man's accommodation, just below his open window, enabling us to overhear all our superiors were saying:

"……..enterprising, I suppose," came the Mate's tones. "Yes. Still we had to do something. The little so-and-so's."

"Anyway, Jim, you know as well as me, it was a bloody good idea and they carried it out extremely well," said the Captain.

"Hmm. When you consider some of the things we got up to as cadets, I suppose." The Mate's unconvincing agreement sallied out of the window. "I know something – two things actually. I'll keep the little devils busy until we leave Aussie. And, I'll be well pleased when sailing day comes in case any rumours leave the ship – unlike my cadets, that is."

"Yes, great. Good job we're well advanced with loading."

We crept quietly away – having heard sufficient.

Arriving for one of my Saturday morning sessions with Mr. Gaskell, shortly after we had cleared the Mediterranean and were halfway through the Bay of Biscay on the return voyage, he told me to come with him and I suddenly found myself heading for the Captain's quarters. I quite obviously blanched visibly for the Mate smiled, asked me what undiscovered sins did I think had suddenly become discovered and, without waiting for an answer, told me this meeting was my end of voyage chat with the senior officers where, top of the agenda, was my professional, personal and academic progress. Captain Henderson-Smyth invited us both to be seated on the settee in his comfortable day room – which I regarded as an optimistic sign. He opened the session by asking the Mate his views concerning my progress since coming on board. Amongst his observations, the Mate stated, reports from other officers and the *Serang* indicated I had settled very well into my chosen profession; he was pleased with the progress being made in all areas of my training on board, and his evidence was confirmed by a series of monthly reports from Keddleston Navigation School on my professional and academic progress to date with them. In consequence I was, overall, 'showing promise.' The Captain nodded his affirmation and said: "to have me serve on board his ship for the voyage had been a pleasure." I looked rather guardedly between the two and, seeing no apparent evidence of past wrongs being re-aired, relaxed and took their comments at face value. It was true, I had enjoyed most things that had happened to me and felt considerably more confident, following my apprehension leaving navigation school.

The Captain smiled again, asking me how *I* felt things had gone on this my first voyage to sea. I blanched a little, but encouraged by his kindly approach, explained that professionally I felt quite re-assured by comments regarding my work and the results from Keddleston. On the personal front, I was honest enough to state I had 'experienced a few hairy moments', and had perhaps 'sailed a little close to the wind on occasions'. All parties present knew what these were and, clearly, felt little could be added to what had already been expressed at any particular time. They skated around further discussion by stressing I was far removed from the innocently naïve young man who had joined in Amsterdam, over a year previously. My professional progress was indeed satisfactory and a report would be made to the Chief Marine Superintendent to that effect, which would probably be followed up during an interview to which all cadets were called at the end of a voyage. He intimated I would probably complete my initial Royal Naval Reserve training, after a short leave, prior to joining another vessel within the Company's fleet. He felt I could be satisfied, but certainly not complacent, regarding my sea-time so far, whilst the pranks in which I had become involved, apart from the Sydney Harbour incident, were largely due to my newness to seafaring. That hull painting incident, however, he was still in two minds about. Part of him was frankly pleased to see my ingenuity, as it proved possession of that particular brand of humour upon which success at sea depended, but he was a bit concerned I had still to learn how to keep a measure of proportion if contemplating future events of a similar kind.

I left the interview with mixed feelings, recognising a possible ambiguity in the Master's closing comments and aware perhaps that even if my colours were not completely flying, then at least my flag remained attached to the mast. When explaining things to Pete, he was totally re-assuring and I was able to venture out on deck, and help complete smartening the ship for arrival at London with liberal coats of freshly gleaming paint, and considerable peace of mind.

As the *Earl of Bath* approached Dungeness Pilot station and I went on deck, again in the pouring rain, I was almost aching with anticipation. Already, over the previous few days, a mounting excitement had been felt, with a bad attack of what Vic termed 'the Channels'. This was a condition that never actually appeared in the *Ship Captain's Medical Guide*. I had eagerly consumed the pages of this august tome earlier in the voyage, whilst fetching some plasters to the bridge for the Second Officer to apply to a cut on his finger, after he had stabbed himself with the sharp pointed dividers whilst doing chart corrections. He was the ship's medical officer and my eyes had been well and truly opened by hearing his discussions with other officers, in the smoke room, concerning conditions which came his way in the performance of this particular duty. The coloured plates in the *Guide* made also their own interesting (if frightening) contribution.

Anyway, psychological manifestations of the Channels were ones to which I was particularly prone as I found myself thinking of meeting with my parents again and, above all, with Sue. Correspondence with her had been consistent throughout the trip and a healthy friendship was developing which seemed to show promise for my forthcoming leave. Replacement of a certain photograph was also necessary. Even Pete was affected by the Channels as he babbled on about meeting with his latest lady of the moment.

We berthed in the Royal Albert Dock in London at half past eleven on a Saturday morning following a change of Pilots at Gravesend. Our passage was noteworthy only for consistently heavy rain. I was called into the Chief Officers' cabin to receive final instructions regarding my leave. There I met his wife and one daughter, along with the son whom I still regarded as having saved my life whilst on passage between Durban and Perth – light years ago. They greeted me cordially, but obviously could not wait for husband and dad to go on leave. Pete was shattered to learn he was to remain on board until Hull and Middlesborough, whilst the ship completed discharging wool in north-eastern ports, before going to the Continent. Afterwards, he was to go on leave and then rejoin the *Bath* for her next voyage to North American, Canadian, Australian and New Zealand ports – potentially a very long voyage indeed on what was commonly known as the 'MANZ' run (The 'M' referring to Montreal). I was to leave the ship after signing-off Articles, packing and ordering a taxi. Saying whatever farewells to other officers encountered, and the wives who had joined for the Continental passage, I went into the ship's office to telephone home.

It was very strange to hear my father's voice after such a lengthy period away. Eagerly, he called out to Mum and we spent a few minutes simply listening to each other and chatting simultaneously. The only practical result, so far as I was concerned, was Dad telling me he would come to the ship and collect me. Astounded at the amount of gear I seemed to have collected, he was uncertain whether or not his small car would take the three of us as well, but knowing it would be impossible to leave Mum at home ("more than the life of either of us is worth," I jokingly stated), he reckoned we would manage somehow. Pete very helpfully took a ship's pass to the dock gate in anticipation of their arrival. This arrangement gave me ample time to sort out my gear. It would be a good couple of hours' drive for them to the docks, via the Blackwall Tunnel, from our home in south-east London.

Once packed, I waited impatiently on our seemingly smaller boat-deck yearning for a sighting of their car as it rounded the adjacent shed and arrived on the jetty. There was an unexpected hesitancy as we greeted each other and I showed them to my quarters. Cargo was not being worked that weekend and the ship was shrouded in uncharacteristic silence. Whilst Pete tactfully shot off to organise some tea from our friendly Purser (our voluntary Captain-encouraged assistance with his ship's paperwork having paid dividends) we took stock of each other in restrained silence. They both seemed smaller and older than I remembered; with wisps of grey in the hair of each, increasingly so at my father's temples. Mr. Gaskell, unaware of their presence, popped in for a few moments to give Pete some final instructions, and his visit eased considerably the stiffness permeating our cabin. Recovering quickly, he was chatty, jovial and witty – 'charmingly urbane' my father described him afterwards – and, as he took his farewell, told me he hoped to sail with me on some future voyage; his voice even sounded warm – as if he actually meant it. Pete helped carry my cases to the waiting car into which we just managed to fit everything and everyone.

Once clear of the docks, we became more relaxed and the conversation ranged from astonishment at the size of the ship on their part (they each thought how large it was) to interesting, yet fragmentary, relating of local news. We each found there was so much to say. Somehow, listening to events being related with such animation, there was a sense of the parochial about familiar names and places. I was genuinely interested and concerned, but could not fully share the intensity of their involvement: not through condescension in any way, but a realisation that it was me who was returning to a different world. I was coming from Hartley's 'alien land' and needed time to revise my attitude towards parents, family members and friends. It was a sobering realisation. The other thing we discovered during that journey home was my natural tendency to use commonplace nautical words in ordinary conversation. It had not dawned on me how familiar were becoming the terms and expressions now used without thinking. Inevitably, of course, there were many which I had to hold in check, but that task came far more easily than previously anticipated. As we drove past only vaguely remembered red London buses, associated traffic and places, into the drive of our home, I began to appreciate that perhaps the sea was now my real world. Eating and talking our way through Mum's welcome home-cooked meal, prior to taking my gear from the car, restored an element of normality. We lingered over coffee, each simply relishing the moment, catching up on even more family and Church news, with me relating some neutral things not mentioned in my letters. With considerable relief, I found how easy it became to change roles from being a cadet on board ship back into being a son.

The first night in my room was strangely disturbing, but I was able to sleep very well. The bed, pictures on the walls, and even the room itself, appeared smaller and oddly unfamiliar, whilst previously considered favourite things of childhood no longer possessed the importance which they had before I joined the Merchant Navy. My books and record player were the only treasured things, and I dipped eagerly into those volumes and music which sheer weight had prevented me taking away.

Two days into my leave came an expected summons from the Kremlin, as everyone on board ship referred to Ellerton Lines' head office. It was a cordial meeting with the Marine Superintendent, during which I learnt of the extremely satisfactory report Captain Henderson-Smyth had submitted, and was allowed to glow briefly before the Company's future plans were unfolded. Royal Naval Reserve basic training was not to be done this time home, but at the end of my next trip. Instead, I was to have another couple of weeks' leave prior to joining the m.v. *Earl of Edinburgh* in Tilbury Docks, Essex, for a voyage to Far Eastern ports. This news of course was received with anticipated excitement as visions of unbridled enjoyment, evoked by my previous officers' stories of a freedom loving way of life in Hong Kong and Japan ran across my mind's eye. I felt it would be interesting to test these tales for myself. He also advised that an edited version of the Captain's voyage report on my progress would be sent home – another Ellerton policy.

But first, I had to continue my leave by being shown around the family once again; this time with far more assurance than my post-Keddleston visits. So many of my relatives commented on my tanned and healthy appearance, and my increased height and stature – that I actually began to believe it. The most important meeting of all was, of course, with Sue. Both sets of parents had followed the path of our correspondence with interest so, by the time I came home, our friendship was virtually taken for granted. Sue had been invited to tea on the second evening and, from then on, we spent a great deal of time together, including most family visits. That tongues were undoubtedly wagging was of little concern to either of us – Sue had become used to having her name linked with mine, whilst for me, within a couple of weeks I would be off to sea again.

Four days prior to my departure, a phone call was received asking me to pop into the Office as soon as convenient – by which, of course, they meant the following day. My joining instructions for the *Edinburgh* were cancelled and instead I was told to report to the brand new *Earl of Guildford* on her maiden voyage, due to load a full cargo of explosives for the Persian Gulf, at the Lower Hope powder buoys in the River Thames. Apparently, dynamite was used in blasting operations as a prelude to drilling. I was to phone the Company's agent in Tilbury who would make due arrangements for me to be transferred by launch to the ship.

My father queried the various earldoms which Ellertons seemed to have created – a question which I had raised with the Mate on the *Bath*. Apparently, when the parent company had been founded in the mid-1800s, there were sufficient seats to justify names but, as the company expanded into a Group, they rapidly ran out of earls after which to name the ships and so adopted a flexible and far more arbitrary system. This included the God-given right to extend their 'regal conferment' and incorporate ports abroad with whom the Company's ships traded – as well as others – at the whim of the Group's directors.

With fond farewells I left home and, by train and taxi, went to the Royal Terrace Pier at Gravesend from whence the Agent's launch took me to the ship. She was less than 5,000 tons gross – considerably smaller than my last vessel – and was lying fore and aft to buoys, surrounded by barges which brought out dynamite and detonators from the nearby Cliffe explosives jetty. I was the only cadet and, after showing my Journal to the Mate, was put on cargo watches with the Second Officer. It was quite clear he was not sure immediately how to employ me, as my presence had not been notified by the Kremlin. The cadets' accommodation on this ship was self-contained, and again situated at the port end of the officers' deck.

I had just turned in that night when there was a horrendous crash and the ship shivered violently, plunging and rearing against her moorings. In the midst of a London dense fog, we had been hit just abaft the fo'c'sle-head by an inward bound Red Star Liner from South America. Luckily, there had been no loss of life or injury on either vessel, but a considerable shaking-up occurred (and not just to the ships). The brand new *Guildford* – pride of the Ellerton fleet – ended up with a deep V in her hull that had nearly entered No. 1 hold. The cargo-passenger liner had a severely dented bow – or 'bloody nose', as the Mate said – more, I thought, in relief than anger. Had the ship been an older vessel, cynics amongst the officers suggested the Company would probably have been delighted to have harvested the insurance value of the vessel.

Thus it was, three days after leaving home, I was back once again, revelling in the drama of how we could all have been blown sky-high and receiving awed glances from all and sundry – especially my devoted Sue, who realised that she might have lost her most ardent admirer. This was a sobering thought to all concerned – not the least myself – but left me quite undeterred and still adamantly refusing to apply for a job in a bank as urged by a certain close member of my immediate family.

Chapter 4

A ROUND TRIP

———

Two days later I joined the *Earl of Edinburgh*, then completing loading for the Far East at the Company's berth in Tilbury Docks, East Branch. She was one of three sister ships, some nine years older than the *Earl of Bath*, 8,100 gross registered tons, with length overall of 497 feet and a beam of 62 feet. She was built by Cammell Laird's, with six hatches – No. 4 a much smaller hold forward of the funnel. The Chief Officer later described it as a 'pig in a poke' whatever that might be. Our first cargo port of call was Singapore and we were to bunker in Aden. Similarly to the *Bath*, the cadets' quarters were starboard side aft on the officers' deck.

Grabbing a taxi from Gravesend railway station to the ferry berth, I boarded an antiquated steamship for the five minutes Tilbury crossing – a trip evoking its own host of memories.

My association with the Thames was comparatively recent and had begun with trips on Harbour Master launches during quiet weekends with my Uncle 'Wag', before I became Keddleston bound. It was about this time that I started visiting the various branches of London docks – ostensibly to take photographs, even though that was merely a ruse to obtain a permit allowing entrance – and even if on occasions there was no film in my camera. I had played things down a little with my parents, to protect Wag and prevent any likelihood of family rows, but these experiences (as well as the African film) had contributed considerably to my desire for seafaring. 'Wag', as he was universally known to work colleagues and family, had been a chief boatman, prior to his promotion as Port of London Authority river inspector. He had in fact been on duty at the time of the collision when I was on the *Guildford*, and had been able to reassure my parents that they were in little danger of losing their son; we had met very briefly when he came on board during his initial investigation.

On launch trips with him, I had acquired a lasting love of this hustling waterway. With over 1,100 ship movements per week, the Thames could modestly boast of being the busiest river in the world. There were craft of all shapes and sizes at every state of tide, but at high water inward and outward bound ships passed Gravesend literally every few minutes, mostly ocean-going cargo vessels representing all maritime flags in the world. Passenger and cargo/passenger liners berthed at Tilbury (both in the docks and invariably on the landing stage) whilst others passed by en route to the Royal and Millwall Docks up river. Every kind of cargo imaginable was carried in specialist ships of all shapes, sizes and functions; high stacked deck-cargo timber ships bound for the Surrey Commercial; hundreds of colliers; a continuous stream of modern and antiquated deeply laden coasters; motor and sailing barges, heading to and from all manner of sized ports everywhere. Much merchandise was carried in dumb (engine-less) barges, strings of which were an everyday sight with their attendant river tugs. A fleet of larger tugs remained permanently moored off – or alongside – Gravesend's Royal Terrace pier, standing-by to assist ships to berth or to leave. A range of ancillary craft with various functions constantly ranged the Thames; harbour patrol service, wreck watching, salvage and river cleaning launches and tenders; customs, pilots, port health, and work boats conveying people in various trades and functions to vessels moored in the small ships' anchorage just outside the main fairway. Tankers – both coastal and deep-sea – abounded, with the latter often moored alongside Tilbury Tanker Repair Jetty, before departing to load at Thameshaven or Coryton refineries further down river, or at the complex of riverside oil jetties in the Purfleet area.

The River Thames at high tide (courtesy Museum in the Docklands, PLA Collection).

Accompanying this vast armada of shipping, I recalled hearing the constant noise, day and night, from ship's sirens signalling alteration of courses, vessels requesting pilots, tugs receiving instructions from their charges, along with sundry whistle signals indicating a variety of needs and operations. Additionally, my eardrums were assailed by crashes and bangs from pneumatic drills, machinery on wharfs, jetties, repair yards, maintenance sheds, demolition berths and the power station across the river in Tilbury. The entire scenario was wreathed in smoke from coal burning tugs, exerting every effort to tow deep laden barges against the tide and emitting dense black fumes in the process; along with coal-fired passing ships, and exhaust from diesel-driven craft. A range of factories contributed their share, chief of which was the cement works in Northfleet. This added its own unique brand of viscous smoke, the density of which caused passing ships to use navigation lights in broad daylight.

I recalled masses of people, hundreds of them, in constant movement. Many worked across the river at Tilbury in various dock-worker posts; pilots, shipping companies' shore-staff, ship maintenance workmen, and ships' crews (like myself) joining and leaving vessels, or taking local leave in Gravesend or nearby London. Passenger and car ferries operated a service of three ships per hour, each way, to meet that insatiable demand for transport over the half mile stretch of water between Gravesend and Tilbury. Most impressive to my mind was the skyline with its uniquely bizarre merging of shapes and structures; cranes, at all angles on jetties and in the docks, nodded agreement as they loaded and discharged deep within ships' holds, contrasting with a forest of masts and derricks from their charges. There was a variety of tall, medium and short chimneys from power stations; awkward looking constructions of warehouses, riverside dwellings, pubs, shops, offices and factories.

Idly daydreaming aboard the ferry I became just another person caught-up in a throng of 'busy-ness'. I lugged my suitcases to a taxi at Tilbury Riverside station, becoming intermingled with hundreds of departing passengers joining the quite new 29,790 gross registered ton P & O liner *Orsova* bound for Australia. She was loading at the landing stage – probably with emigrants under the popular Government Assisted Passage scheme, to Australia and New Zealand; with a thriving liner trade similarly engaged from Liverpool to Canada.

By now, I was becoming accustomed to reporting to Chief Officers so, having made myself known to him directly arriving on board, I received instructions to report back after stowing away my gear. Taking my Journal – up-dated with the latest explosives saga, that included a photograph of the ship which London office had given me – I trundled along to his cabin. Mr. Drury was rather thickset and recently promoted from Second Officer. His greeting was firmly friendly and I found myself hearing instructions similar to those on joining *Earl of Bath*. One other cadet had signed-on Articles, but had been allowed home for a couple of days (perhaps a promising sign of a sensibly benevolent authority) and would be re-joining next day, prior to completion of loading. The bulk of cargo had been taken on the Continent and, because Tilbury – although a very busy port – was a transit dock with limited warehouse facilities, we were completing with a range of manufactured goods for tween deck loading only. He believed we would (hopefully) sail on the following morning's tide. Meanwhile, after unpacking, I was to find the Third Officer who was on cargo watch out on deck somewhere.

I unpacked and changed and eventually ran to earth Matthew Synnott, in No. 4 tween deck, where he was talking to the *Tindal* about dunnage. I made myself known and was very reassured by the reception. Although Ellerton's Group was large, the officers generally kept within individual companies and so knew each other, either from having sailed together or, frequently, meeting in sundry ports abroad, or even having been pre-sea trained at the same nautical colleges where mutual sporting fixtures, and the like, abounded. He knew the officers with whom I had sailed on the *Bath* – apart from the Captain (of whom he had heard) and Pete Dawson. The other cadet was about a year my senior – called Austen Greig or "Scruff" as he had been commonly known at Pangbourne – a nickname gained from his unconventional (by Pangbourne's standards) way of wearing uniform. That evening, I went back to Gravesend with Matthew for a wander around, taking in a drink and a John Wayne Western, *Rio Grande,* in the local cinema: an uncomplicated and enjoyable final evening ashore in the UK, which deepened our new friendship.

Loading completed on schedule and Austen arrived in time to start work at 0800 on that day so we were ready for sailing as forecast. Whilst he did Movement Book and flags I was on the fo'c'sle working with the crew, handling mooring ropes and backspring, as well as taking a towing wire from our forward tug. After reading my journal, Mr. Drury reckoned it was time to develop my training programme into more practical stuff during stand-by, which was interesting if quite heavy work but, as with all Asian-crewed ships, there were enough of us to cope. As we cleared the locks, I was told by the Mate to man our telephone, which was rather awkwardly situated in the very eyes of the fo'c'sle head. I was to remain with him and the Carpenter on the river passage in case the anchor was required. Eventually, we passed the ill-fated explosive buoys and were soon abeam of the major tanker jetties, on the port side at Thameshaven and Coryton. Mr. Drury discussed the collision incident with me but, more interestingly, told me he had served his time aboard tankers prior to joining Ellertons, so was able to point out ships of the various major companies. Shell boats were the predominant representatives, with names derived from the Latin for various shells. Those alongside began with the letter 'H' such as *Hima* or *Hyalina*. The BP refinery was just around the corner, in the Isle of Grain, and we saw a number of their tankers arriving and departing this very busy terminal. I was intrigued by the information he gave me and (again) liked the look of these sleek-lined, rather attractive ships. Tentatively I enquired about sailing on them: what it was like on board, the voyages, conditions of service and lifestyle, so he filled in the intervening river passage by telling me of his experiences. He obviously picked-up my keen interest, so suggested I should ask the Chief Superintendent for a 'taster voyage' on a crude or product carrier of another Company associated within the Group. He thought there could be little harm in my doing this and if, by the end of this voyage I was still interested, he would sound out the situation on my behalf.

Tilbury Docks (courtesy Museum in the Docklands, PLA Collection).

I spent a great deal of this trip working with the deck ratings, interspersed with cleaning out the wheelhouse. Austen also did far more deck work than either Vic or Pete had done, not being so advanced into his cadetship as they with theirs. This *Serang* was again pleasant and friendly and working with his crew presented few problems. We found ourselves on stages or Bosun's chair, painting funnel, whistle and mast stays; silvering holds and, whilst at various anchorages, re-cutting with white paint, load-lines, draft marks and the ship's name. There was ample opportunity for bridge work with the duty mates after day work and, indeed, this was actively encouraged. With Pangbourne and an extra years' sea-time behind him, Scruff was well advanced with his mathematics and navigational theory, so he was allowed to go onto the bridge with the Chief Officer's morning watch to take star sights. He was also stood-down after breakfast and at noon to 'shoot the sun' and work out the ship's position with the Second Officer, Mr. Bryant. Mr. Drury advised that, once I could understand sufficient theory, he would encourage me also to commence taking sights.

The Bay of Biscay was really rough and, once again, my stomach and I disagreed about any movement other than lying in my bunk. This, of course, was certainly not allowed, so I spent a few days feeling very ill, but turned-to anyway cleaning out both wheelhouse and sundry other parts of the Mates' deck stores. Up forward was definitely the worse place to be and my experiences of illness on the *Earl of Bath* were again repeated. The ship plunged and reared unpredictably, adopting simultaneously a twisting corkscrew motion that threw me off balance and had me hopping around dangerously wherever I happened to be working – a most unpleasant experience.

By Gibraltar, I had again become accustomed to the motion and, although it was rough for the entire Mediterranean passage to Suez, the trip was bearable. It was almost 'old hat' to pass through the Canal, Red Sea and Aden approaches. Again, we cadets were allowed ashore and, on this occasion in Aden, I purchased a radio, and tape recorder, along with some blank tapes and pre-recorded music. These were comparatively new exports from Japan, but considerably enlivened our off-duty time. The crackle of atmospherics and intermittent fading of the BBC's Overseas Services Radio News, with its regular programme for merchant seaman, became very much part of my new found maritime freedom. The fading invariably occurred just as a significant news item was scheduled and there was, equally as invariably, the over-riding of whatever was being broadcast, by the staccato song of Morse code, as Sparks rapped out his frequent messages. The Merchant Navy programme included record requests; although I never knew anyone to have theirs played. The Mate warned me that my purchases in Aden had taken me perilously close to becoming in debt to the ship, and accordingly advised caution in my future spending.

I practised semaphore and Morse signalling with Scruff and, as the voyage progressed, went to the wheelhouse to use our Aldis lamp to communicate with passing ships. I became quite adept at the call sign and exchanging information such as 'What ship?' and 'Where bound?' along with subsequent voyage details of cargo, mates and the like. Learning Morse code had proved easy, so far as sending was concerned, but receiving still required some assistance, either from Scruff or the duty mate, helping me interpret symbols flashed whilst receiving. I questioned why the code had not been rather more logically arranged and worked out a system which appeared easier to remember. Unwisely, mentioning my theory to the Mate brought, perhaps not surprisingly, a response along the lines of 'the entire World is unlikely to adopt the Caridia code, just to please you, so you had better turn-to and learn Morse's version of the damn thing.' This rejoinder, however, was accompanied by a penetrating look, leaving me to think that perhaps he had not entirely disagreed with me. Scruff's response however was not so cordial, it was, in fact, totally unprintable. I suspected, had he been of the same ilk as Fulbright in Keddleston, it would have been accompanied by a hearty clout.

A cadet 'speaks' to a passing ship by Aldis lamp (courtesy BP plc).

The Second Officer tests cadets on the Collision Regulations (Crown copyright/MOD).

Weekly meetings on this ship with Mr. Drury followed a similar pattern but were on Sunday mornings. My knowledge of the Collision Regulations increased and the Second Officer took to instructing us on a Tuesday morning, discussing Rule of the Road situations, characteristics of lights, shapes and sound signals. He also dealt with any mathematical or ship construction problems we had encountered. The Chief Officer allowed us this time off immediately after stand-easy and the sessions lasted until lunch. This was in addition to our regular Tuesday and Thursday afternoon sessions whilst at sea. Even at the time, we both recognised being well spoiled by Ellerton's progressive cadet training policy. Keeping up my correspondence course was time consuming but, with such positive encouragement from the Chief and Second Officers, and with obvious benefits resulting from my studies which I could start applying practically, the time devoted to this was welcomed. Scruff was really helpful with his enhanced knowledge and, in return, I was pleased to help him memorise his Rules for relating to the Mate at his weekly meeting on Friday afternoons. He was far more practical than me (which was not too difficult), but I possessed a skill in perfecting line drawings of hold interiors, shipboard machinery and navigational theory diagrams which I was willing to share – and many became the additions to his Journal which were done in return. Working thus to each other's mutual advantage we got along very well together.

Discharging in Singapore was straightforward and brought its own reward of two little envelopes tucked into two cadets' shirt pockets – devoid this time, I was relieved to find, of the accompanying pat on the cheek. The Mate winked as he gave us permission to go ashore that evening after cargo work which I interpreted (rightly or wrongly) as 'don't worry too much over your Aden purchases'. We visited the Happy World, an interesting and delightfully uninhibited 'play ground' for want of a better description. Things really came alive in the late evening but, true to my loyalty to Sue, I never became too involved, even though Scruff fell by the wayside and, en route to Hong Kong, found himself seeking out the Second Mate for medical attention. The Chief Officer was not very pleased with him and he went before the Captain for further discussion of his sins.

Unlike the *Bath*, we cadets saw the Master only from afar. Captain Mitchell always came into the second senior officers' saloon sitting, rarely spoke to either of us, and never came to the smoke room, sharing film shows or other relaxing pursuits with his officers. He was not at all hostile when our paths did cross, in fact, was really quite pleasant, but practising an isolation policy was simply his particular style. Scruff and I had been invited to join the officers, as we had done on previous ships to play chess, cribbage and darts, as well as using the pool and participating in deck games. Once again, my crib skills came in useful and, for a while, I topped the ship's league table before being ousted by the third engineering officer – a veritable dragon of a player. My dubious contributions to our occasional Sod's operas also seemed much appreciated.

Hong Kong was a bustling, thriving maelstrom of diverse shipping and cargoes. We went alongside in Kowloon to discharge and were quickly festooned with dock workers who, equally as soon, cleared our cargo. This was not before a tailor came to the ship directly we arrived, measured most of the officers for suits, brought these back the next day for fitting, and delivered the finished product early on the third day, just prior to sailing. I ended up with a light brown two piece of good material, well sewn and a perfect fit, for a tenth of the price in England. I was well satisfied and felt very much a man about town.

Whilst still alongside, Ellerton's homeward bound *Earl of Leicester* berthed at an adjacent jetty. I felt Scruff agitated for us to board her with an almost indecent urgency which initially had me rather baffled. On the way to their vessel, he explained that this was the system in the fleet and enabled us to drink their booze, instead of paying to entertain them. I refrained from comment as I could think of little sensible to say – part of me agreed with him, but the other part felt we were being a bit mean. Either way, it felt quite strange to be discussing similar features of seafaring life in another ship's smoke room and cadets' cabins, exchanging news and gossip about the fleet, experiences and cargoes – yet conducting this exchange with different faces above our similar white uniforms. I asked casually if the other cadets had heard of Peter Dathan, and found that one of *Leicester's* cadets had completed a coastal voyage with him the previous year. He appeared to be getting on very well with his cadetship and life at sea generally. Yet again, I resolved to write to him, later on.

Amidst the bustle, I still found time to go ashore and drink in the sights of Kowloon and and then made the short crossing to Hong Kong Island on the Star ferries. It was in Kowloon that I popped into a chandler's shop, passed accidentally whilst wandering, and bought a left-handed sailmaker's palm. The Mate was quite impressed with my purchase. He had not seen one before, but was accustomed only to the conventional right-handed ones. The *Cassab* gave me odd bits of canvas, sewing twine and beeswax, and encouraged me to learn how to use the thing. I went on the second evening with Mat and Sparks, to Aberdeen fishing village on the other side of the island, to sample its floating restaurant. It was quite an experience. A kitchen sampan came alongside our boat and the cook took the fish we indicated, despatched this, and prepared it in front of us. Not a meal for the squeamish, but extremely tasty, especially washed down with a bottle (or two) of what was described as 'a local light white wine'. Scruff was also taken ashore, but by Mr. Bryant during the day, to visit the port medical officer.

Coincidental with the completion of cargo, came a typhoon warning – 'timely, to say the least', as the Mate put it. The Captain without hesitation decided to face this by putting to sea. The first indication we received was the viscous-like appearance of the heavy swell, as we set course for Taiwan and our next port of discharge. Soon the seas became considerably angry; the crests broken by hurricane force winds to merge in scattered confusion over the deepening troughs, whilst salt laden spume ran in streaks along the diffused waves. The sky darkened and sheets of wind-blown rain blotted visibility often to just a few yards. I was sent to the wheelhouse to act 'as an extra pair of eyes', a delightful euphemism for better known lookout duty. The Captain looked up as I entered the wheelhouse and stationed me on the starboard side. The senior *Secunny* was already on the wheel and Mat, as officer-of-the-watch, was stationed by the telegraphs. The Master reassured us by saying that we would not experience the full force of the typhoon by going through the eye of the storm and (hopefully – as he put it) 'coming out the other side', because we were on the periphery. Outer limits or not, the wild seas beyond our comfortably warm domain were very frightening. I duly reported a light suddenly observed off the bow, which turned out to be a passing small dry cargo vessel. She pitched and rolled like a wild thing, frequently lost to view in the trough of quite mountainous seas, only to appear a few minutes later, barely supported along her length, and her propeller periodically clearing the water. Amongst the maelstrom she looked very insecure. I do not know what we looked like to her officers, admittedly much longer in hull and heavier in tonnage against her tortuous labouring, but she was making very heavy weather of things. We also saw a Chinese junk which seemed like a cork on top of the water – the Captain told us these were the most seaworthy craft in existence and it was extremely rare for one to founder. Being made largely of timber they simply floated on top of the waves regardless of how high or severe these might prove – safe or not, I was hardly filled with envy watching them being thrown around the ocean, feeling that the ships may well have been able to take it, but what about the crew?

Suddenly, we heard a monstrous groan from our main deck, and the entire ship shivered and shuddered. I wondered what on earth was happening and even Mat looked decidedly nervous. The Captain smiled and told us not to worry as the noise was caused by our ship's deck plating giving to the powerful longitudinal stresses to which the hull was being subjected in our part-loaded condition. He told us that, under such circumstances as we were experiencing, the time to worry would be when we did not hear this sound as it could possibly mean one of the bulkheads might give way, resulting in the ship breaking at the point of intersection between two hatches. 'Mind you,' he added, 'you probably would not have time to register much ...', his voice ending on a rather whimsical note. I tried to look comfortable in the light of this information, but think my appearance was a little wan to put things mildly. Strangely enough, I did not feel seasick at all – perhaps being too scared even to think about being ill – in which, I felt, there might be some kind of medical moral.

Over the next day or two, the sea gradually quietened, but the swell accompanied us until we took the pilot into Kaohsiung. We were soon tied up alongside and I was stood-down from for'ard to help rig the gangway. With the clearing of the ship, work started immediately – continuing until completion of cargo. I reflected this was a far cry from the attitude exhibited by Australian dock workers who, even in my limited experience, came out on strike at the drop of a hat which had ensured our prolonged stay in their ports.

Scruff and I were allowed shore leave by the Chief Officer, following dire warnings to my cabin mate to pay closer attention to his choice of friends than he had in Singapore – from which, it was firmly pointed out, he had yet to recover completely. Our sortie was limited to a quick look around those parts of the city adjacent to the wharf, which I found totally fascinating if rather too hectic for words. We made an almost mandatory trip to the Missions to Seamen's building which was predictably quiet for that time in the afternoon. Over a beer, we met up with a Bank Line Fourth Officer who was on a tramp ship just along the wharf from us. I was horrified to learn that had been out of the UK for three and a half years. He had started tramping as a first-trip deck apprentice and had been promoted uncertificated officer on the strength of accrued sea-time. The Third Mate had been hospitalised some seven months previously in South America, which had given him his opportunity. He pointed out graphically how his presence on the ship had saved the Company money because they did not have to fly out a replacement officer. I say 'graphically' guardedly. This guy was really worked up, and even Scruff was subdued as we listened to him recounting his experiences. Clearly, being away from home for such a lengthy period had affected his moral sense and completely eroded his social skills. He was quite unable to have a normal conversation without swearing. He even interjected an oath by splitting words into two, a past master if ever I heard one. I wondered how he could possibly manage to conduct himself when finally he took leave, and grinned wryly imagining him over dinner with his parents, requesting his mother to 'pass the ------- salt'. My mind baulked at the task of visualising her reaction whilst, forecasting his likely performance at the vicarage tea party, had me in upheavals of silent mirth. The stories he related, in such a matter-of-fact way, possessed a uniquely spicy brand decidedly all their own. Overall, he came over to us as quite an engaging character, uplifting in a way, causing us both to laugh in astounded amusement as we trundled our way back on board. We both felt however that, in the light of his experiences, he was not a particularly happy mariner.

We were had a surprise on approaching our ship and seeing a number of suitcases, both by the bottom of the gangway, and being carried up in the arms of the Goanese stewards. Someone was clearly joining the ship and we were totally mystified to know who – Taiwan not being one of the usual places for officer replacements, especially sandwiched between the far easier accessed Hong Kong and Japan. I asked the *Secunny* what was going on and he told me that a passenger had joined us. It was true that *Earl of Edinburgh*, in common with many of the Company's ships, had accommodation for a limited number of passengers, but rarely carried any.

Entering the accommodation, we saw a tall, angular looking woman, probably in her mid-thirties, standing talking to Les, our Purser. Mat told us she was a nursing sister who had just completed a three-year contract and was taking local leave by visiting Japan and the Philippines, before flying home to London, upon our return to Hong Kong. She had been the only woman amongst hundreds of men working on a ship demolition site – for which this port was internationally famous.

To say she took the vessel by storm was truly an understatement and, in my comparative innocence and inexperience, she appeared quite frightening. Her lifestyle having made her totally uninhibited – almost a female equivalent of the Bank Line Fourth Officer. As we were soon to find out, she possessed a penetratingly deadly sense of humour leading the Mate to describe her, in resigned tones, as 'battle hardened and weary'. In vocabulary and flair for words, even our most hardened engineering officer blushed to the roots of his hair. She sat at the centre table in the saloon with the senior officers so we juniors saw her only in the smoke Room. Apparently, as the Old Man came towards his seat, she commented on his 'lovely knobbly knees' – a comment which did not exactly endear her to him. He was in a bit of a quandary concerning what to do, as the Company had been only too happy to agree the passage arrangements, and the table seating could not be changed. Basically, he had to put up with things – an attitude that caused considerable guarded merriment amongst his officers.

My introduction to her over coffee that evening was disconcerting, to say the least. She came over and introduced herself holding in her hand an oval shaped purse, with a slit down the middle, which she opened and closed as she was talking. I found this disturbing, to put it mildly, and had difficulty in concentrating on what she was saying. Out of the corner of my eye, I could see Scruff, Sparks and the junior engineers laughing gleefully at my obvious discomfort. She was talking with just the merest wisp of a smile on her face, so was clearly aware of the effect she was having not only on me, but also on the others. I managed to draw my eyes away from the offending purse and stammered some kind of response. She asked me in quite matter of fact tones, 'if I were still at the pulling stage?' but I was saved answering by Mat, who quickly (and to me thankfully) exercised his public school skills by offering her another cup of coffee from the tray at a nearby table. I escaped quickly before she could draw second breath. Sharing our leisure time was plainly going to be something of an eye opener – even to our travel hardened officers.

One of the juniors, 'slightly in his cups', became a little argumentative over an issue raised naturally in conversation. He was not offensive in any way, just a little loud, but 'our Booboo' – a corruption of her name Barbara – simply looked him in the eye and asked him, "Why don't you shut your ------- trap, you drunken ------ ". The shock alone had the desired effect, leaving him open mouthed, which promptly attracted additional derogatory comments. I heard the Mate telling the Second Engineer that he thought 'she lacked certain social skills' – a masterly understatement. Following our meeting with the Bank Line mate, I wondered if this behaviour passed as an acceptable norm in polite Taiwanese social circles.

She was excellent in the sick bay needless to say, and when one of the 'arg whallahs' (as our Deck *Serang* laughingly and derogatorily referred to engine room ratings) sustained a deep cut on his hand, Booboo offered to deal with it. She was 'three-parts cut', as Mr. Bryant assessed her condition, but cleaned and stitched the wound competently, balanced between table and medicine locker, support she considered necessary against the motion of the vessel. That the sea was like a millpond at the time, with low swell, was sufficient evidence for the Second Mate to rest his case. Such was her prowess, however, that when he took his 'in port sick parade' to the local MO (along of course with the still suffering Scruff), the doctor complimented him on what he thought had been his work. Her skill was obviously far superior to the rough and ready norm witnessed by the doctor from far too many navigating officers co-opted (often unwillingly) into his profession.

Whilst at anchor in Osaka Roads, our first Japanese discharge port awaiting berthing instructions, I did my first solo anchor watch. It went without incident and I busied myself checking our anchor bearings against the Decca Navigator and radar and, occasionally for something to do, taking visuals bearings. I watched the Signal station for any messages directed to our ship concerning coming alongside, but was off watch when these finally arrived. We were at the general cargo jetty for two weeks off-loading. Scruff was 'discharged by the doctor' – to coin his own delightful euphemism and was, once again, warned by Mr. Drury concerning his choice of friends.

Our Asian Carpenter met his own Waterloo when he was arrested by the Japanese police for 'unsocial conduct'. Overcome by passion in the early hours of our first morning in port, he conducted his amorous adventures in a telephone booth of all places. The Mate was summoned to the Agents and had to attend a summary hearing in the local Magistrates' Court where Chips was fined the equivalent of two weeks' pay. It was most unusual for Asian crew to become involved in any misdemeanours of any note so Chips prestige was raised to elevated heights in the eyes of the officers – apart, that is, from the Old Man. Mr. Drury privately considered the incident hilarious and he saw Chips in a new light far removed from the petty officer who looked after our anchor windlass during berthing operations. He handled his varied deck duties with much competence, including the daily soundings of all tanks to check for any unsuspected ingress of water into empty tanks and to see that levels in others were as they should be. Chips did also a multitude of mending jobs around the accommodation and on deck.

Nagoya was notable for a serious accident, which added considerably to my experience. I wondered if there would ever be an end to the series of incidents and mishaps which charted the progress of my seafaring to date. We came alongside the jetty at two o'clock in the morning in pouring rain. Mat was in-charge on the fo'c'sle for stand-by, thus extending his professional experience, and was supplied with Scruff to answer the telephone, relaying orders from the bridge. On this occasion, something was seriously wrong with the phone line causing considerable communication problems. We had a tug made fast to the starboard bow and the anchor walked out ready for dropping, when Mat and Scruff between them misunderstood an order from the pilot. I was doing the Movement Book and telegraphs in the wheelhouse, and the Chief Officer was on the telephones, gaining bridge experience in preparation for eventual command of his own. He reported to the Captain and Pilot that there was a lot of telephonic interference and voice distortion, so the Pilot (perhaps unwisely) shouted an order which Scruff and Mat interpreted to let go the anchor. The Third accordingly motioned to Chippy who, eager to make amends for his indiscretion in Osaka, promptly took off the brake allowing the seven-ton anchor together with its mass of heavy cable, to drop from a height of about twenty-five feet. Unfortunately, the tug was so close to the flare of the bow that the hook promptly fell onto its stern. There was enormous crash, clearly audible to us in the wheelhouse, and the tug sank to the bottom of the harbour, parting the towing wire in the process. With the subsequent loss of restraint, the ship smashed into the jetty bows on, causing an indentation to the quay and some damage to the stem. The Mate dived out of the wheelhouse and rushed to the fo'c'sle, but there was little constructive action left open for him to take. Mat and Scruff were severely shaken by the event, especially when it transpired that two of the tug's crew had drowned. The Harbour Master's launch was soon on the scene, rescuing survivors, and another tug was called to steady the ship as we careered around the berth. It took quite a while to bring us under control and alongside. Mr. Drury remained for'rard, whilst Mat and Scruff were stood down. They were both far too upset to play any further part in the operation. I did telephones, additional to my usual duties, which kept me busy until we were eventually in position and made fast.

To say things were pandemonium was putting it pretty mildly. Harbour authorities, police, Company Agents, an Assistant Marine Superintendent flying out from London, insurance representatives, all besieged the ship as we lay on the berth with our battered bow. The Captain, Mate and senior engineering officers were kept very busy and, in the midst of all of this, I was summoned to the Old Man's cabin with Scruff and told to prepare for transfer to the *Earl of Salisbury*, which was due shortly, to load for Australian and New Zealand ports, thence bound for the United States and Canada. We both received the news with mixed feelings. Too much time in port failed to be reckoned, by the Board of Trade Marine assessors, as qualifying sea-time for our Second Mates' examination, so clearly the Company had a duty to ensure time on board was spent sensibly. Scruff secretly welcomed the chance to leave this particular ship, whilst I was happy and enjoyed being on the *Edinburgh*. It was different to the *Bath*, but none the less useful as an experience. Yet, simultaneously, I welcomed the idea of visiting the ports for which the *Salisbury* was bound. Still, regardless of our thoughts and feelings on the subject, we had no option but to conform to requirements and prepared to gather together our gear. It was not known how long it would be before our ship could make repairs.

As it happened, the problem was solved quite unexpectedly. The heavy industry dry dock locally had been expecting a tanker for her annual survey but, in the way of tanker trading patterns, she had been delayed with a gas-freeing problem, so we were offered her place in the queue. Luckily, owing to the slow speed at which we had hit the jetty, our stem damage was not too complex and would be only a three or four day job to sort out. Accordingly, we cadets were able to remain on board, giving me at least an opportunity to experience a dry-docking, with the extra material this provided for my Journal. Officers and crew lived on board for the brief period, but Booboo was taken to a hotel ashore by the agent. The only problem for us was having the heads locked, which entailed a considerable trip ashore whenever nature called.

Nearly three weeks after our infamous arrival in Nagoya we sailed for our next Japanese port complete with newly painted and renovated bow. Mat remained on board, the Pilot's part in the debacle and the faulty telephone line having saved him almost certain dismissal – if not prosecution in Japan – much to his relief. He was given a reprimand for failing to look over the bows to see if it were clear, prior to dropping an anchor, and was subdued for quite a while afterwards. The deaths of the Japanese tug-boat crew clearly preyed on his mind. We all had to sign depositions concerning our versions of what had occurred and these were left with the British consul; there was however a possibility that we might be called to return to Nagoya and to give evidence in court.

Yokohama was an extremely busy port in the western part of Tokyo Bay, some eighteen land miles in distance. The Missions to Seamen provided a minibus, which one of the chaplains drove, for a sight-seeing tour that included lunch – at a very reasonable cost. The Chief and Third Officers went on this, along with some off-duty engineers, and we cadets were invited at no charge. I found Tokyo to be a thriving city – with countless hundreds of people milling around – apparently quite pointlessly.

Too tactful to say so, I suspected the cost for this was covered by the Mate's perks on the Japanese coast. We knew he had gone into a huddle with the Agents, both in Osaka and here, but regarding the exact nature of this transaction, I neither knew nor cared. I received also an unexpected monetary bonus from the purser for doing some of his port forms, prior to arrival in Japan. Using cadets for such duties seemed a policy of Ellertons (although not peculiar to every ship) and, strangely enough, came our way directly from the Captain, not the Mate. My typing had become fairly proficient, if only two-finger style, and it was no real hardship for me to help out. I worked also in the Old Man's office on occasions doing his voyage reports, and sundry non-confidential paperwork, usually for onward transmission to the Company's Superintendent, in the Kremlin. His report on our Nagoya incident made interesting reading which I was sufficiently tactful (and sensible) to keep to myself.

A national holiday in Tokyo (courtesy NBC Inc., Japan).

Leaving Yokohama, we proceeded to Otaru, on the northern island of Hokkaido, and commenced loading for the UK and the Continent. We were now officially homeward-bound and the references on all ship's papers became 'Voyage 19-Home'. Otaru saw another moment of glory for our Carpenter who was brought back to the duty mate on board, having been arrested by the Japanese police for urinating over the municipal flowerbeds, whilst under the influence of alcohol. The poor long-suffering Mate found himself attending yet another Magistrates' hearing and bailing him out once again. Whilst this caused great amusement to us officers, it led to a veritable eruption from the Captain, resulting in the stoppage of all leave for Chips. He was to prove one of the most colourful of all the Lascar seamen I was ever to meet.

Our arrival in Kobe corresponded with my eighteenth birthday and, as a treat, I was taken ashore by the off-duty officers for a celebration. Accompanied by Booboo, we adjourned to an illustrious dimly lit joint called the *Cherry Club,* a name which – with characteristic painful bluntness – she associated as appropriate to my good self. I was far too befuddled by drink to worry overmuch. The club was as sleazy looking a place as I had ever imagined, let alone visited, and I was immediately intrigued by the beer-mats on our tables. They consisted of match-stick figures in poses that, on first appearances, seemed to be fighting. It was only, following a closer look, that I realised the stances were in fact far more amorous. As ever, in such bars around the world, immediately on entering we were met by an appropriate number of girls who made us welcome – in the manner to which my colleagues were clearly expecting. I wondered if the girls arrived at the correct number by accident, and speculated what would happen if they ever fell short of numbers and whether or not they had any kind of reciprocal arrangement with an adjacent bar.

A unique line in beermats from the Cherry Club in Kobe (Author's collection).

My reflections were interrupted by the arrival of a tray of drinks. We had enjoyed a tot or two prior to coming ashore so were already very much in party mood. I sat with Booboo. She had proved universally quite popular, if to be given a guarded reception at times. The problem was you never knew what she was going to come out with next, in fact, the more outlandish the utterance, the more demure she looked. As it was my birthday, I was treated with endless rounds of drinks – mostly indefinable looking liqueurs in a range of different coloured and shaped glasses – each possessing its own unique kick. My colleagues (inevitably aided and abetted by Booboo) urged me to celebrate in style and 'pop up to the next floor rooms'. Scruff, all too well aware of the Mate's beady eyes on him was a model of decorum, at least for the initial part of the evening. I found 'my girl friend' looking at me with a delightfully admiring expression, having already told me a dozen times how much she loved me. By two o'clock in the morning, I was decidedly 'woozy' and suddenly found myself looking at her in a strangely new light. On legs that were far from steady, she dragged me to the forbidden quarters but, even before we reached the landing, knew I was about to become extremely ill. Wrenching away from the wench, I just made it to the toilets, where so many kindnesses bestowed upon me by generous ship-mates became totally wasted. I was really ill, being left with a throbbing headache, dry mouth and sore stomach. Coming back to the table, I was in time to witness Booboo admiring the ornamental ash-trays and demurely asking the waiter if she could be allowed one as a souvenir. He agreed and, as she opened her cavernous handbag to put it away, I caught a glimpse of another two which she had already knocked-off. She gave me what I interpreted as a sympathetic look, but which could equally have been a warning to keep quiet about the illicit ash-trays. Anyway, I sat down again, before I fell down, and waited for the proceedings to end so that I could return to the ship and my bunk. Scruff, meanwhile had vanished, only to re-appear suddenly wearing a look of supreme satiation. As the Mate was by then well in his cups, it seemed my erstwhile cabin mate had got away with what seemed like yet another indiscretion.

It was nearer 0600 before we made our way back on board. I felt like death warmed-up, but still had to turn-to with an equally shattered Second Mate for cargo watch. I am still not completely certain just how efficient we were between us, but fortunately the cargo we were loading was open-toed flip-flop slippers, of a type just becoming universally popular, that were bound for the Continent. We loaded two thousand cases of the things in No. 5 tween deck, so the supervision was not over demanding. Following just three hours sleep, when I felt like having another twelve, stand-by was called along with my summons to the wheelhouse.

There I was greeted with another of life's surprises. I saw Scruff neatly drawing vertical lines in the Movement Book and expected him to pass this over to me. Instead, the Mate, just before he went for'ard, told me to take the wheel under the supervision of the duty *Secunny*, and steer the ship out of port. Over the trip in the evenings, whilst sharing the watch with Mat, I had been allowed to knock-out the automatic pilot – or, Mad Mike, as it was universally called – and steer the ship manually, especially in crowded waters and rounding headlands. With treble the necessary hours to qualify for a steering certificate already clocked-up, the Chief Officer clearly thought it time for me to put my newly found skills to more positive use than 'merely careering around the bloody ocean'. Mat did flags, telegraphs, phones and book, whilst Scruff went to the fo'c'sle head with Mr. Drury where, under supervision, he took charge of moorings and tug. With a spinning head, I managed to steer effectively and respond to uttered commands without too much intervention from the *Secunny*.

Our passage back to Hong Kong was enlivened by two colourful events in the engineering department – one medical and the other social. One of the juniors had for the entire outward voyage bored us mindless with his constant harping on the virtues of Japanese Geisha girls. Apparently, in Kobe, he had finally spent a couple of nights ashore with one of these desirable creatures and, three days out, the inevitable happened. Very shame-faced, he reported to the Second Mate with parts of his anatomy heavily swollen and darkly-coloured, and in considerable agony. He was so bad that the Captain took him off-watch and seriously considered calling in at Okinawa to make use of the American medical authorities based there. Booboo was consulted and offered to nurse him in the officers' sick bay, having given her opinion that the junior would last until HK. The Old Man clearly thought that subjecting him to her ministrations would prove sufficient temporary punishment and agreed with this advice. The Chief Engineer however was not so charitable and the blistering he gave the unfortunate man could be heard all over the ship – to the entertainment of us all.

The social incident came to our wider attention by accident. The Fourth Engineer was sunbathing in his trunks on the boat-deck when one of his colleagues – obviously in the know – went over towards him casually and, suddenly before any of us realised what was happening (including the poor Fourth), stretched out his hands and pulled down the Fourth's trunks whilst he was leaning over the rail looking at the *Chusan* – a passing P&O liner. To our amazement, two very large coloured eyes, neatly tattooed one on each buttock, winked back at us. To say we laughed is putting it mildly – we hooted. We rolled all over the boat-deck in merriment; our caustic comments ranging far and wide. It transpired that whilst ashore 'in his cups', he decided to liven up his life by having a modest little butterfly engraved on his middle back. Succumbing to the drowsy effects of the tattooist's couch, he fell asleep to find, on awakening, that he was the proud possessor of a full-blown decoration which admirably illustrated the advanced skills of this craftsman – together with a monstrous sized bill.

Booboo left us in Hong Kong to await her flight back to the UK, the junior left us temporarily to go to hospital, and the Purser left us en route to Booboo's hotel with the Agent to collect a sundry array of coat-hangers, ashtrays and half his saloon cutlery, all of which she had 'borrowed' as souvenirs of her exciting trip. We took in her place a retired British army Brigadier who, in the words of the Second Engineer (obviously an expert in immediate psychological assessments) 'was as queer as a coot'.

I was allowed to take a day off to go to Macau by ferry, a visit much anticipated after reading, in the ship's library, a brand new book by Simon Kent, entitled *Ferry to Hong Kong*. It was a fascinating trip and I returned tired but contented. Scruff had a slight debacle when fixing a 'toilet chute' over one of the outlets in the ship's side, necessary to prevent waste dropping onto the sampans, lighters and junks working cargo below. His lashing to the rail was not perhaps as professional as it might have been, with the result that the heavy metal chute fell onto the sampan below, frightening the life out of the crew as it narrowly missed them, and almost sinking the boat. It took considerable persuasion, a bottle of whisky and two hundred cigarettes from the ship's bond to pacify them and restore working relationships – a price that he paid willingly, following his contribution to the debacle in Nagoya, from which he had still not fully recovered. It seemed the "nether regions" were fated to be particularly accident-prone for Austen.

We were soon loaded and I took the helm for our departure, without a duty *Secunny* standing-by. By tacit agreement the Second Mate, on duty in the wheelhouse whilst Mat took charge on the after deck, was keeping a discreet 'weather eye' on my progress. Fortunately, his intervention was not required and my confidence increased considerably as a result. I also rigged for the first time on my own; the ship's Chernikeeff log which, towed astern, registered the ship's speed through the water. In practical terms, I could by now also supervise small groups of the crew in rigging both gangway and awnings, and take charge of fire-fighting parties during fire and boat drills. Mr. Drury's supervised planning was taking shape with the result that my confidence increased daily.

We called into Manila for our final cargo topup which was notable as being probably the only Missions to Seaman club in the world where the girl serving coffee, beer and sundries behind the bar also offered her favours as a marketable commodity. I could not believe initially what it was she was suggesting but with raucous giggles, Scruff explained, and so made her intentions more apparent. I think he regarded me as being extremely naïve at times, whilst I wondered rather sardonically, whether or not she might have suggested we used the Mission Chapel had I expressed positive interest. I was however reluctant to put this to the test.

The Brigadier was a pain during the homeward trip – more like a 'bitch on heat' – as the Mate described his antics. We wondered how he had possibly reached such senior rank without getting himself court-martialled on the way. He took a fancy to Scruff, myself, the most junior of engineers and even made sweeping passes at Mat. He also made improper suggestions, as the newspapers refer to such antics, to his cabin steward. The poor Goanese had the life frightened out of him and would not go into the cabin unless the light was on and the door open. We could hardly ignore 'Freda' (as he was nicknamed) as circumstances necessitated us all using a common smoke room for relaxation, but I made certain I was never alone there in his company. I was probably quite safe, but was reluctant to put too much to the test. The dangers of experiencing foreign parts suddenly acquired a new meaning.

Soon after we cleared Pulo Weh, at the northern tip of Sumatra, and settled on course for the 2,500 or so mile trip to Aden, we received orders to call in at Columbo and load a consignment of tea in the after-part of some tween-deck hatches, which had been left empty upon departure from Hong Kong. We had to wait for completion of the cargo, due to a delay never satisfactorily explained by the Agent, so took the opportunity of going out to the Mount Lavinia hotel for a relaxing afternoon swim. Only the duty mate was left on board whilst the rest of us bundled into a series of taxis for the journey. The junior Third and Fourth Engineers were late leaving the ship so followed later but, on the way, their taxi driver suddenly stopped and demanded more money. It was not a wise thing to do, for the two officers threw him out of his own taxi and drove the thing to the outskirts of the hotel, where they promptly abandoned it. They never said anything to us about the incident until we had returned to the ship, but I suspect the knowledge that a posse of Singhalese police might be popping-in at any moment may have detracted a little from their enjoyment. I was not entirely sure of this, as they were a pretty hard-bitten pair. For the remainder of us, the time was an unexpected idyllic period – the sand was white with palm trees sweeping gently to the bay – "It's just like the travel brochures, sir", I suggested unwisely to the Mate, receiving in return a quite unprintable answer.

My correspondence course was progressing very satisfactorily and I was beginning to understand more of the navigational theory and mathematics behind celestial observations. As a result, soon after we cleared Columbo on passage across the Indian Ocean to Aden for bunkers, Mr. Drury allowed me to try my hand at sextant observations by taking morning sights of the sun, working these out by the Marcq Saint Hilaire method, and following this with a latitude by meridian altitude observation at noon local time. My methods were quite correct, but I received the mother and father of a rocket from Mr. Bryant, supervising my efforts, for column jumping. This was all the more of an embarrassment because the Captain entered the wheelhouse whilst I was on the receiving end, and although an interested listener, refrained from adding his own comments. I never made that mistake again, but adopted the far more orderly approach necessary for examination requirements. So far as accuracy was concerned, my intercept on the morning sight was rather large, and eventual position a little too far to the south-east. Other than the mechanical error however the effort was not deemed a disaster and I was allowed to put my first sight under the heading of progress. From then on, a point was made of going to the bridge in the evening, where I was introduced to the mysteries of star identification, preparation for taking azimuths at sunset to check the magnetic compass error, and eventually the working of sights. It was amazing to discover that, of the countless billions of stars in the firmament, only fifty-seven (plus of course four planets) were sufficiently recognisable and bright enough for navigational use. That part of me the Mate classified as romantic was certainly appeased by the magnificent names given to some of them – *Mirfak, Almilan, Miaplacidus, Dubhe, Zubenelgenubi* and the amusing *Nunki* – to name just a few. The Mate explained the Arabic origins of many – leaving me with an unspoken reflection that there might also be a romantic side to his make-up.

Using a sextant correctly was important to the accuracy of sight reduction of the sun and stars, and occasionally the moon (Crown copyright/MOD).

A deck cadet reduces the sight to obtain a fix from the sun (courtesy BP plc).

Plotting star sights with the Chief Officer (courtesy BP plc).

Just before we reached Socotra, I saw what I thought a phenomenal sight, which even the Mate agreed, was unusual. There was a distinct line across the ocean where the wind suddenly ceased – with one side having the water flat mirror calm, whilst the other showed only a very slightly ruffling.

It was about that stage of the trip when Scruff and I decided on a little premature preparation for our own smuggling operation. We had both built-up quite a stock of varied bottles of spirits about which we had to keep quiet, because cadets were most definitely only allowed a limited quantity of beer per week. Late one night, we entered No. 5 hold by the inspection hatch and, each armed with powerful ship's torches, broached the stack of flip-flops bound for Hamburg. We attacked the thirtieth row from the after-part of the stack, fourth column in, and third carton down. Taking out the flip-flops for disposing over the side, we inserted our contraband liquor, along with four hundred cigarettes each, following which we replaced the stack. We thought it pretty unlikely that the Customs rummagers in London, or wherever we docked prior to signing-off, would have the time to wade through this lot, so felt confident of it being available whenever we wanted to smuggle it ashore.

I took the helm entering and leaving Aden and for part of the passage through the Suez Canal, receiving the accolade of a compliment from Captain Mitchell. Just after we left the Suez, my end of year Merchant Navy Training Board annual examination became due. For this, I was installed in the Chief Officer's study and for the three hour duration was supervised by an off-duty mate. I managed to keep my cool responding to the questions, even when I found myself up against the time limit for the final answer. Scruff told me he had been assisted discreetly by the Third Mate when he confused a trigonometrical ratio, but my supervision was under Mr. Drury – so no assistance came my way (reminding me of the chart work exercise aboard the *Stenwood Navigator*).

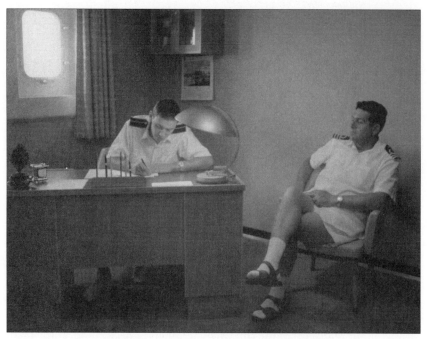

The Chief Officer invigilates an examination (courtesy BP plc).

The entire crossing of the Bay and the Channel from clearing Gibraltar to off the pilot at Dungeness was like a millpond. Needless to say I experienced the Channels once again and, with a sigh of relief, found myself phoning home once we were alongside Millwall Dock in London – our first port of discharge. Another end of voyage interview ensued with the Master and Mate, as we proceeded up the Kent coast, upon which would be based my report to the Company. It was a constructive and cordial occasion, from which I learnt my orders were to remain on board and do the coastal trip. This was visiting Middlesbrough, Hull, Antwerp, Rotterdam and Hamburg for completion of discharge, then returning to the Royal Docks in London, where the ship would commence loading for her next deep-sea voyage. I was to leave her there and await further instructions. It was hinted that my preliminary Royal Naval Reserve training of ten days or so could be done, prior to doing another deep-sea voyage. Austen was to proceed on leave and re-join upon our return to the

UK in some six weeks time. I had been away again for over a year and had clocked-up (including my three months at Keddleston) almost two and a half years' sea-time towards Second Mate.

Discharging general cargo in London's Royal Victoria Docks
(courtesy Museum in the Docklands, PLA Collection).

The quiet of the evening in Millwall docks was in complete contrast to the frenetic pace of activity during the day, when hundreds of dockers worked numerous ships at every berth, busily engaged working cargo. I reflected that loading and discharging ships was a highly labour intensive business, involving hundreds of dock workers on quays, in barges, down holds and on deck – often with a number of complete gangs serving three or four hatches concurrently. The bash and crash of railway engines and wagons, road traffic and endless creaks from cargo gear and cranes were silenced. It was too late by the time we were stood-down that first evening to go ashore and, anyway, Scruff and I had far more important business of our own to attend to. After the officers had sorted themselves out, and either gone ashore or were keeping duty watch unobtrusively in the smoke room, we went into No. 5 tween deck to recover our contraband. Scruff wanted to take his on leave, whilst I was going to take mine home with some deep-sea gear, unwanted round the coast, whilst taking an overnight local visit next day allowed me by the Mate. To our horror, we saw our flip-flop stow had become dislodged from the forward end, and was just a maze, with hundreds of haphazard cartons littering the deck. We ran panic-stricken to the after-part, counting frantically once we arrived. Luckily, the stack had fallen from row forty, so our carton was quite safe. Working quickly, we recovered it and shared out the spoils in our cabin. I stashed mine among my tropical clothing and, ordering a taxi next morning, whilst keeping fingers well crossed, safely passed the police constable on duty at the gate. All went according to plan and I arrived home well-stocked for my later leave.

Another cadet joined the ship, of similar seniority to me, who had completed the one-year residential course at Southampton University's School of Navigation at Warsash, following three years at a minor public school somewhere in Shropshire. James Eastlake's father was not only a Captain with Ellertons, but was Master of this particular coastal and continental voyage. Clearly, organising mutual leaves as a family unit was difficult, so the Company – in a typical gesture – arranged for his mother also to sail for the trip. We junior officers both found it rather droll when James used to announce, in the smoke room after supper, "that he thought he might as well pop-up and have a drink with the Old Man". We both agreed that this situation would not have been permitted on deep-sea voyages, the ramifications being potentially too complicated. The Mate had no say in the matter, but rightly of course, did not allow the situation to affect his organisation of our duties.

Our work proved far more casual than that experienced over deep-sea voyages. For a start, we did very little deck work on passage due to the short interval between ports. Most of our time at sea was spent on watch – James with the Mate, whilst I was turned-to with the Second Officer. Sea passages to Middlesbrough and Hull became periods of intensive activity doing coastal navigation and radar work under his supervision. He was not really 'cadet friendly' and, as I thought ahead to when he became promoted to Chief Officer, guessed cadets deep-sea with him might have a pretty thin time. I was tolerated because the Mate dictated work loads, but much of his attitude was curt and detached. He warmed as the various sea passages progressed, when he saw my interest and noted my reasonable proficiency. Needless to say, I gained a great deal in experience, learning and confidence, so was not as nervously perturbed by his manner as I thought might be the case. It was fascinating to run course lines, checking these against the Decca Mark12 Navigator and Kelvin-Hughes radar. The highlight was when I detected and identified a Westminster Dredging Company's vessel on collision course, off our starboard bow, and was allowed to determine the action we should take and then give appropriate commands to the *Secunny* to avoid contact, afterwards putting the ship back to her course-line. It was the first time I had actually done collision avoidance as an exercise from start to finish.

Other highlights developing both my training and experience were being left alone in the wheelhouse keeping a number of anchor watches, going both fore and aft on stand-by doing telephone duties, taking the wheel (again) for a number of port arrivals and departures and handling the windlass to let-go the anchor. My Journal was filling rapidly with a mass of significant data – a far cry from the elementary drawings of hatch construction and fo'c'sle arrangements from just a couple of years previously. Usually, whilst in port, we turned-to with the *Serang* and worked manually alongside the ratings opening hatches and rigging derricks for use, or swinging them out of the way, allowing shore cranes to work cargo. We went ashore in both UK ports, but nothing of any particular note occurred – just pleasant evenings spent in quayside public houses.

Visiting the continental ports of Hamburg, Rotterdam and Antwerp, we were allowed ashore frequently, but again experienced no adventures of any particular note. In both Rotterdam and Hamburg we were taken ashore, one evening in each, by the Captain and his wife after we had cleared with the Mate that we were not required on board for duties. They were thoroughly relaxed occasions, once I had overcome the diffidence of sharing my social life with the ship's Master and his family. I found it quite interesting to compare differences between the various ships' Captains encountered. On other evenings, our time-off was shared with the officers who remained on board, invariably ending-up enjoying a 'Sod's Opera', or going ashore for a casual walk around and a drink. It was in Antwerp that James and I found a bar that provided us with a thoroughly unexpected evening's entertainment. After buying our beer, and thinking of moving to another more lively place, one of the locals suddenly began playing an accordion, whilst everyone else started dancing to a variety of what sounded like marching songs – whatever, we also were encouraged to participate, and finally left the bar at about three o'clock in the morning, arriving back on board just in time to prepare for 0600 departure.

For our arrival at Tilbury, I was on the wheel for the entire time from when we took the Gravesend pilot, through the locks to 'in position alongside', until made fast and stood down. We berthed at three o'clock in the morning, so I turned in until later that day. My instructions were to proceed on leave until summoned for my end-of-voyage interview at the Kremlin. James was remaining on board and doing the following deep-sea trip with Austen, so I was able to reassure him by relating my experiences with his senior cadet out in the Far East.

My leave was notable for its own particular crop of interests. My parents threw a small family party celebrating their silver wedding and my success to date as a mariner. Many of the family were present, including paternal grandparents (both Mum's had died some years previously), a few assorted aunts, uncles, cousins and one of Mum's maiden aunts. It became quite a social gathering numbering about fifteen people, whom we just managed to fit into our lounge, with an overflow into kitchen and front room. I was late arriving, having come directly from Millwall Docks where the *Edinburgh* was still discharging. I arrived in uniform – to the delight of my parents and Sue. Inevitably, the wine flowed, and a grand time was being enjoyed by all. Much of the animated conversation centred upon my seagoing career and I revelled in relating a number of considerably edited experiences. Needless to say, Uncle 'Wag' needed little encouragement to contribute nautical anecdotes from his own wartime sea-going, plus a few from his present job at Gravesend. Sue listened with cousinly interest and the increasing closeness of our developing friendship.

The general conversation drifted towards the Clean Air Act which was currently being discussed in Parliament. It was attracting widening public interest due to associations being investigated between smoke pollution from numerous sources and the increasing density of London smogs. Gravesend Reach, with its high density of shipping, was a natural target and, recently, a Clan Line ship had been the subject of a test smoke emission prosecution.

Maiden Aunt Jenny had to ask me (as an acknowledged expert on all matters maritime) how ships managed to create such dense emissions. As a deck cadet I did not have a clue but, with the wildness of youth, was in no way going to admit this. Carried away by my ensuing explanation, I suddenly became aware of an unnatural silence, broken only by an agitated rattling of bone china cups in saucers. Mystified, I suddenly noticed two things; Uncle 'Wag' had left the gathering, and was creased with silent laughter in the small hall connecting lounge with front parlour, whilst a look of unadulterated horror was etched onto my mother's face, matched by one of interested surprise on that of my father's. I went back over my previously uttered comments and went quite cold, realising I could not possibly have said something like, "Well, the engineers open up the ------- boilers below" and so on. Attempting to rally my thoughts, I realised that I most certainly had, so could only conclude lamely with a remark to the effect, "that is how it happens". The stillness could be cut with a knife, broken only by dear Uncle 'Wag' returning with a plate of peanuts and offering these around the shocked circle with tongue-in-cheek aplomb, asking everyone if they would like a nut.

Gradually, conversation returned to normal, but I fear mum had encountered her own version of a Joycean epiphany with the realisation that Jonathan was no longer her innocent little boy. Sue could not stop laughing as I escorted her home later that evening: she clearly considered the incident hilarious. My father and I were to experience our own epiphanies a couple of evenings later, as I was leaving home to visit Sue. Dad was closing the garage doors and as I went past him, quite unthinkingly, commented to the effect that the weather was "------- cold this evening, Dad". He responded in similarly exotic agreement, but it was only halfway down the drive I realised what we had both said. Glancing back, Dad was standing with his hand frozen to the door, looking in my direction. We exchanged speculative glances, but no future mention was made by either of us to the incident. Upon relating this little gem to Sue, she thought with a characteristic grin, that going away to sea had done something for me. I was left pondering how the Bank Line officer, met in Kaohsiung, was faring in comparison.

Meeting casually an old school friend, now working ashore in the London Corn Exchange, we agreed that a drink in the local pub one evening just prior to the end of my leave might be a good idea. He was with a couple of other school colleagues, and although we commenced on a cordial note, once we had covered mutual interest exchanges, it soon became apparent we had little further in common. Seafaring was plainly a different world to their lifestyle. They could not understand my way of life and clearly thought the incidents which were quite the norm to me were exaggerated to the point of incredulity. In turn, I found their careers mundanely unexciting and their concerns with everyday affairs frankly boring. It was not a successful occasion. I was particularly peeved, considering the time wasted that could otherwise have been spent with my Sue.

My leave was not totally negative. Apart from the smuggled booze, the gifts I brought home were extremely well received – particularly the ill-fated bone china tea-set purchased for Mum and the electric shaver for Dad – along with my anniversary present of an engraved silver-plated fruit bowl. Mum had asked for a photograph of me in uniform so, overcoming my aversion to photographers, this duly arrived. Sue was so impressed she also wanted one – necessitating a further order. I had bought her a musical manicure set, portraying a dancing ballerina, with which she appeared very pleased. We spent a great deal of my leave together; I suspect thoughts of the family were secretly consistent with ours – sharing a view that we were becoming fairly serious.

I was home for one day before being summoned to bring along to an interview my journals for inspection by the Chief Marine Superintendent himself. I had not met that officer since my selection board whilst at Keddleston, so was quietly apprehensive. As it happened, there was little to fear. He took me through my cadetship to date extremely thoroughly and I had to support many of my comments with close references to Journal entries. He expressed the Company's pleasure with my training and appeared happy with all voyage reports and commented particularly on the neatness of my Journal. I was much applauded for my success in the MNTB examination taken aboard the *Earl of Edinburgh* in which, he was delighted to inform me, I had fared very well. He also picked up Mr. Drury's comment (which frankly I thought my ex-Chief Officer had forgotten) concerning a 'taster voyage' on one of the Group's tankers, but said he preferred me to remain within my present Company, requesting a transfer once Second Mate's had been passed when tanker life could be tried as a junior officer. As forecast, I was now to do my RNR Britannia Royal Naval College, Dartmouth course and should go home to await joining instructions from the Admiralty.

Chapter 5

SURVIVAL

———

My orders for RNR training stated, in delightfully quaint language, that 'By Command of the Lords Commissioners' I was to travel by train to Portsmouth, using the enclosed travel warrant, where service transport would take me to report aboard HMS *Beautiful,* a Naval shore base, for 'basic training as a Midshipman, Royal Naval Reserve'. Glancing at the pompous conclusion to the letter, with its indecipherable signature assuring me, 'I remain, Sir, Your obedient Servant', I wondered what had happened to the forecast course at Dartmouth. Accepting the change in orders with a philosophical shrug of the shoulders, I recognised by now, as an established Navigating Officer Cadet, Merchant Navy, my role in life was to become accustomed 'to being frigged around', a term elegantly expressed by Scruff following one of his meetings with Mr. Drury.

Travelling in uniform, it was easy to meet up with other midshipmen at the barrier to Platform Two on Waterloo Station. With a little time to spare, due to a train cancellation, we went into the nearby News Theatre and hooted with laughter over the antics of Tom and Jerry, and others, during the best part of an hour-long picture show. Much refreshed and completely relaxed, we joined our train and exchanged news and views about our respective Companies. These ranged from P&O Lines, Orient, Clan Line, Furness Withy, City Line, Elder Dempster, Palm and a number of tanker outfits, predominant amongst which were BP, Shell and Texaco, all very reputable companies. I met also two other Ellerton Group cadets, both of whom were new to me.

Upon arrival at Portsmouth, there was no one to meet us on the concourse or outside due, we suspected, to our planned train being cancelled. Spending a few moments wondering what to do and then, deciding we ought to at least do something; I phoned the Naval base and was put through to the Guardroom HMS *Beautiful*. Abruptly, I was told that, as we had missed the transport, we should find our own way to the barracks; an order which created something of a hiatus amongst us. I put down the phone and duly reported this little gem to my fellow midshipmen. Our collective reaction was wild, abusive and unanimous, resulting in the station staff threatening to call the police unless we quietened down. Suitably subdued, I was elected to phone again and suggest that as we were Merchant Navy cadets, with limited financial resources, a fleet of taxis was quite out of the question. This comment was met with stony silence so, pausing to take a deeper breath, I enquired that if no service transport appeared available, was it the Royal Navy's recommendation that we catch the next London train, and thence go home. There was what is known in the trade as another pregnant pause, combined with a stillness that, even above the chatter of my colleagues, seemed almost tangible. The voice then suggested that we should await a service coach.

About twenty minutes later, a blue-painted bus with the words 'ROYAL NAVY' painted in white letters pulled up. From the front emerged a RN Chief Petty Officer, complete with glistening white belt and gaiters and a run of badges on his lapels. He was clearly not a very happy mariner and enquired who it was who had phoned. I was immediately (and joyfully) thrust forward by my erstwhile friends. He asked my name, giving me a very meaningful look as he did so. We were then directed to board the coach. It was a good fifteen-minute drive to the base, which turned out to be what the RN refers to as a stone frigate. Once inside the gates, we were checked in individually at the guard room and told to muster outside once this process was completed.

It was then that a whirlwind exploded upon us as the Chief, aided and abetted by two others of the same type, stormed out a string of commands which soon had us in three more or less straight lines. The party was obviously over even before it began, and set the pattern for ten days during which everything was done 'at the double and, preferably, sooner.' We were marched to a bleak barrack room which, we were told, was to be our accommodation and was laughingly known as the gunroom 'seeing as you gentlemen are Reservist Midshipmen – the lowest form of all known 'uman existence'. We were certainly made to feel very welcome. I had asked the marine super at Ellertons whether or not Dathan was to be a member of this course, but he confirmed Peter had already completed his training at Dartmouth during a previous leave. Neither of us had quite got around to despatching the promised letters. It appeared, not only in ecclesiastical circles was the road to hell paved with good intentions, the thought so succinctly expressed by a wayside pulpit in our local Church.

Our Divisional Officer's briefing reminded me very much of Captain Mobb's talk on our first night at Keddleston. In fact, my nautical college experiences were to prove invaluable during the next ten days. How I blessed our long suffering drill instructor there and the patience with which he had put us through our paces on the square. He was a paragon compared to the team of Chief Petty Officer instructors who were now our mentors (or tormentors – which I considered a more appropriate term). We were told that our course was the first for RNR Midshipmen to be run at HMS *Beautiful* and was very much experimental. We were still left unclear why this had been transferred from Dartmouth but, as the training continued, learnt that two of the Chiefs had been appointed from there for temporary duty, bringing with them their skills in Merchant Naval RNR deck cadet training. This proved little consolation. I, of course, was immediately labelled a 'sea lawyer', but felt that the RN had little love for our group anyway, so was not too perturbed.

We became integrated with other RNR cadets who had joined earlier and were told off into three squads of sixteen Midshipmen, referred to as Port Watch, Starboard Watch and Middle Watch. Port Watch's gunroom was an old Nissen hut, colder than that at Keddleston, and all three watches used part of a hut near the galley for our meals. Reveille was at 0600 with a first rigorous uniform inspection parade at 0630 – so we had to get a bit of a move on. Breakfast was half an hour later, following which we cleaned our quarters, were inspected again, and then drilled in a manner that was stupefying to our, by now softly conditioned, Merchant Naval temperaments. I was impressed at the speed with which our instructors learnt our names and also by the epithets they attached to them whilst we wheeled and performed gyrations to their bellowed commands. I felt the secret for survival was to become detached and treat the process as quite impersonal – a mode which fitted me so successfully that I was soon the target of more individual attention – being frequently urged, "Caridia, shake your bloody ideas up, you dozy cretinous little item", to the muffled sniggers of my fellow squad members. Strangely enough, being 'a bit dense at times', as Chief Mitchell described me, especially when it suited me, I gained considerable comfort from their support. After all, I was not the only one to fall foul (both literally and verbally) of the Chief's abuse. The result of course was a rapidly acquired determination to concentrate more closely, thus to cope with the rigours of this daily hour-long torment, which I recognised as being our instructor's intention.

The remainder of our training was very interesting, if not without its pitfalls. Lectures were given on naval writing, during which we learnt how to use impersonal military forms of address – making the 'Your obedient Servant' of the appointment letter take on a less hilarious meaning. Talks followed on naval practices (a delightful euphemism to my mind), rank structures and the range of ratings' trade badges, together with insights into naval communications, seamanship and navigation exercises. Much was necessarily elementary, but I could see the logic behind the classroom theory. The practical work was really good; swimming, boat-work in sailing and small power-driven craft and voyages in the Solent aboard motor launches, during which we ventured into the Channel for combined fleet manoeuvres. Port Watch gunroom rang at night with shouted commands such as 'Corpen Two' and 'Take Station in Line Ahead', as we 'sent up' the training as much for light relief as to retain our sanity. I was told, by our DO – acting as the officer-of-the-watch during our training cruise – to tell him immediately the set and drift of the current being experienced at that point in the Solent. By now, accustomed to experiencing 'bull-dust and gaiters', I realised he had no idea, but had set the task merely to flummox me. Going below, I made a great show of consulting tidal atlases, comparing tidal streams and squinting myopically at tide tables; made up a set and drift and duly reported this as 'gospel'. It was, as I suspected, immediately accepted, to the surprise of my fellow navigators, and I duly received a high grade for my proficiency.

It was on the fifth day that I was placed on a charge. I had a severe attack of diarrhoea from something obviously eaten the previous evening and, as a result, had to go on sick parade, along with the paraphernalia involved of grabbing a small pack and fitting everything into this in case of being detained. I had reported to the duty Chief before parade and was duly excused in order to 'report sick.' The doctor was late arriving and so I sat waiting, as patiently as possible – a term which appealed to my sense of humour – and finally left the sick bay with a bottle of 'jollop' and instructions to report back to my squad. Before doing so, I returned to our gunroom to replace my overnight bag, and was seen doing so by one of our Chiefs. He bawled the hell out of me; told me that I should have gone directly to class with my bag, and placed me on a charge. After lunch therefore I was duly marched before the DO and listened, with a little wry amusement, as my crime was read out: 'In that Midshipman Jonathan Caridia, Royal Naval Reserve, was absent from his place of duty without prior permission.' The inevitable rocket was duly fired and hit its target. My punishment was 'to be admonished' which merely meant that the charge had been added to my record. The CPO repeated this as 'demolished. About turn. Quick march'. I was hard put to keep a straight face (and so avoid further trouble), before being dismissed to rejoin my squad and take part in the afternoon's activities.

We were marched everywhere and each half-day a midshipman was delegated to be the class leader, otherwise the course would be of insufficient length for us all 'to have a bash'. His job was to conduct the squad between classes in safety, looking out for officers to whom the correct salute had to be accorded. Inevitably, I met my Waterloo, recalling the words of a certain Chief Officer concerning a lascar carpenter on a recent voyage. Following on from my sick bay charge earlier that same morning, I felt this was not my day.

Marching my squad to their class, a wrong turning was taken so we got lost. Passing the Commodore's quarters in a vain effort to find my bearings, I failed to catch sight of this personage and order the squad to "Eye's Right" giving him his due. The midshipmen called *sotto voce* warnings, but failed to make clear what precisely they were being *sotto voce* about. The first I knew something was amiss was hearing a stentorian voice shouting at my class to halt. The second thing I knew was that one of our training chiefs who, wondering where on earth his class had disappeared to, ventured out of his nearby lecture-room looking for us, only to walk directly into an erupting, purple-faced uniformed Commodore who promptly blasted him into oblivion for failing (unjustly, but what the Hell, 'that's Service life') to keep his squad under control. Needless to say, the benefits of his misfortune were duly passed on to me, with considerable interest, and I was saved only by Chiefy suddenly noticing, out the corner of his eye, that the remainder of my class were collapsed with silently hysterical laughter. We did not laugh for very long as we were marched onto the parade ground, after instruction that day, to be "smartened up". We were drilled solidly for two hours – collapsing afterwards to our bunks with very little pre-sleep chat. Our only consolation was that the Chief had also been deprived of his comforts for the same period.

The next day, the Base Commander joined our Divisional Officer to address the squad prior to classes. Obviously, the Commodore had lost little time in relating events, so we received a considerable shake-up from these august personages which lasted for all of ten minutes. By now, we were far from bothered by the excesses of the Royal Navy and merely listened in fascination as this gaitered officer, with half a peak of gold braid and a walking stick, ranted uncontrollably about our short-comings, followed by a further volatile dressing down from the Lieutenant Commander. We suspected that future courses would be in for a far more rigid reception than we had experienced, and subjected to a far tighter discipline overall. Our collective opinion deducted we had probably got away with things rather lightly. As the course leader for that fateful afternoon, I received my own singling-out and was placed on yet another charge – something about 'Idle in performance of duty' this time, but being a far more hardened personage than a certain naïve Keddleston cadet, took the full force remarkably philosophically. In the midst of this blasting, I reflected I could hardly have picked a more important person to upset than the Base Commodore.

On the water next day, two of the sailing boats had a collision – somebody's application of the collision regulations pertaining to vessels at sea was faulty – resulting in both boats capsizing, one being sunk, and two cadets narrowly escaping drowning. The incident occurred in Portsmouth Harbour, near to channels which disappeared into waterless creeks at low tide, whilst the mechanised safety boat was rescuing a cadet who had 'lost his wind' (another delightful Naval expression) a few cables to the south. They were eventually dredged out, but the result was an official inquiry, which lasted a couple of days, resulting in countless interviews, reams of paper work, interrupted classes and (inevitably) the administrating to our course of a further rocket from the long suffering Base Commander and our Divisional Officer.

We had to take turns in practical leadership tasks which gave our Chiefs more headaches and us compensatory laughter, as well as additional 'nausea', as the RN referred to what the Merchant Navy called 'aggro'. Our squad was split into smaller groups, based around our watch system, and we were given a number of varying sized planks of wood, lashings of rope and various assorted Bosun's gear, as we referred to the sundry items. One person was nominated to take charge of a task, brief the remainder of his team, and then 'get on with it'. Benson, a pretty hard bitten Furness Withy apprentice, was told to construct a raft, based on a series of empty forty gallon drums, ropes and planks upon which the remainder of us and our gear, had to paddle across a stretch of deep, smelly water. The CPO stood by taking notes and timing his efforts with a stopwatch. We went to work, under Benson's direction, and forty minutes later – some twenty minutes after the time limit – we had constructed a raft that would have crossed the Atlantic. The Chief constantly remonstrated with and badgered Benson, but to no avail. The Middy had the bit between his teeth and nothing, not even the most impressively darkened threats from Chiefy, could stop him. We followed Benson's leadership with quietly subdued laughter, as our CPO became increasingly irate, and then joined him on board to cross the ditch with perfect safety. CPO Darnley was livid – accusations of disobedience to commands – uncontrollable behaviour – were the most minor of threats which sailed across Benson's ears – and ours, by association. He too was placed on a charge – something about 'Disobedience of Lawful Commands', I believe.

My task was to send a weighted barrel across the narrow part of this same ditch. I had never done anything like this before, and soon found that much of the gear available was superfluous. I did the wise thing and kept detached from the team, by holding a watching brief and directing my team into counter-balancing the planks adroitly enough, allowing use of the ropes to best advantage. We eventually got the barrel and everyone across just within the time limit set. I felt I came out of that particular role with flying colours, receiving for a change quietly approving smiles from our Chief. The assault course was not completed with quite the same proficiency. I was team leader for this, but a couple of my team had considerable difficulty lugging the log we had been lumbered with across the scrambling net. Eventually, we managed the task, but only after Driscoll – a P&O cadet – managed to break his index finger in the process. As team leader I was of course, in the Navy's eyes, responsible – resulting in another rocket from my DO, but with no charge on this occasion.

Eventually, our ten gruelling days came to an end. We passed out with a parade and march past, with the Base Commander taking the salute. He was still not a particularly 'happy mariner' though and I suspected our course had done little to cement harmonious relationships between the two services. Following a few farewells, we boarded the coach and left the Royal Navy – some, I suspected for good. Whether or not I would be included amongst that latter number was frankly a matter of some indifference. I was allowed to count the time towards Second Mate's, but knew the training had little further relevance towards my career. In fact, thinking back on the local train home, I decided my ten days RNR training had proved expensive to the nation both in manpower and resources. The only fathomable result, from my point of view, appeared to be a hardening of my attitude towards authority which bordered dangerously close to insubordination. Common sense told me, were I a regular Royal Navy Midshipman at Dartmouth, my future career would have been in considerable doubt. As it was, the worse thing that could happen would be an adverse report to Ellerton's.

Chapter 6

FINAL LEG

———

Following my return home, I was called into the London Office for a chat with one of the Marine Supers – a Captain Atherton, recently brought ashore from command of the *Earl of Johannesburg*, in preparation for better things. As he had been put in charge of cadet training, I wondered to what extent he might feel he had achieved his brief, but was shown into his study before the thought could develop. Following a warmly cordial greeting, he asked about my experiences at HMS *Beautiful*. He listened carefully, smiled ruefully at my being placed on two charges on the same day, but expressed little surprise that the RNR and I were 'possibly a little incompatible' – a delightful phrase which endeared him to me immediately. I could even imagine serving under his command. The Company awaited my training report and would come back with the RN's viewpoint on my success (or otherwise) as a Midshipman, Royal Naval Reserve in due course. Meanwhile, we discussed matters more relevant to my career with Ellertons.

I left eventually with joining instructions and a travel warrant appointing me senior cadet aboard the brand new *Earl of Melbourne*, currently loading all five hatches for her maiden voyage in Manchester and thence bound for London, Las Palmas for bunkers and African ports. She was 6,100 gross tons, 445 feet in length overall and a beam of 52 feet. Completed at Glasgow the ship was a motor vessel with a service speed of 17 knots. The cadet's accommodation again on the officers' deck, starboard side, had a slatted wooden door separating us from the Third and Second Officers' cabins – not that this was ever to be closed.

I went home for a further few days' unexpected leave. Two days later brought another summons to Ellertons. My RNR report had arrived and (surprise, surprise) there was a change in my joining instructions for the *Melbourne*. The next day I duly reported in but, as Captain Atherton was engaged on other business, I was shown into the waiting room and given a cup of tea and a tin of biscuits. Idly flicking through a copy of the Company's house magazine, my attention was suddenly riveted by an article about the *Earl of Bath*. Due to be scrapped, a potted history of my old ship was set out in all its glory. From this I learnt of her impressive, but mundane Second World War record for most of which she had been requisitioned by the Royal Navy, and had served the fleet in various stations around the globe as a maintenance vessel for motor torpedo and gun boats.

Engrossed in this information, I realised to my horror the level of biscuits remaining in the tin had lowered rapidly. The tin was about half-full (a pessimist would have said empty) – so perhaps it had been unwise of the well-meaning secretary to have left me and this magnificent bounty together. She returned before I could complete the task of hastily jamming on the lid in an attempt to hide this social error. Casting a baleful look at both the tin and myself, she uttered a thinly-veiled sarcastic comment that she was pleased to 'see you have already enjoyed lunch', before showing me into an adjoining office where, once again, I found myself seated opposite Captain Atherton.

To my surprise, my progress with the RNR had not been a total disaster, but The Lords Commissioners of the Admiralty considered I might 'need a little more training', prior to being Commissioned, if I obtained a Certificate as Second Mate. I was not so sure about the lack of confidence reflected in their emphasis on 'if', but mused how everything concerning my future maritime career seemed to hang in the balance on this particular qualification. The tacit impression gained was that my Superintendents were not particularly bothered by my RNR adventures and that it would be largely up to me whether or not I eventually 'took papers', to use the common expression.

So far as joining the *Melbourne* was concerned, I was now required to meet her in Liverpool where, following successful sea-trials and handing-over, she was due shortly to load for her maiden voyage. Remaining up north, we would transit the ship canal for Manchester cargo, after which we would head for Glasgow, finally completing in King George V Dock, London. Our African ports had also been finalised; we had cargo for Cape Town, East London, Port Elizabeth, Durban, Lourenço Marques and Beira. It was good to know where the ship would be heading, and memories of exploits in LM and Durban flashed across my mind, but I felt better able to cope now, and indeed looked forward to re-visiting these ports. The junior cadet was a first-tripper straight out of nautical school, Howard Elbourne by name, another in the series of non-public school cadets whom Ellertons were regularly appointing. He had a highly successful academic record and was awarded the sextant (which I just missed at Keddleston) by the Honourable Company of Master Mariners. It seemed 'the venture was proving successful' as the Superintendent said, in what I now regarded as his customary dry tones.

Following a ten hour train journey, caused by countless delays due to adverse weather, the train finally hauled itself into Lime Street station in the midst of a thick snow storm – from whence a taxi, slipping and sliding on icy roads, took me at a snail's pace to join my ship.

Taking my gear up the gangway, assisted by the *Secunny* who showed me to my quarters, I reported to the Mate. I was immediately impressed with Mr. Greenly's manner and approach: he fell into the typically Elllerton mould of senior officers. Casually, he told me to get my gear stowed away and, as little was happening until the next morning, to relax on board for the evening. It would shortly be supper-time so I was pleased to take his advice. We met again in the smoke room over coffee and, after looking through my Journal, he told me something about the trip and what was required from me over the forthcoming voyage. I was to continue deck-work in the mornings with Howard and the crew but, more importantly to me, would be regularly on the bridge with him during his four-to-eight afternoon watch. The new cadet would not be joining until Manchester and it was my major responsibility to help him settle. I would work with Howard and the crew until we took transit of the canal outward bound, when I would be up for'ard with Mr. Greenly, whilst Howard went to the wheelhouse.

The remainder of the evening was spent playing cribbage – the Third Mate Graham Dow and I, versus Sparks and the Fourth Engineer. We won six rounds, but lost the evening's contest, the game finally being interrupted by the entry of our Second Officer, Mr. Flood and the Second Engineer. Inevitably, we ended up having a Sod's Opera in a junior engineer's cabin to the great delight and edification of all. I turned-in eventually, well past midnight, grabbing a few hours sleep prior to turning-to with the *Serang* at 0800 next day.

At 0900, I was called by the Mate to meet the Master and sign Articles. It had been related the previous evening by the Second Engineer that Captain Thurlow was 'a bit of a character'. Apparently, he had previously held command of one of the Company's larger cargo liners, but had 'fallen by the wayside through the demon drink'. I was therefore interested to meet him. His crime, it seemed, could not have been that serious or he would have been dismissed by the Company, not just demoted. The interesting addition to my knowledge was that those in considerable seniority to me also had warts of their own with which to contend. He greeted me in a friendly manner, enquired of my ships and service to date, and hoped I would learn a lot more in advancement of my career aboard his ship.

As I returned on the main deck, my attention was attracted by the noisy bustle around me. Amidst its snow-blanketed surrounds, the port suddenly seemed to have awoken. The previous evening, Mr. Greenly had told me there were normally around 250 deep-sea and coastal ships berthed in Liverpool and the surrounding area, with numerous assorted tugs, barges and sundry craft milling around. On considering the density of shipping in London, and what I had heard of other British main ports not yet visited, the magnitude of the industry in which I had become involved was brought home to me. It was in such a reflective mood that I reported to the *Serang*. As each hatch became partly completed, we lowered the derricks, making them fast by preventers, one on each port and starboard side, with the runner fast to the bull wire hook on the hatch, in readiness for loading in Manchester. Everything was new, and the wires were particularly stiff and difficult to handle.

I was taken off this work for a while to go with the Second Officer, *Tindal* and three *Secunnies*, to take deck stores from a delivery lorry and load these onto a pallet for lifting aboard by crane. Being a new ship, there was a complete lorry load for the deck department alone. Taking a couple of *lascars* onto the jetty, the midships accommodation and funnel towering above us appeared almost ethereal in thin white coverings.

It was bitterly cold and my fingers were frozen even through my working gloves. Ice bedecked everything and a thin covering of snow muffled the clanks of cranes and winches, with occasional flurries blotting out the immediate landscape. Working with the driver to sort out as near as possible homogeneous (I learnt this new word from the Mate) loads to assist stowing, I commenced supervising the crew and before too long, using the nearest shore-side crane in between cargo slings, we had sent two pallets onto the main-deck where the *Serang* was working the remainder of our deck crowd. We were well advanced with a third, piling this with drums of tallow, varnishes, oils and white lead, when suddenly a voice shouted at me and, looking up in surprise, I saw a stevedore telling me to off-load as the pallet was wanted for cargo. Assuming that the second mate had already cleared the lift with the crane driver I stood for a moment, mystified. The *Tindal* came along, but had little to add to the proceedings, and there was no sign of Mr. Flood. The stevedore glowered and I tried to explain that the Second Mate had things in hand, but to no avail. The lorry driver stood an interested spectator, the stevedore was becoming increasingly unreasonably angry and redder in his face (which at least kept him warm, I reflected inconsequentially) and the crew were looking at me in anticipation, clearly expecting me to come up with something positive to solve the situation. I glanced for help from the crane driver only to realise he was reading a newspaper while waiting for the next cargo lift; clearly my salvation did not lie in that direction.

There was nothing for me to do, but suggest to the ratings that we take everything off and give the stevedore back his pallet – anything for a quiet life. But then I thought a bit and suggested to this irate dock worker that perhaps a gift of one hundred cigarettes might help make the pallet more readily available. He agreed immediately, but brought us over a cargo net for use instead, into which we proceeded to off-load the stores. In the middle of this transfer, the Second returned with the delivery notes that he had been checking with the *Serang* on deck, for later matching against our requisition in the Mate's office. He glanced around and asked me what was going on. With some trepidation, I related what had happened, and to my relief he smiled agreement with my actions, suggesting additionally that the bargain struck had been a good one as the normal price in kind for borrowing any stevedore's equipment was twice what we had agreed.

Mr. Flood had previously negotiated a standard fee to crane drivers of two hundred cigarettes but, as a large amount of stores was involved on this occasion, added also a bottle of whisky. It was a useful cover for emergencies when our own derricks were swung to keep them out of the way of shore-side cranes, or were being used for cargo, yet the ship still expected to store. The bounty was kept in a joint 'float' kept especially for the purpose and operated by the Chief Officer, Second Engineer and Purser. It paid dividends; the alternative was for the crew to lug them up our gangway – not an impossible task but difficult to achieve, and potentially dangerous, with both arms full and our gangway swaying alongside the hull. An interesting sequel to this event was that the pallet remained unused, precisely where it was, for our entire stay in Liverpool. By the time we sailed, it was partially hidden by five inches of encrusted snow.

We had taken the pilot aboard and tugs were advancing towards us; the main-deck had been cleared, and the Mate and most of the crew were already on stand-by fore and aft. Graham had tested the bridge gear and was doing the Movement Book, whilst I was supervising raising the gangway with a couple of the deck crew. We were literally minutes away from sailing. Suddenly, a snow covered apparition appeared along the jetty lugging two large suitcases. We all looked in some surprise but, travelling in uniform, it could only be a cadet. Sure enough, Howard Elbourne stood nervously looking upwards until I lowered the gangway again and sent the *Secunny* down to help him aboard. Leaving his gear at the top of the gangway, he joined us as we went for'ard, and showed Mr. Greenly his joining instructions. Plainly, these had been altered by the Kremlin without their notifying us. Less than twenty minutes later and he would have missed the ship. With wry smile, the Mate agreed with my jaundiced comment that Captain Atherton was slipping into his superintendent's role extremely efficiently. I was stood down and told to take him to our quarters, then lead him into the wheelhouse, place him under the control of Graham, and return to my duties for'ard without delay.

Taking Howard to our cabin, and talking casually on the way, I recalled memories of joining *Earl of Bath* in Amsterdam; my reception, and subsequent kindnesses shown towards me. In Howard's face were reflected echoes extending over two and a half years of my original uncertainties and, for the first time, I realised my progress since those hesitantly nervous days. I understood also something deeper concerning Victor's possible feelings on meeting me, which helped me re-assure Howard that all officers would do everything in our power to help him settle. There was no time other than to dump his gear and take him to the wheelhouse where, introducing him simultaneously to the Captain and Graham, I beat a hasty retreat to the fo'c'sle, before arousing the Mate's ire.

We left in a snow storm and entered Eastham Locks. This allowed the fifteen feet or so tidal drop to level out before commencing our thirty-six mile ship canal passage. It was three days before Christmas. The *Earl of Melbourne* fell comfortably within the canal's maximum 15,000 gross tonnage but, as the height of our funnel and top-masts exceeded seventy feet, the Company's thirty ton crane removed the top two sections of the former, whilst we lowered the latter. This was the first time I had experienced these operations and was impressed by the fluency with which they were conducted – particularly considering the newness of the ship's gear. I looked up in my seamanship books the procedure for lowering top masts so had at least a notion of what happened in theory, but removing part of the funnel was then a complete mystery. Working under the Mate we did the mast-tops, but here the newness of all the gear proved a handicap which then, and over the subsequent voyage, created a raft of problems. Once the crane lifted away half our twenty-six ton funnel, the bare pipes poking from the remainder looked bizarre. Combined with shortened masts, our ship acquired a decidedly unfamiliar naked look. The sight of half a Strick line funnel, and a similar portion from a Palm Line vessel, looked quite incongruous on the quay. I imagined a scenario in which the wrong half was returned to the wrong ship.

Whilst we took tugs fore and aft to help centralise us in the canal, Howard was stood down to stow away his gear for after all, as the Mate confided in me, there was little he could practically do for the moment. That Mr. Greenly should exchange confidences was a new experience that made me feel very much accepted. It brought re-assurance that, as I progressed through my cadetship and gained seniority, enhanced relationships developed with the senior deck officers. Again, the situation made me see Vic in a new light. There was an additional knock-on effect not previously considered, but which had come to light during storing and raising the gangway. I was now expected to supervise working the crew with whom I had previously been working alongside, yet remained still a cadet. This entailed exercising considerable tact, especially with the *Secunnies* who were after all, leading hands.

I spent the Canal passage in warm comfort inside the wheelhouse doing the Movement Book and telephones. The duty mate was for'ard, but either the Master or Mate was present with the pilot and his quartermaster. It was a fascinating passage. We passed a number of moored cargo ships and assorted deep-sea tankers, representing more of the multitude of diverse flags with which I was becoming familiar. The hooting of tugs and assorted craft seemed muffled in the snow, whilst ubiquitous steam and motor powered cargo, tanker barges and coasters, dredgers and solo tugs returning to Eastham for further duty, contributed thick smoke-storms of their own which mingled with the continuously falling snow. Crossing underneath railway arches possessed singular interest; the bridge loomed ahead and it seemed as if the monkey island must almost certainly catch on its underside but, of course, we sailed under perfectly safely. The pilot confided that if we had not been fitted with serviceable radar equipment we might not have undertaken the canal passage in such restricted visibility, but would probably have anchored in the Mersey until conditions improved.

I was on stand-by for'ard with the Mate whilst coming alongside Latchford Dolphins, awaiting a couple of outward bound ships to pass (including the *Manchester Spinner*), and again for entry into the locks leading to Manchester docks. I remained there, doing telephones and helping with tugs and moorings, until we were made fast alongside one of the Company's regular berths in No. 8 dock. From when we had left Knutsford Bridge, the wind had blown a strong Force 4 with continuous driving snow, so by the time we stood-down and returned to our accommodation, the Mate, me, and Mr. Flood from aft, were all completely frozen. Being invited to drop into Mr. Greenly's cabin with the Second for a warming tot was much appreciated – 'to keep out the cold you understand Caridia, but don't expect this on a regular basis, my son'. As I sat with these officers, accepted without familiarity, I reflected this was a further highlight of a voyage and new relationships only just begun.

Returning to the cadets' cabin, I found Howard standing by our desk looking at photographs of his parents. He had been stood-down from the wheelhouse and was clearly wondering where he was; what he was doing, where he was going – and which to sort out first. I showed him around our quarters and pointed out the officers' accommodation and facilities open to us cadets telling him, in the process, of the general set-up and procedures expected of him as a first tripper. He seemed very quiet, which I put down to shyness, but soon perked-up when we were in the saloon and the crisp white-coated steward came to our table with the menu, inviting us to order supper. Afterwards, adjourning to the smoke room for coffee, we met other officers, enjoying their banter and relaxing aboard for the evening, as the weather was too foul to encourage much of a run ashore.

Christmas and Boxing Days were spent lying idly at our berth celebrating in traditional fashion – especially enjoyable as cargo watches were not required and there was little else for us to do. We enjoyed a traditional Christmas dinner, with all the trimmings together with free wine for all, including us cadets, supplied by a benevolent Company. Finishing a drink in the Third Mate's cabin afterwards, to which all and sundry had been invited, one of the junior engineers tipped the dregs of his glass over the head of our Radio Officer. Sparks retaliated with a glass of water and, before we fully appreciated what was happening, a wholesale water fight broke out which involved virtually all officers (deck and Sparks versus the engineers) and spread rapidly outside to the boatdeck. It finally involved rigging hoses, buckets and a general wash-down. The highlight of the evening for me was watching the duty *Secunny* on the gangway looking aghast at his officers belting around the decks in freezing weather, wailing like banshees, and smothering each other with icy water. His laconic comment as I passed, "Ah, it is the Chrisemus, Chota Sahib", was very revealing and led me to ponder how, as a devout Muslim; he could possibly relate events taking place before his eyes with a religious festival. I think Howard, very much an involved participator, was left wondering about the nature of the service he had joined – clearly events for which his nautical college had hardly prepared him. Still, as we took hot showers afterwards and invited him to join our full scale Sod's Opera in the Electrical officers' cabin, I think he took a less serious view of his new found professional lifestyle. On Boxing Day evening, the engineers invited some nurses to the ship for an all-night party, which widened his (and my) education considerably more. I suspect his letters home might have been similar to those which were not sent by me immediately after my African experiences.

The following day saw a moderating of the weather and resumption of loading. It remained bitterly cold as Howard and I worked with the *Serang* battening down hatches as they were completed, housing derricks, securing cleats, stowing wires and preparing the vessel for our sea passage to Glasgow. We loaded cars into the tween decks – brand new Triumphs and Land Rovers. That evening Howard and I went ashore, and saw *The Captain's Table* – a maritime comedy, with John Gregson, set aboard what looked suspiciously like an Orient Line ship, enjoyed a fish and chip supper and generally became better acquainted. Like the weather, he too gradually thawed.

As expected, I was on the fo'c'sle with Mr. Greenly for much of the outward bound canal passage, standing by the for'ard tug, and chatting informally. It remained bitterly cold, but there was no further snowfall. He left me with the Carpenter for a while, having told me to contact the bridge if necessary, which added another boost to my confidence, but later returned allowing me to stand-down for a warm-up. At Eastham, we soon reclaimed our funnel parts, raised the topmasts again, and set course for Glasgow in a blinding snowstorm resulting from yet another deepening depression. The only consolations were the ship looked like a ship again and we had commenced our maiden voyage.

Glasgow was not the best place for a shore leave – with its drab stone buildings encrusted with soot and grime – and, of course, the pelting rain which had replaced our snow, following a slight increase in temperature. We loaded Nos. 2 and 4 lower holds with general cargo and No. 3 tween deck with good Scotch whisky. The duty mate kept alert by the hatch coaming and both of us cadets were placed on consecutive watches in the tween deck, as security guards until all two thousand cases had been taken aboard. With such desirable cargo the probability of pilfering on a grand scale was not only high, but 'off the Richter scale for stealing', as the Mate told us. (Knowing as I did the extent of Chief Officers' illicit dealings abroad, I wondered if his tongue might just be in his cheek, but kept very wise counsel.) All involved had to keep their wits well and truly about them in the face of various attempts by the dock workers to distract our attention and so broach the cargo. The process made an interesting interlude from customary deck work. Luckily, we considered our joint efforts had proved successful and we gave ourselves a pat on the back as the last dock worker disappeared empty-handed down the gangway and we closed the hatch in preparation for sailing.

On the coastal passage to London, as promised, I was put on watch with the Mate and spent much of the time doing coastal navigation, radar work and collision avoidance. It was interesting, exciting and hectic – but great fun. The radar had a few teething problems, with a number of picture losses whilst changing ranges. Sparks was called out frequently and his curses of frustration over the thing became a delight to hear, contributing magnificently to our entertainment. For much of the time, the Mate left me to get on with the navigation and Decca work directly, but frequently checked what I was doing. He told me he had 'a vested interest in my doing the job properly' and then related a lesson learnt from a recent tanker investigation. This had demonstrated how the Master and navigating officer of that unfortunate ship were enjoying 'a slight disagreement', regarding a policy matter, and unwisely had left the navigation of the tanker to the cadet. He accordingly made an error in his calculations of set and drift of the current with the result that the tanker gradually – some might even say, regally – ran gently aground onto a shoal. The Master and duty mate were 'taken to the cleaners', each having his certificate of competency suspended. Plainly (and correctly), Mr. Greenly had no intention of allowing me to place him in that invidious position.

When we were off watch, he called me into his office and I looked with interest whilst he explained the construction of the ship's cargo plan for our loading in London's 'KGV' dock – as it was referred to colloquially. We had cargo space in Nos. 1 and 5 holds, as well as No. 2 tween deck, into which we were to load machinery and dumper trucks, condensed milk, toilet bowls and five cased glass chandeliers, each apparently worth a few thousand pounds which were destined for the High Commissioner in Durban. We were also taking on two pedigree dogs for Beira, which were to be housed in kennels built on the boat deck, whose care was to be entrusted to us cadets. He then went one step further by giving me a rough copy of a cargo plan together with tonnage and stowage details of the cargo to be taken. Then, despatched to the cadet's study, I devised my own version of loading, using a colour coding on the basis of our ports of discharge, and with regard to the stability of the ship. Once my version was completed it was taken to the Mate and, in a moment of truth, his copy and mine were compared. In the ensuing discussion I was closely questioned about differences between the two versions, whilst he examined shortfalls in my plan, then explained how mine could be improved, and more importantly, highlighted its failings. This was a major step forward in my training and was consistent with the current stages of my correspondence course.

I took the helm for berthing alongside in the Royal Albert Dock, London (there had been a change of orders) from the time we took the river pilot on board off Gravesend until when the ship was in position alongside. My only break occurred when the ship was in the entrance lock for forty minutes or so, whilst the water levels evened. Howard was on the Movement Book and clearly taking interest in everything happening around him. Cargo was not being worked until 0800 next day so, after being stood down, he and I went ashore to one of the local pubs – a venue known to merchant seamen colloquially as the 'Bent Arms'. It lived up to its reputation that particular evening with a vengeance, as *Bloemfontein Castle,* a Union-Castle passenger liner on the African run, was in the adjacent King George V dock. After fighting our way to the bar, and returning with drinks, I suggested that it might be prudent just to listen and enjoy, but remain silent in our pleasure, the cabaret spontaneously laid on by the 'Queens', or effeminate stewards, out for a last night ashore. The barman more than had his work cut out to contain the antics from this lively and uproariously hilarious crowd. The language and styles of speech were witty, totally unrestrained and largely unprintable, although nowhere near as extreme as witnessed in bars abroad. I saw reflected in Howard's disbelief much of my own earlier shock on being exposed initially to the wilder excesses of human frailty and depravity. I had long since ceased wondering what my mother might have made of it all in such situations, viewing these now in the light of a seasoned campaigner whom nothing could shock, even if numerous surprises still occurred. It came within the category of 'an enlightening evening' and left Howard talkative, yet consumed with amused wonder, as we made the journey back to our own ship.

The next day, a junior Second Officer arrived to assist the mates with problems arising from our new gear. There were no mechanical faults, merely the newness of everything, as we had found with the mooring wires and topmasts, plus a number of other things which required closer attention than might have been the case with established equipment. This appointment released the Mate for day work enabling him, until Cape Town at least, to sort out new wires and mooring ropes with the crew, as well as countless other deck jobs. The new officer turned out to be none other than Julian Blandford, Third Officer from my first ship *Earl of Bath.* We greeted each other warmly; he already knew the senior Second and had met the Master on a previous coastal voyage. There was much to discuss.

I was allowed ashore for a final overnight stay at home which was both unexpected and thoroughly enjoyable. I phoned Mum, who contacted Sue, enabling us to spend a thoroughly relaxing family evening chatting comfortably in what was now regarded as their front room. We also drank some beer which Dad brought over from the 'Two Brewers' across the road. I reflected this pint and the company were a little different to the circumstances of my last drink, but then, of course, so also were many other things. There were no longer references to steady jobs in a bank; Mum seemed to have accepted my chosen way of life as being precisely that and, in consequence, had let-go of both me and the past.

Returning to the ship via the Woolwich Ferry next morning, I noticed how ships' masts, funnels and superstructure, towered over houses in the short dumpy streets leading off the main road, en route to the dock entrance. Loading was completed without any particular delay or problem and, three weeks after arriving in the Royal Albert, we sailed at three o'clock one bitterly cold February morning.

Howard was seasick for much of the time after we had cleared the Channel and did not really improve until we were well past Gibraltar. I did what was within my power to help, but there was precious little that could be done. I was also far too busy taking bridge watches with Mr. Flood, who was now keeping the Chief Officer's watch and had taken my good self in default. Instead of turning-to in the mornings with the *Serang* and Howard, once we had cleared the Bay of Biscay, Mr Greenly gave me a paint measuring device and the task of going everywhere on the ship testing that thicknesses were consistent with the manufacturers' specifications. This duty was boring, but different, and one I would hardly be likely to do in the future, unless sailing on a brand new ship again.

Also, for variety, I renewed signal halyards and looked after both lifeboats and their gear. Once at sea, for our first fire and boat drill, the Mate put me with his boat, placing me in charge of the entire operation; mustering the crew against the boat list (including drawing these up, under the Third Mate's supervision), lowering it to the embarkation deck and the recovery. I was again given my small party of crew to run, either with stretcher drills from any part of the ship, or fire hose control or, worst of the three, running the smoke helmet party. It was all good experience for Second Mate's. Widening my experience, I was turned-to with the radio officer for a 'look-see', as the Mate called it – even if Sparks referred to the session as 'seeing how the other half lived and worked'.

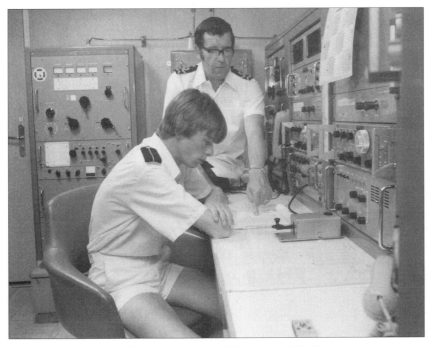

Working with the Radio Officer (courtesy BP plc).

Lifeboat drill (courtesy BP plc).

Las Palmas offered a brief opportunity for cadets' shore leave and the buying of presents. There was also some bartering of ship's stores with the Agent for a few cases of dry sack sherry, one of which was opened in our cabin over a card game with off-watch engineers and drunk out of half-pint beer tumblers. It represented a far cry from that delicate sipping which accompanied pre-luncheon drinks at home. I have to confess a lamentable lack of finesse at this stage of my cadetship but, of course, had the consolation of knowing Howard was being trained in his maritime skills to the correct level of perfection. As the game progressed, spades began to look suspiciously like clubs, and we ultimately turned-in decidedly the worse for wear. The next day saw us both on deck with severe hangovers, having consumed five bottles of the stuff between four of us.

Leaving behind the Gulf of Guinea, some thousand miles from land off the River Congo, a generator caught fire in the engine-room and the ship was called to emergency stations, potentially at least for real. Cries of 'never a dull moment' were once more heard wailing around the accommodation from anxious and frustrated officers. I was on the bridge with the officer-of-the-watch and Master, anxiously awaiting news – more anxiously in fact, because we had nothing better to do than wait. This was by far the worst part of it, for personally I should much rather have been kept busy. At one time, Sparks was placed on stand-by to transmit a distress message and both the Mate, Chief and Second Engineers were working flat out down below fighting 'a particularly vicious fire', as Mr. Greenly described it later, wiping his brow and doing admirable justice to a couple of pints. By that time the emergency was over, everyone had breathed a big sigh of relief, and was enjoying a celebratory tot.

The Mate experienced his own unique problem during this emergency. He unwisely stood too closely whilst supervising one of the *Lascar* seamen handling a fire extinguisher. Reflecting on my *Stenwood Navigator* days, I was led to wonder if standing too close was a senior officer disease. The seaman correctly upended the thing, bouncing it on the deck, to allow the cap plunger to break the acid bottle. As the nozzle received pressure, it twisted unexpectedly to point upwards, leading the foam jet to burst up the leg of the Mate's shorts. With a yelp of shock, he leapt backwards, striking his head a glancing (but not serious) blow against a bulkhead obstruction in the engine-room. The Second Engineer with him was creased with unrestrained laughter as he related this gem to us in the smoke room. We cadets kept very much our own counsel but, in the privacy of our cabin, gave free rein to our own laughter. It was not quite so funny afterwards, for we were given the job of cleaning out the used extinguishers and refilling them.

Howard became a major concern as we approached the African coast. Once he had recovered from his sea-sickness, he was turned-to with the *Serang's* happy crowd, but was displaying a marked reluctance to do dirty jobs on deck. Not that there was as many as normal aboard a ship, because running and standing gear had had no time to become spoiled. The *Serang* reported him to Mr. Greenly and, although I was not over-bothered with the details, knew Howard received a quiet dressing-down and an explanation why deck work was necessary. It did not do much immediate good though and both parties mentioned their various concerns to me. My role as senior cadet put me in an invidious position. I discussed the matter quietly with Julian. He advised there was little for me to do, other than help Howard settle into these obviously unexpected duties required of him, and keep the Mate informed regarding the cadet's wider welfare. At the same time I had to keep the *Serang* happily re-assured that the situation was in hand. Howard's main complaint centred on the amount of time I was allowed to spend on the bridge and doing my host of other jobs around the ship. Obviously, the reasons for this were explained to him by all parties, and we could do little more. The problem was one which ultimately Howard alone could resolve.

My meetings with the Chief Officer continued as on previous ships, but now with an increased impetus. I found it easy to express my concerns to him; working the crew, Howard, and the new difficulty of maintaining my Journal which, this trip, was becoming increasingly tedious. Mr. Greenly said of the latter that this was a good sign – rather akin, as he put it, 'to the sparrow becoming ready to leave the nest'. I had additionally to produce a Sight Book – complete with workings showing the ship's daily run, and my crop of sextant observations and amplitudes. Collision Regulations coverage was extended to include discussions on numerous situations, the avoiding action necessary, and word-perfect support of my decisions from the relevant rule. This was interesting, but Mr. Greenly was a truly hard taskmaster and all hell was let loose if my concentration wandered and I made a silly mistake. At nautical college we used to refer to our tutorials as being 'action packed' hours – those aboard the *Melbourne* were more realistic and proved very nerve wracking on occasions. I received considerable assistance from Mr. Flood, both supervising my correspondence course and whilst on the bridge. Regarding working the crew, as opposed to working with them, the Mate considered this would 'come with experience'. My studies intensified considerably as I entered this more senior phase of my cadetship.

Cape Town was our first port of call and, in keeping with what I learnt was a coastwise tradition, the junior officers bought a Land Rover which we lugged all around the African coast for use in every port at which we called. Nobody had vehicle tax or insurance, but we did boast one international driving licence between us. I became quite adept at driving the thing, after a few scrapes, dents and gear crashes. I shuddered even then to think of the consequences of an accident with another vehicle or worse, but still joined the others in living (if not driving) dangerously. I am not quite sure what Captain Thurlow and the Mate thought about this – nor the Chief Engineer, for that matter, seeing that most of the officers involved were in his department.

It was whilst alongside an Ellerton berth in Duncan Dock that I saw a massive supertanker moored off the New Eastern Mole directly opposite my cabin window. She was (like ourselves) the brand new, *Universe Apollo*, which at over 114,000 deadweight tons and nearly 1,000 feet in length (virtually twice the length overall of *Melbourne*), was one of the last large tankers to be constructed with midships accommodation. After this date such very large ships were built with 'everything aft'. My mind was captivated by the sight of this vessel, and once again I found myself wishing to serve on these ships. Sharing this view with the other officers, however tentatively, did not bring much consolation, with the general view held being largely negative. Julian recalled my interest previously, but was not over-enthusiastic at the prospect of serving aboard tankers himself. It was not possible to go over to visit her, which I would have enjoyed doing.

We did visit one marine institution known internationally to seafarers – that classic clip joint, 'Del Monico's Bar'. Fortunately, (or unfortunately, depending on viewpoint), our berthing coincided with two of the larger Southampton-based Union-Castle Line mail ships – one outward and the other homeward bound. Their presence guaranteed the place to be a riot. Even as we were disgorging from our taxis and about to enter, we saw the police proceeding to clear it, for reasons never made clear, although conjecture was rife. We beat a hasty retreat in case we were caught up with the mass exodus. It seemed that random customers were being arrested as they came out and were being taken away in large vans. Our group considered we had experienced a very narrow escape, so quietly came back the next evening after cargo had stopped for the day. I had heard much about this bar during the voyage, and it certainly proved different to other clip joints visited elsewhere in the world; what I would call more 'raw' – for here were neither exotic decoration nor delicate girls. Women there most certainly were, and in abundance, but with a hard-faced, business-like professionalism; possessing as much sex appeal as my maiden aunt's aspidistra in her front lounge. Intermingled with the girls were seamen of just about every nationality under the sun. Any behaviour seemed acceptable. I made certain Howard and I stayed very close to the door so we could hop out rapidly if things went awry. The noise was deafening – music, shrill oaths, diverse languages, cluttering glasses, broken bottles, arguments and general conversation in bellowing tones. A man of indistinguishable nationality was vomiting all over the floor, having failed to make the toilet – even charitably assuming he was heading for it – two others were shaping up for an unspecified, but pretty obvious confrontation. We did not stay long, but discreetly bailed out – able to say we had at least sampled the place – for whatever merit that might earn us either in this or the next world. Howard was horrified once again and I shuddered to think what he might write in his next letter home.

The VLCC Universe Apollo broke the 100, 000 ton barrier in 1959 (courtesy World Ship Society).

Discharging the whisky from No. 3 tween deck, we were amazed to find that twelve cases had been broached and, apart from a few bottles, the contents removed. The Scottish dockers were, it seemed, far more subtle than we gave them credit for. Julian and I pinched the remainder, took it discreetly to his cabin, and shared it (more or less equally) whilst on the coast. We had to enter the details in the Mates' cargo loss book for onward transmission to the Company's insurance brokers.

I was on bridge watch with Mr. Flood for the passage to East London where the pace of life was very calm after Cape Town. The only incident of any note was watching parties of prisoners from the local gaol being marched to work at various sites throughout the town. We completed discharge and, after belting around the outskirts of the town in our jeep, unobtrusively left as quietly as we had entered.

Dock scene at Port Elizabeth (courtesy Art Publishers Pty).

In Port Elizabeth, the Agent arranged for a party to visit a banana plantation a few miles inland. Julian, Howard and I, along with Mr. Flood, and the Electrician representing the 'Ginger Beers' department, took advantage, and certainly enjoyed an evening which was different. Following a massive meal, washed down with a potent local brew, our host invited us to visit his workforce in their village about a quarter of a mile's walk into the jungle. We were each given fiery torches and urged to use these not only to see where we walking, but also to sweep the path before us, and bushes alongside, in order to frighten away black and green mambas, the resident's pets. We needed little urging. The first indications of approaching the village were noise and smell and we soon caught sight of a clearing with small collections of mud huts, each group having a large fire burning unevenly outside. The workers were dancing sedately and singing a plaintively haunting, gentle, melody. Suddenly, this burst into harsh chanting, accompanied by a more intense, fervent even, thundering of drums, and an agitated dance of frenzied orgiastic movement. The experience was primeval – quintessentially African – and one I found vaguely disturbing. As we entered one of the huts, at the invite of the smiling worker, the sight of a battery-operated portable radio, stuck precariously on a bamboo shelf, met my eyes. Civilisation encountered in such bizarre surroundings was incongruous to say the least, and was the subject of much thoughtful chatter on our way back to the ship.

Howard was settling better to deck work now to the great relief of all. Although I had experienced much kindness as a junior cadet, I had never fully appreciated how unobtrusively caring were Ellerton's officers. In my slightly senior role things were now evident to me, the existence of which previously I had probably been only vaguely aware. There was much genuine concern expressed regarding his welfare, much of which brushed off on me. It was a pleasure to keep an eye on him 'from a distance', as it were, for he rarely got into scrapes, but merely jogged along with what he was asked to do, making the best of his work. Like me, he also had his correspondence course to attend and it was good to help him, but only when asked. We both became involved in new practical skills, learning how to sew canvas to cover the wicker anchor ball and Not Under Command shapes. My sewing (using my left-handed palm) was described as a 'little rough and ready' but, like my ill-fated attempts at splicing, the finished article, once camouflaged by a coat of black paint, was sufficiently respectable for ordinary use. Looking after the dogs was in a way straightforward, but time consuming; they were lively and I found them rather aggressive, but Howard got on quite well with them.

Working with Howard on coastal and the deep-sea passages, I found myself teaching other duties, similar to those which senior cadets had offered me as the junior. I showed him lifeboat maintenance routines and, during boat and fire drills, unravelled the mysteries of the compressed air breathing apparatus, including wearing the thing. He was an able pupil, far more practical than my good self. We also worked together painting areas of the accommodation, working with the *Secunny* on a painting stage, the mechanics of which I had at long last mastered.

It was good to return to Durban once more and dock almost next to our previous berth. Once again the same Agent visited and, once again, familiar envelopes were tucked into two little shirt pockets, with a similar admonition. I had no idea what the Mate had bartered this time round, but suspected that paint was probably top of the Agent's shopping list. Either way, we lost no time going ashore and spending it, once more at the Officers' Club and the 'XL' restaurant. Howard received the explanation regarding the source of his bounty with the obvious crop of misgivings which I had had previously and, like me, they failed to take root. I did wonder what would happen if anyone complained, how they would set about this and what might be the outcome. I discussed this with him, over our usual T-bone steak meal with all the trimmings. With our mouths full of illicitly earned food and wine, the discourse acquired a mildly humorous slant as we imagined Chief Officers, now in their nineties, along with numerous Captains even older, hauled before a magistrate. I do not recall our fantasies giving us indigestion.

Cadets painting the superstructure (courtesy BP plc).

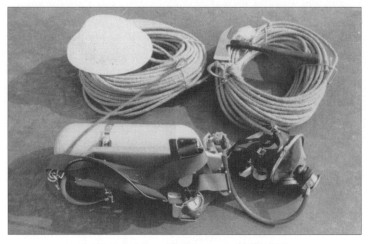

Compressed air breathing apparatus (Shell IT&S).

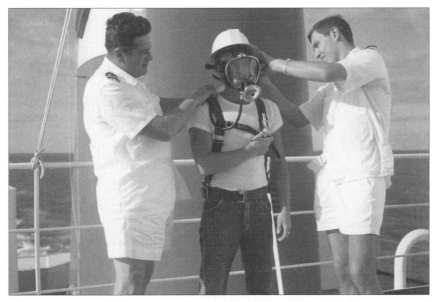

Fitting breathing apparatus (courtesy BP plc).

Cadets servicing lifeboat equipment (courtesy BP plc).

When we came to discharge the chandeliers, shortly after arrival, an interesting (albeit expensive) 'chink' came from the wooden packing cases as they were moved gently along the tween deck. The inevitable had happened; they were each smashed to pieces. The Third Mate sent for the Chief Officer to have a look, followed shortly by the shipper's representative, the Agent, the Master, the Chief Officer again, and an insurance assessor. Costing in excess of one thousand pounds sterling each, a considerable sum of money, all parties concerned with their transportation glanced warily at each other and strove to transfer the blame onto one another. Eventually, a 'Note of Protest' was drawn up and brought before a Notary Public which firmly blamed God or, more specifically his action in producing a spell of rough weather, along with the notorious Cape Rollers, experienced as we approached Cape Town.

As a new ship to the Ellerton fleet, a shipboard dinner and dance was organised by the Agent for cargo shippers and their families, which included some local dignitaries – 'Hangers-on of the Agent', we deduced cynically (and probably not too far from the truth). The event was held on the after part of the boat deck, to the disgust of the Purser who was expected to do all the organising and, of course, catering. All officers were expected to participate as hosts and, as this was a formal affair, we were dressed either in full mess kits or, for us cadets whose finances baulked at such expense, 'collar dogged' No. 8s, with shoulder straps indicating our respective ranks and providing splashes of colour. Howard and I were seated at the bottom of a table opposite two very beautiful young ladies, daughters of one of the major shippers. Our Asian stewards were immaculately dressed in whites, with blue corded shoulder lanyards and matching cummerbunds which, with the starched tablecloths and shining cutlery, produced an effect of considerable smartness. All of this gear had been loaned for the occasion by one of the Company's larger cargo liners moored in our old berth – which happened to be our Captain's previous command. About this, a tactful silence was maintained – after all, there was no need to spoil the event by a side-swipe – least of all from any of his officers who valued their promotion prospects – and certainly not from cadets who valued their lives.

The wine flowed liberally, relaxing the occasion admirably and a good time was had by all. The entrée was chilled Cantaloupe melon served with cinnamon and, engaged in animated conversation, I took a neat spoonfull of this stuff only to cough it all over the table cloth. There was what was known in the trade as 'a pregnant pause'. Suddenly, the situation appealed to my sense of humour, liberally blunted by wine, and caused me to burst out laughing. This at least broke the ice of embarrassment and managed to go some way to smoothing over my *faux pas*. Luckily, the girls saw the funny side of things, but it proved an awkward moment and, momentarily, put me back some years to the days when *gaffes* of this nature were rather more common than they had been recently. I was understandably quiet for a while, but was soon drawn back into the conversation by the very understanding girl opposite me. As the evening developed, and wine flowed even more freely, she and I found ourselves dancing ever closer, with thoughts of my Sue becoming blurred in the background. The inevitable happened as Yvonne and I found ourselves moving snugly close, with rapidly beating hearts and a rising excitement. It had to happen, of course – frustration was doomed to be my middle name – for a large maternal figure appeared out of nowhere gently suggesting the girls, Howard and myself, joined the family for coffee.

The parents were very understanding and tactful, and we were both invited to their home the following day for lunch. This worked out well as it was a Sunday and no cargo was being worked. Mr. Greenly knew the shipper quite well, from days when he had served on the larger passenger ships and had carried the shipper and his wife, on an occasion when Yvonne's parents had come back from a UK holiday. He was more than happy to allow us both local leave, so we were collected mid-morning after a couple of hours deck work. We met the girls later in the week for afternoon tea in town and so began a delightfully innocent, but fun filled friendship that lasted until we sailed for LM. Mother however made very certain (for some reason) that neither daughters nor cadets were left alone for any length of time.

I kept well clear of L.M.'s 'Green Door Club' on this occasion, but Howard was taken ashore by Julian and the engineers and returned in a terrible state, reminiscent of my adventures there. Mr. Greenly observed his condition with the cynically jaundiced eye of a man who has seen it all before (as undoubtedly he had) and merely suggested I keep an eye on him and make certain he was turned-to for work next morning regardless of shape or state. It proved not an easy task, but one I regarded with detached dry humour, as after all I had also travelled that particular path.

Mr. Flood, our esteemed senior Second Officer, for some reason best known to himself, purchased a small African grey parrot and paid us cadets a princely sum to look after the thing, with particular emphasis on keeping its cage clean. I never ceased to wonder at the antics of senior officers. The ship was fast becoming a menagerie, with every whim of these blasted dogs to cater for as well.

For the entire voyage we had taken them for walks along the boat-deck, cleaned up after their 'daily business', so off-duty officers would not have to 'bronzy' lying in their social errors or whilst they played deck quoits. We had fed them, changed their water, kept their kennels clean, given 'tender loving care' whilst they had been seasick and generally amused them. Howard was more of a dog lover, but even his patience was wearing a bit thin. Beira was eagerly anticipated when their adoring owners would come to claim them and so restore our boat-deck to something approaching normality. Anyway, in an unguarded moment, one of the beasts slipped its lead and escaped. We spent a hilarious time chasing it all round the main deck trying a retrieval operation, but to no avail. Our crew and officers considered the event extremely funny and the latter at least offered us all kind of helpful suggestions as we belted around the ship trying to recapture the thing. The Mate was not very pleased with us and I, in particular, received a royal rocket for what he saw as our combined error. In the end, after three hours of freedom, we managed to entice it, slobbering with love and luckily also hunger, back to the fold. Beira was a welcome sight as we handed them over. The grateful owners were clearly impressed with our efforts as they slipped Howard and me twenty pounds each in local currency – a very welcome and unexpected bonus that helped us see our canine friends in a more charitable light. With a bonus from the Purser, for continued assistance with his port forms, and a sub from the Mate, we were managing extremely well with finances on this trip.

We used the jeep to full advantage at each port. In Durban, four of us had travelled into Pietermaritzburg for a Sunday jaunt and thoroughly enjoyed a tipple or two upon our arrival. The standard of driving on the return journey left even more to be desired than usual, but we managed to return to the ship in one piece. Part of the adventure was running over a number of snakes that unwisely chose our moment of passing to cross the road. In Beira, a few of us went out for a picnic in the thing, taking advantage of unexpected leave granted due to a delayed copper ingot cargo from up country. As the Purser came with us on this particular venture we lacked not food or drink, and spent an enjoyable day far from civilisation swimming in a small lake and sun bathing.

It was in this port that the master gyro-compass caused some problems. I joined both Messrs. Flood and Blandford as they applied their joint skills to discover 'what was what', aided by me of course, who stripped away the metal covers enabling these eminent surgeons to operate. In the course of doing so, I learnt considerably more about how it operated than in six weeks of correspondence course. It had been promised throughout the voyage that I would be shown its workings, so considered this gremlin rather opportune. The gyro-compass was also serviced, enabling me actually to see the cosine groove, for example, instead of just reading about it. Eventually, the fault was discovered in the form of a large piece of grit that had become lodged inside the works. Three hours to find it, five minutes to correct it, another five to replace the covers – and then twenty four hours to re-start it, and allow it to settle.

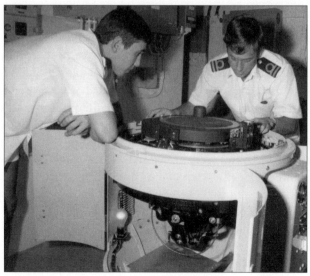

Second Officer servicing master gyro compass (courtesy BP plc).

Once loaded, we began the return journey via LM and Durban to Cape Town. Howard and I met our girl friends in Durban for nothing more than an enjoyable family time, leaving the officers to enjoy their customary wilder excesses, based essentially round the Nurse's home at Addington. Yvonne and I managed a meal at the XL restaurant one evening, far from parental supervision, and even went swimming amongst the sand dunes – love at last it seemed was to have its way as we lay naked, kissing, cuddling and drying off on the warm secluded beach. At the moment of what should have been impact, however, and to the unbelievable frustration of us both, my feet slipped in the soft sand. She was livid with me and we parted on estranged terms – to put things mildly. It seemed that, in certain circumstances, I could do little right, so cut my losses and on returning back on board, decided once back home I would propose virginal engagement to my 'fated to be, ever faithful' Sue. Howard and the officers, needless to say, thought the incident hilarious. They had been regaled with the details from Yvonne's loyal sister – with whom Howard had experienced even less opportunity for seduction than I with Yvonne.

On arrival in Cape Town, the juniors ditched the much-abused jeep by simply parking it down a side street and walking away. It had served its purpose. On a previous voyage they had unwisely driven that vehicle into the dock, but the splash (not surprisingly) had attracted so much attention that the police had been called. The officers made themselves very scarce, whilst divers were called to the scene, thus providing entertainment for the juniors who took more than a morbid interest in events from the after deck of the ship. They were even more bemused when a police sergeant came aboard enquiring if any of them had seen anything suspicious. Mr. Flood was becoming increasingly agitated – not about the jeep as he had enjoyed his share of the pleasure from this vehicle – he had a problem more acute.

His parrot had initially lived in the chartroom where we used to talk to it in friendly, coaxing baby-talk and even the Master was agreeably acquiescent to its presence, jabbing it occasionally (unlike the rest of us, of course) with the chartroom pencil. But, 'Tommy' as he unoriginally called the bird, remained tantalisingly mute. Life continued as usual around the African coast until suddenly, one morning, the parrot found his voice. In very clear speech he proudly displayed his vocabulary; a mixture of helm orders, navigational terms, cargo jargon and people's names, all innocently interspersed between bursts of quite appalling language. This aroused new interest in the bird, but Tommy found himself relegated to his owner's cabin by a shocked and irate Captain. The crew continued his education by teaching him the same unmentionable words, in fluent Hindi. A somewhat confused state of affairs developed, proving to the Second what we cadets knew all along – namely, his bird was more damn trouble than it was worth.

Mr. Flood's problem was exacerbated for, having applied for a permit from the Ministry of Agriculture to bring it into the UK shortly after acquiring it, by the time we sailed from Africa there had been no response. He was left in a bit of quandary.

Being due to re-sit part of his previously failed Masters' certificate this time in, he had to leave the ship. As no one on board wanted to take on the parrot, our Captain was adamant that, like the Second, it should also go, but to bring it ashore without a permit would be illegal. So he was left wondering what to do. There was no lack of advice from his fellow officers – much of which proved either illegal, impossible, impracticable or unsavoury. We cadets kept very quiet, after all this was senior officer territory, but (once again) our private thoughts and conversation were our own.

Howard and I had our individual voyage interviews with Captain and Mate. He had settled more readily to the life now, so finding himself enjoying things, had decided to remain at sea to complete his cadetship – a move which received wholehearted support from his seniors. He was to go on leave prior to appointment aboard another ship. My voyage had been quite successfully devoid of professional incidents, with the result that my reports to Company and parents were likely to be positive. I was to remain on board the ship with Howard and proceed on leave from Newcastle and re-join the ship in Tilbury, following her coastal and continental voyage, prior to sailing again for the African coast. Howard was particularly pleased as Newcastle was his home port.

On arrival in Millwall Docks, the Second's permit had still not arrived so he had to do some fast thinking. Two berths along was the *Earl of Staffordshire*, wherein resided a friend. Accordingly Tommy, complete with perch and chain, was without ceremony man-handled along the jetty. The 'friend' however declined the offer, so the long-suffering parrot was hawked among the dockers, allowing a few more expletives to enhance its repertoire. They refused to have the bird and the Second was forced into taking the risks attendant on smuggling it ashore for sale to a pet shop.

The next day a taxi was summoned and the driver informed of the plot. He was one of the vessel's regular cabbies and agreed to take Tommy through the dock gates, past the policeman on duty, if somehow the bird could be kept sufficiently silent whilst alongside the constable. Things, already slightly out of hand, escalated from this moment. The Second tried an aspirin but (surprise, surprise!) the effect was nil. A double tot of whisky in its drinking water proved equally futile and so he decided to tape his beak with adhesive plaster borrowed from the sick bay. This proved impossible and amidst a flurry of feathers, seed, curses and squawks, from both parrot and owner, he had to admit defeat. Then came another idea. Chippy was sent for and agreed to make a wooden box into which Tommy was eventually bundled, continuing his harangue about the degrading mishandling to which he had been subjected.

The taxi was duly called, Tommy's temporary home placed on the seat next to his equally agitated owner and the journey to the dock gates started. Fate had apparently not yet played all her cards; a dock worker, not looking where he was going, stepped out in front of the taxi. The driver braked sharply, Tommy's box slid forward, the lid opened and the parrot flew out, through the cab window and onto the jib of a nearby crane. The verbal expression of his feelings matched exactly those of the Second Officer who clambered from the taxi and up the crane's ladder. Tommy, still cursing avidly, waited until his owner had almost reached him before leaving his refuge to fly further along the quay. Almost paranoid with frustrated anger, the Second climbed down the crane ladder and started going along the dock after his elusive bird. Freedom had its own reward, it would appear for, with a final stream of pure vitriol, Tommy solved everyone's problems (except perhaps his own) by flying high over one of the cargo sheds and out of sight. It was with a mixture of frustration, relief and almost regret, I suspect, that the Second re-entered his taxi to drive through the dock gates and out of my life. We onlookers returned to our ship to be met by an interesting, if astonishing, sight. Pacing backwards and forwards along the starboard bridge-wing was the Captain, with a familiar small feathered figure preening himself contentedly on his shoulder. Tommy it seemed had recognised home and landed on the bridge where the Master was pacing in the manner ordinarily associated with watch-keepers even (or especially) when tied to their ship with very little to do. The parrot's obviously distraught condition had touched some deep instinct within Captain Thurlow's bosom, to which unaccustomed friendliness, Tommy had responded immediately. The happy outcome was that he was officially adopted by the Master and, while not exactly signed-on ship's Articles became, as it were, a fully fledged member of the crew. Howard and I were re-assigned a bird-cleaning role – unpaid this time – leaving us yet again to ponder the idiosyncrasies of our senior officers.

We docked in Newcastle at twenty hundred with the ship due to sail next day. Howard suggested I come home and stay with his parents and continue my journey after breakfast, a suggestion I accepted with alacrity. His excitement reminded me of my first return home and I shared his pleasure as he unpacked suitcases and distributed presents to the family, simultaneously showing things he had purchased over the voyage. One of his acquisitions in Durban (which had driven me partly mad in the process of experimentation) was a set of two small bongo drums. These he proudly dragged out of his case to show loving parents and adoring elder sister. In retrospect, this was not a particularly wise move. The junior engineers, aided and abetted I suspected by Graham and Julian, had filled the things with anti-VD kits (commonly known as 'Dreadnoughts') and French letters. These cascaded in a stream cross the fitted lounge carpet to lie winking at us accusingly. The action proved a conversation stopper for, to say there was a pregnant pause, is understating completely the tense atmosphere created. Howard's jaw dropped in his white face; his mother and sister looked equally horrified, whilst sinking back into my armchair I pretended not to be there. Unfortunately I was. The scenario reminded me of my Clan Line ship *faux pas* – and proved as much consolation. Responding with an accountant's quickness of mind, Howard's father at least partially saved the day. Looking at his abashed son, in the process of falling over himself in his haste to retrieve the things, he enquired if Howard had enjoyed a good voyage or 'was he anticipating a good leave?' With a wry smile Howard stuffed the offending articles back into his case, mumbling something incoherent. The remainder of the evening was an anti-climax.

I was called by Captain Atherton to the Kremlin two days after arriving home. The Company were pleased with my progress to such an extent that I was to be promoted uncertificated Fourth Officer for the remaining seven months of my sea-time, prior to sitting for 2nd Mates' Certificate. Contrary to popular belief, I was not to return to the *Melbourne*, but was to come ashore for three weeks and take my radar observer course at a London school of navigation. As the course commenced in just two days' time there was not a great deal to discuss about the plan. Ellertons had booked me in, paid for the course and put me on study leave, so I was not left with any choice. As it happened, I wanted to do this particular course so was not unduly concerned. On the contrary, it proved instructive and interesting and again proved a good opportunity to meet with other navigating cadets and exchange news and views about conditions in our various companies. We proved a quite serious lot in many respects, but mellowed considerably as we worked together in teams on the radar simulators, sweated considerably at plotting targets and took turns to command our own ship. The simulator proved extremely realistic and, once we had some theory under our belts, we spent days at sea aboard the radar training vessel, exercising our skills in the Thames estuary to the great edification (and doubtless horror) of approaching ships. The practical sessions were reminiscent of my days aboard the *Stenwood Navigator*, and brought memories of LBB's dulcet Scots tones to echo in my ears. The end of course examination was not exacting, but taken quite seriously.

Practical radar plotting exercises (Crown copyright/MOD).

A return to Captain Atherton, upon successful completion, left me being appointed to the *Earl of Ripon*, another new and near-sister ship to my last vessel. She was currently commencing loading for the Far East in Tilbury. My joy was complete as I went home and arranged for the tailor's to add a thin gold stripe to my uniform sleeves retaining, as I was still technically in my cadetship, the cadets' gorgets on my lapels. My parents shared my excitement in more ways than one for, mindful of my promise in Durban, I proposed to my Sue – who simply said, "Yes, please." So it was as a newly appointed, engaged to be married, young officer that I set out for Charing Cross railway station and the familiar trail to Gravesend.

Undoubtedly permanently wholesome truths reside in the Bible and particularly in the Book of Proverbs. I was to learn an immediate lesson, 'Pride goeth before destruction…and a fall'. History, if not repeating itself, certainly covered a stretch of familiar ground, as echoes of the *Bath* and a certain *joie de vivre* on the part of a sixteen year old cadet, returned to haunt me. I reported on board the *Ripon*, was given a cabin of my own, and duly accepted as a near equal by my fellow navigating officers. The Chief Officer, Mr. Abel was hard-pressed as he and the Second, Mr. Withers, were currently the only deck officers; the deep-sea captain was not yet aboard, so Mr Abel was also senior officer. The shortage of officers meant that I was greeted warmly. My efforts on cargo watches were satisfactorily performed, but two days' later, I was given the job of using the Asian crew for loading four tons (some eighty sacks) of rice for use as ship's stores, with all three crews – deck, engine and catering together. This was always a delicate duty to supervise as both deck and engine ratings felt that provisions should be loaded by the catering crew without their assistance. The official view was that, as they helped consume the stuff they also should help carry it, but whatever the rights and wrongs, it certainly led to my downfall. The Purser saw the delivery notes checked off and the stuff stowed in the dry store below, whilst my job was to organise the ratings into a chain gang and hump it from lorry to store. My problem was, I could not be in three places simultaneously and had no petty officers to assist, merely being given a collection of far from happy ratings from all three departments. The inevitable happened, and resulted in a trail of rice from broken sacks leading from the lorry, up the gangway, along the companionways and to ladders leading to the store-room. The crew simply fooled about in those areas where I was unable actually to see them. The Mate took one look at what was happening and 'went ape' as the current expression was. He took immediate control himself and, clearly unimpressed by my ability at crew control, re-organised them and quickly finalised the loading.

The knock-on effect was that my credibility with the crew was considerably undermined, leading to a discussion with the shore superintendent, and then a visit from Captain Atherton – who was called to the ship. The outcome was fair, but firm. It was decided I should be transferred to the *Earl of Gloucester*, returning from the Continent and due to load for African ports in Swansea. It was appreciated that whilst my confidence 'had taken a bit of a knock', as Mr. Abel and Captain Atherton jointly read my situation, I should not be too over worried, but put the incident down to experience and learn how the Mate had re-organised the crew. It was suggested I ask to do the same operation with another crew as soon as possible on my newly appointed ship.

Suitably chastened, I set off for Paddington and South Wales, stopping off overnight at home and confessing all to my parents. They were understandably supportive, but the humility was rightfully mine. It remained with me as I reported on board the *Gloucester* and diffidently explained what had happened, to Mr. Strode the Mate. His reaction was refreshing to put things mildly; he listened, looked at me, burst out laughing and agreed that I should organise the crew for the loading of all deck stores, especially the collective voyage rice, as these arrived. He also told me not to dwell on this incident – it was really pretty minor in comparison to some of the clangers I would undoubtedly drop in the course of my officer career – thus providing just the re-assurance needed.

True to his word, running the crew for stores loading and deck work came my way pretty frequently and a lesson was soon learnt. Once at sea, I was placed on permanent bridge watches with him, understudying and taking charge as much as possible. I was also put in charge for'ard and aft during stand-bys, under supervision from the duty mate concerned. My confidence and competency were increased considerably as a result. No further discipline problems resulted with the crew. Other distinct advantages accompanying my promotion were the single cabin and a share of the officers' steward, a place at their table in the saloon, and a natural acceptance from senior officers with whom previously I had barely been on nodding terms.

We had cargo for east African ports including en route, machinery for Aquaba, bunkers from Aden, and general cargo for Mombasa, Beira and L.M, proceeding to South African ports once again for loading. It was an uneventful voyage apart, that is, from a hiccup from the Mate which, ironically, proved to be one of the clangers that I had been warned against. We had to off-load a number of cases bound for Mombasa in order to access those for Aquaba. They had been loaded out of sequence in the tween deck to ensure the stability of the ship. The approaches to this port entailed passing an area of narrows, which the pilot wanted to navigate during daylight, which led to a most undignified rush to complete discharge. The result was that three cases were accidentally left on one of the pontoons used to receive all the cargo discharged in Aquaba. The incident was not noticed until Mombasa when it was suddenly discovered that these cases were missing. An unproductive search of the remaining holds led to the realisation. Captain Auderly-Jones was not impressed by our combined efforts – particularly those of his Chief Officer – as he had to cable the Kremlin, requesting a later Africa-run ship be diverted to pick these up and deliver them on our behalf. I was certainly continuing to learn, not only professional lessons, but not to regard my chosen profession too lightly.

I liked Mombasa. The approaches to Kilindini Harbour involved a couple of miles of quite intricate pilotage, during which I took the helm thus enjoying a refreshing stand-by instead of playing with the customary moorings and tug wires. Discharging our cars, fire engines, tractors and bagged cement proved a lengthy process, not least because numerous bags had split, so that our cement cargo turned out to be almost bulk. This gave plenty of opportunity for time ashore; the place impressing as being pretty 'laid back.' My pleasure and leisure were assisted by an increase in the perks given me resulting from the Mate's bartering, another benefit of my promotion. In the Mission, we met several more deck cadets and officers as, over the pool and a few beers, varied experiences were exchanged and careful condolences expressed.

We proceeded to Durban to load hundreds of cases of tinned fruit and a variety of general cargo, including rum, cotton goods, skins and hides, and jams. Peter Driscoll the Third Mate, and Roger Deering, the Second Officer proved admirable company ashore and on board. They were very senior in their respective ranks, each being due for promotion next time in, and offered me considerable help professionally, together with many useful hints for the examination room – especially the dreaded orals, which now loomed ominously over my horizon. We had identified the more serious weak areas in my knowledge, during watches with Mr. Strode, who took every opportunity to help develop these into strengths. I was becoming more quietly competent in cargo, anchor and bridge watches as a direct result of the encouraging support from these three officers – to whom I was already acknowledging gratitude.

We lowered the boats to the water line in Durban Harbour and I took complete charge of the entire drill, including pulling them across the bay to the vicinity of the whale-flensing yards. There were a number of sharks here attracted by the blood and rotting flesh from carcasses. For once, I did not have constantly to remind the crew to keep their hands and especially fingers inside the boat. This time they sat on their thwarts rigidly upright, as fins came fleetingly alongside and the ugly snouts of hammerheads occasionally broke surface less than a couple of feet from the boat's side. Observed from such a low angle, the experience proved quite salutary and very frightening. Coming alongside the ship, to hook-on falls and hoist the boat into its davits, was really quite safe as there was invariably so much noise from tugs attending ships and other sundry power-driven craft, whose propeller vibrations tended to keep the sharks out of the immediate way. The crew still hooked-on pretty sharply though, being, for some reason, anxious to return in board.

We left Durban to call in again at Aden, not only for bunkers, but to lift aboard a number of tanks and some ammunition from the military authorities based there. An army ordnance major came on board accompanied by a number of lieutenants and NCOs. We were to use the ship's heavy lift gear to take on board eight Centurion tanks, towed out on pontoons by tugs to the moorings. Together with spares, each weighed sixty-five to seventy tons and we loaded them to port and starboard of Nos.

2 and 3 hatches. There was also a number of armoured cars and scout cars to be taken on board, together with something in excess of five hundred tons of assorted ammunition into the tween decks. We were invited ashore to the officers' mess for a formal meal, with lashings of assorted wines and after-dinner port, coffee and liqueurs. We were finally poured back on board in the early hours of the morning, having made arrangements to return the compliment in our own saloon and smoke room the next evening. Only Roger was totally *compos mentis* for, being teetotal (a rare thing indeed in the Merchant Navy), he readily undertook officer-of-the-watch deck duties in port. The engineering officers shared this hardship between them, to the obvious chagrin of a couple who had to miss out on the fun. Certainly, none of our engineers were teetotal. Even Captain Auderly-Jones came ashore with us, sharing our collective disgrace, but in the more exalted company of the lieutenant-colonel in command of the base. Consequently, it was with extremely 'thick heads' that we eventually sailed.

Once loaded, our passage through the Suez Canal looked pretty impressive with our deck cargo of tanks and armoured cars – perhaps, we thought, they might have proved useful a couple of years earlier when a certain colonel decided to nationalise this previously British owned asset. We stopped off in Plymouth to discharge our armaments to the Royal Ordnance Corps, who apparently repaired the things prior to shipping them out again in another of the Company's fleet. However there were no mutual exchanges of hospitality with the military officers here.

I was relieved immediately upon arrival in London and, following an interview with Captain Atherton, was told to report for a twelve week 2nd Mates' Certificate course in London and attempt the examination upon its termination. It was good to be home again on paid study leave – the longest period ashore since commencing at Kedddleston – more than four years previously.

My signals and navigation skills, and my mathematics and seamanship theory were quite sound, so my first pre-certificate course was an intensive session on derrick rigging and rope work. Sitting with the rest of my class over lunch and chatting away animatedly, as is the wont of hungry students, the person on my left side in the refectory nudged my arm, asking for the pepper. Still talking across the table, I absently passed this to him only to hear a very familiar voice saying, "Gosh, it's Jon Caridia" – it had to be, and it was – Peter Dathan from Keddleston days! Great was the rejoicing and an adjournment to the nearest pub ensued where we stayed until thrown out at fifteen hundred. He had of course changed, but the familiar person remained clearly identifiable. There was much to discuss, including the number of times our paths had nearly met as we compared our ships and voyages, matching dates and experiences. He knew of my disinfecting saga as apparently this had gone around the fleet pretty quickly, passed and relayed by numerous radio officers – making my name something of a by-word. Of such fame (or infamy) I was blissfully unaware. He was doing signals at present, but it seemed we would meet up for theory lectures and teaching during the following weeks. We arranged to go for a drink the following

Saturday, when we could fill the gaps of intervening years. The lectures were a hoot. I do not think the college could have arranged a greater number of characters amongst such a small class if they had scanned the oceans intentionally. There was never a dull moment; one student was a cartoonist of exquisitely delightful skill and ingenuity, consequently our wrestling with stability problems was lightened considerably by a sequence of cartoons.

Another character made a point of arriving late every morning, throwing open the door with such enthusiasm that it crashed back on its hinges, and greeting everyone present by crying at the top of his voice, "Good morning, girls". All the long-suffering instructor could do was join in the laughter with the rest of us, before again picking up the threads of some complex formulae. Another trio regularly took off for the pub immediately after lunch, not to be seen again until the pubs closed. Following our meeting that first Saturday, Peter and I very much towed the party line and knuckled down to serious study, although we still enjoyed the occasional "do you remember" and "did you know so-and-so at sea?" chat, usually over lunch.

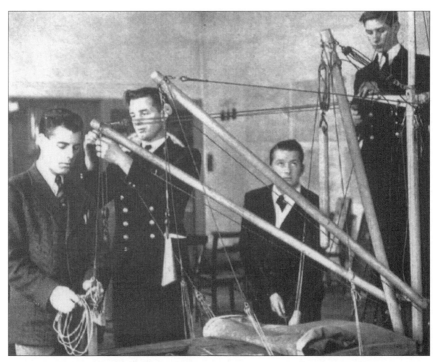

Deck cadets on study leave rigging model derricks (Crown copyright/MOD).

Our lecturers were acquainted with the latest examination requirements and were quite *au fait* with the penchants and vagaries of the examiners. This was particularly true because some of the master-mariner staff *were* the examiners. Consequently, whilst there was no air of complacency wafting over the classrooms, there were certainly gentle breezes conducive to relaxation. The signals part was taken separately; semaphore included, where the general melée was happily conducive to surreptitious assistance by one to another, particularly as this method of signalling was rarely practised at sea. In fact, the only times I ever saw it used at all, was when we cadets went through the motions (literally) on the boat deck between ourselves. It was never used in practice aboard any of the ships upon which I served. Similar opportunity for discreet cheating applied to the Aldis lamp Morse test. This was not so necessary because most of us were quite proficient in this area, having contacted numerous ships and shore stations whilst on passage.

Then came the series of written papers and, with them, our first shock as we realised they were to be sat in a hall on top of a busy post office overlooking a street market. Whatever induced the Board of Trade to select such an enterprising place was beyond the wildest imagination of any of us. We had expected a quieter venue, but had to make the best of it. The examination followed a strict menu which included papers on navigation principles and practice, ship construction, seamanship theory, cargo work and mathematics. We had no indication at the time of how we might have fared. We then discussed with the examiner arrangements for us to call in individually and take our dreaded orals. Those who lived furthest from the centre were invited to attend first – which seemed logical enough, but as I lived about an hours' travelling away, I was unfortunately one of the last to be tested. I re-lived again, but with enhanced intensity, similar tenter-hooks experienced aboard my training ship when I was chosen to navigate from Calais to Tilbury landing stage.

My first impression was that the oral examiner looked very human and he certainly put me at ease initially by asking questions about the ships on which I had served, their equipment in every area, and various professional practices. The pace quickened, with questions that asked me to compare various seamanship and cargo work practices between the different vessels. After a pause, a discussion arose from answers given in my written papers – although he was sufficiently generous to tell me that I had scored very highly on both navigation papers and achieved creditable performances on the others. This was followed by a host of questions on chart work, seamanship and the sextant, which were largely taken in my stride. He then passed me a short length of rope and asked me to make a back splice. This was the moment I was not particularly looking forward to because although the theory was known, I still retained my two right hands of Keddleston days. Fortunately, the rope had been used so many times for back splicing that it almost did the job itself. All I had to do was to thread the willing strands back onto themselves in the usual manner. It was similarly so with the eye splice he asked me to make in some wire. Luckily, I had practised rigging derricks frequently in the college and had done this so often at sea that this hurdle was taken in my stride.

I was about to congratulate myself on not perhaps being so obtuse practically as I had thought, when he showed me a cobra mooring rope – an intertwined (almost cat's cradle) mixture of wire and rope, enquiring if I could put an eye splice into this. This length clearly had not been used before so, with beating heart, I simply told him that I could not do so. To my surprise, he smiled and retorted that if I had said I could, then he would have asked me to do it. Breathing returned to normal and we started probing on the Collision Regulations. I detected that the tone of the examination had now taken a very serious note. He bowled the questions and numerous potential collision situations and I batted back the answers – amplifying these as instructed with specifications concerning characteristics of lights, shapes and relevant sound signals under all conditions of visibility. I was particularly thankful to the training sessions with various Chief and Second Officers. I may not have enjoyed them at the time, but now they more than paid dividends, especially when the exchange increased considerably in tempo.

The final question seemed almost predictable as he offered another scenario, "You are on the bridge of your ship in the English Channel at night when through the mist you see six red lights in a vertical line dead ahead. What is it? And what action do you suggest taking?"

I did some very quick thinking – one of the reds would be the port sidelight of a vessel, two more would indicate she was Not Under Command, and the remaining three could presumably only represent a ship constrained by draught. So, she was clearly a power-driven vessel which, for all six reds to be seen in a vertical line, would indicate she was port side open and, as these were in a vertical line, I was seeing her beam ahead. Consequently, I would hold my course and speed and watch to see how the situation developed. I passed this on and he smiled again, telling me this had been something of a trick question. He paused – looked and then, shaking my hand, congratulated me on passing not only my orals, but my 2nd Mates' examination. He wrote something briefly on a slip of paper – which I found to be the magic 'P' – and handed this authority to me, enabling me to order my Second Mate's Certificate of Competency.

It was true. I had passed. Suddenly, three months' at Keddleston navigation school, seemingly now light years away, four years' sea-time as a deck cadet, and the final course ashore, seemed so worthwhile. I immediately phoned Captain Atherton at Ellertons to receive his congratulations. He also advised me that the Company always paid a £200 bonus to newly qualified officers and immediately offered me a Company Contract for a further two years' service with the Group (a subtle difference this time, I noticed) as Third Officer. My phone calls home and to Sue, were the kind of calls made by any successful young man to his parents and fiancée.